BECOMING ALICE

BECOMING ALICE

A Memoir

Alice Rene

For Karen
to enjoy!
Alice

iUniverse, Inc.
New York Lincoln Shanghai

BECOMING ALICE
A Memoir

Copyright © 2006 by Alice Rene

iUniverse books may be ordered through booksellers or by contacting:

iUniverse
2021 Pine Lake Road, Suite 100
Lincoln, NE 68512
www.iuniverse.com
1-800-Authors (1-800-288-4677)

The views expressed in this work are solely those of the author and do not necessarily reflect the views of the publisher, and the publisher hereby disclaims any responsibility for them.

Some names and other identifying characteristics of persons within this book have been changed in order to protect their privacy.

ISBN-13: 978-0-595-40339-4 (pbk)
ISBN-13: 978-0-595-84715-0 (ebk)
ISBN-10: 0-595-40339-5 (pbk)
ISBN-10: 0-595-84715-3 (ebk)

Printed in the United States of America

To the Memory of Norbert and Jenny

Contents

ACKNOWLEDGMENTS

I am indebted to my grandsons, Cameron and Andrew, both of whom have used the experiences of my early life to fulfill class assignments. Their fascination with this true and personal story led me to believe that it might be of interest to others.

I'd like to express my appreciation to Jack Grapes, whose writing classes gave me the confidence to undertake this project, and to Tristine Rainer, for her contribution to my understanding of the genre of memoir. To those in my writing workshops, Claudette Young, Kathleen Auth, Audrey Bishop, Jean Castaing, Jody Avery Smith, Rhoda Novak, Rochelle Linick, Jim and Doris Vernon, Mario Speiser, Shlomo Kreitzer, Richard Goodman, and Liz Ellenberger: I thank you for your suggestions and advise. A special note of gratitude goes to Dr. Shlomo Raz and June Behar for adding their expertise to my work. Lastly, a special heartfelt toast to my husband, Bob, whose support and encouragement made the writing of this story, like all of life's adventures, a joy.

PART I

From My Window

"Get away from there. Don't let them see you." Mama grabbed my arm and pulled me away from the window, her brows pushed down over her eyes. I didn't know why she was so angry. I was only looking down the street for Opa, hoping to see him coming to play with me. A cool breeze blew Mama's beautiful mesh curtains over my head, as if they were fishnets thrown out at sea. Perhaps she thought I might ruin one of the crocheted round pieces she'd sewn into them. She was so proud of the way they looked—she told me once they reminded her of the stars in the sky on a sparkling, clear Viennese night.

I liked playing chess with Opa. At age five, I couldn't always remember how each piece had to be moved, but somehow, we made a game of it. When I moved a rook like a bishop, or a pawn like a queen, his eyes would dance and he'd say, "No, Illy, no. You must move it like this." And he'd move the piece the right way. After letting me move pieces this way and that, without any plan whatsoever, he managed to let me win. Then, with a wounded, defeated look on his face, he'd say, "*Ach*, you did it again! You beat me again!"

But Opa wasn't there. Instead, I saw many people streaming out of their apartments onto the sidewalk. In the distance I heard music. Was it a march? Yes—it was a march—and I was excited. I heard the trumpets blasting a catchy melody with short, crisp notes, which I started to hum in my head. I thought I heard a band like the ones I'd seen in the Prater. They came closer and I forgot all about Opa.

At last I saw them under my window—men in uniforms that didn't look anything like those I'd ever seen before. These uniforms were muddy brown instead of sky blue or grassy green. They weren't decorated with two rows of brass buttons and gold fringes on the shoulders. The men in these uniforms wore black leather belts and black straps crossing their chests, from one corner of their waists to the opposite corner of their shoulders. They wore black knee-high boots on their feet and caps with shiny, black visors. The only colors I could see were the red armbands with white circles that had black, hooked crosses inside them. Some people watching the parade waved flags that looked like the armbands. I couldn't understand why they were so excited about men in such ugly, drab uniforms.

But the beat of the music made me jump up and down as the band passed by. It was followed by rows and rows of men lifting their feet high in the air, pounding their heels onto the pavement as if they were hammers—their chests were puffed out—their chins held high. All our neighbors were smiling and cheering and waving their arms. The excitement made me hop like a rabbit—until Mama grabbed my arm and brought me to a standstill. Her face twisted into a knot. I'd never seen her like that before. I didn't understand why she was so frightened.

Rebuff on the Trolley

Everything changed after that day. Mama changed. Papa changed. Even our maid, Betti, changed. She no longer baked cookies, no longer smiled and chattered like a magpie. Mama didn't do her crocheting or needlepoint anymore. Papa didn't take me to the gardens of the Prater to feed peanuts to the squirrels. And he didn't bring me chocolate bars, saying they were for me, but then eating them himself, before I could get to them.

Then one morning, Betti was gone. Mama said, "She can't live with us any longer."

"But why not? Doesn't she like us anymore?" I loved Betti and needed her.

"*Ach*, Illy, she likes us all right, but ..." Mama stroked my hair and looked at me as if she were in pain.

"Then why can't she be with us?" I felt like crying.

"Because it's too dangerous," Mama said, walking out of the room. "Now don't ask so many questions."

I didn't know what "dangerous" meant, or that it was against the law for Betti to work for us. But Mama wasn't in the mood for any more questions.

Betti did come back to our apartment though, sneaking in like a burglar, making sure no one saw her. She helped Mama clean and cook and sometimes went shopping for her. One time when she was going out, I begged to go with her. I'd been kept inside so long, I felt like a caged animal. I bounced up and down. "Can I go, Mama, can I go with Betti?"

Mama looked at Betti, who had cornflower blue eyes and milk white skin, and said, "I guess you'll be all right, seeing that you'll be with her. The fresh air will do you good."

It was spring, and there was a chill in the air. Betti dressed me in a navy blue wool jacket and a gray pleated skirt. We were almost out the door when I ran back for my favorite stuffed toy, a golden bear with shiny, black beads for eyes and a tongue of pink felt.

We waited for the trolley on the corner of Austellungstrasse. A few blocks down the street we could see the giant Ferris wheel in the Prater. Shiny steel bars shot out from its center like the spokes of a huge bicycle tire. At the rim, a line of

5

red wooden boxcars filled with people rose high into the sky. Whenever I'd been on the Ferris wheel, I'd had the most fun when it stopped at the top and my box-car would swing back and forth. I could see the whole city spread out before me.

"Let's go for a ride on the Ferris wheel, Betti, let's go." I pulled on her hand in the direction of the Prater.

"No, Illy, there's no time. Besides, here's our trolley." She helped me up the two high steps into the coach and I forgot all about the Ferris wheel. The electric trolley was just as much fun. With its bright gold lettering, the ding-dong of the brass bell, and the uniformed conductor at the controls, it was like riding inside a giant toy. The conductor seemed like one of my brother Fredi's toy soldiers with the gold braid on his hat, the shiny lapel insignias, and the two rows of brass but-tons down the front of his chest. I scampered into a seat next to Betti.

The trolley lurched forward, its small, round metal wheels screeching along the tracks in the street. It wasn't long before I was out of my seat and in the aisle, holding my golden bear under my arm. Across from us, a smiling lady with silky, white hair said, "What a beautiful child."

I took a step back to lean on Betti sitting in her aisle seat, tucked my chin into my jacket, and smiled. A lady with a striped feather in her fedora, who sat behind us, said, "What beautiful long curls." A few more smiles broke out on other faces in the car. The white haired woman followed with, "What's your name?"

"Ilse. But Papa calls me Suzinka." I said.

"How old are you?" the striped feather lady asked.

"Almost six," I said, enjoying the attention.

In the row in front of us, a girl wearing a black-and-white school uniform turned around and said, "Where do you live?"

"71 Austellungstrasse," I said, but saying the word must have sounded like something else, because everyone in the car laughed.

The uniformed girl, still laughing and looking at my jacket, said, "Ilse, where is your swastika pin? Why aren't you wearing it?"

"Because I'm Jewish," I said, waiting for smiles and laughter. I got neither. The smiles disappeared. No one asked more questions. The girl in the school uni-form turned around in her seat. The white haired woman looked out the win-dow. The striped feather lady opened her purse and pulled out a handkerchief.

I went back to my seat, set my golden bear down in my lap, and buried my face in his soft, warm fluff. Betti looked at me as she'd done so often when I'd hurt myself, and pulled me onto her lap. I'd learned that it wasn't good to be Jewish in Vienna in that year those men in mud-colored uniforms had marched down my street.

Kitchen Conference

Mama, Papa, Fredi, and I were in our kitchen eating breakfast. No one spoke. Outside our window the chestnut tree's ribbed leaves hung limp, waiting for a breeze to wake them. A pair of light brown finches hovered in midair before floating down onto a branch like a couple of feathered eggs. Then all was still again.

The kitchen was my favorite place in the apartment. It was where I spent most of my time, engulfed in the aromas of fresh breads, roasting chicken, and brewing coffee. Betti would sing while she cooked; sometimes she taught me nursery rhymes. But Betti wasn't in our kitchen anymore. It was Mama who fixed breakfast, and she wasn't singing.

Fredi, his raven-colored hair slicked down, was in his uniform ready to go to school. He had his normal half-sad, half-mad expression on his face. He hated school. He feared the teachers, who punished the students for the slightest thing, and was afraid of the kids, who picked on him. At home Mama consoled him, but Papa yelled at him for not standing up for himself. Fredi wasn't anything like Papa, who was born a fighter. He fought with his sisters, his classmates, and anyone else who got in his way. Papa even had his nose broken in a fistfight when he was only a little boy. He said nobody bothered to fix it—that was the way it was for everyone growing up on his father's farm way out in the country. That's why it was big and flat and wide—wider than anybody else's nose I'd ever seen.

Fredi stuffed the last bite of breakfast roll into his mouth and washed it down with coffee He reached for his schoolbooks and said, "I'm going."

Papa looked up from his morning paper and said, "Be careful." He hardly moved his lips when he spoke, which is what he did when he warned us kids to stop doing something bad.

"I know," Fredi said.

"Maybe he shouldn't go to school by himself," Mama said, still in her housecoat and slippers. "Maybe I'll go with him."

"I'll come, too," I said. "Can I?"

"No, you can't," Fredi said. "That's ridiculous, having my Mama and my baby sister take me to school." Fredi picked up his books. "I'll be all right."

He was already out of the kitchen when Mama shouted at his back, "Be careful!"

Papa went back to reading his paper, his finger crooked into the handle of his coffee cup. He was dressed in his suit pants, looking like he was ready for work. A heavy gold chain, attached to a watch in his vest pocket, hung across his big belly in a deep U. I loved winding the chain around my fingers when I sat on his lap. I waited for him to look at the time, put on his suit coat, and say, "I've got to get to work." But on this day he only lifted the half-empty cup to his lips.

"Aren't you going to be late for the hospital?" I asked. Papa always saw his hospital patients first before spending the rest of the day in his office, next to our apartment.

"No, Suzinka, I'm not going to the hospital." Papa's heavy-lidded eyes were glued to his newspaper. Two fingers moved up and down the handle of his coffee cup.

"Why aren't you going to the hospital today?"

"Because they won't let me see my patients anymore."

"Why not?"

"Because ..." He paused, his eyes studied me a brief second. "You ask too many questions. Go along and play now."

I didn't move. "If you're not going to the hospital, will you take me to the Prater to feed the squirrels?"

"No, Suzinka, not today." Papa stared at his coffee. I fell back into my chair.

Mama cleared the breakfast dishes and sat down next to Papa. "We're out of food," she said. Her eyebrows pulled together on her forehead into two lines. "I'll have to go out shopping. I told Betti not to come anymore. I'm worried about her. I'm afraid someone might see her and report her to the Nazis. I don't want her to get into trouble."

"And I don't want *you* to get into any trouble. No—you won't go out. I'll go. Just tell me what to buy."

"But how can you go? How does it look for a man—and a doctor yet—to go shopping?"

"What does it matter what it looks like, with everything that's going on in the streets these days? I'll go."

Papa came back carrying two string bags full of groceries and hoisted the heavy load onto the kitchen table. He lowered himself into a chair, as if his legs couldn't hold him up anymore.

"Bobi, what's wrong?" Mama's voice was high-pitched.

"They've frozen all Jewish bank accounts. We can't get our money out."

"*Ach, mein Gott!*" Mama sat down next to Papa. She bent forward in her chair, her fingers laced together in her lap. "What'll we do? I don't have much more than a few *Schillinge* left ... maybe enough to last a week."

"I know. I know." Papa looked at the floor in front of his feet. "I guess we'll have to sell some of our furnishings like everybody else is doing." He was quiet for a moment. "Our Persian rug should be worth something."

"You can sell my golden bear, Papa." I ran to his side. "It must be worth a lot."

The corners of Papa's mouth moved up, but there was no smile in his eyes. "No Suzinka—we wouldn't sell your bear. That's the last thing we'd sell."

"We could sell the rug, I'm sure," Mama said. "But how much would we get for it now? Every Jew in Vienna is trying to sell his belongings on the black market. The market is flooded. People get next to nothing for their things."

"I know. But we have no choice. We'll have to take whatever we can get."

Papa looked at Mama and said nothing, their eyes speaking that secret language they had between them that I couldn't understand.

"You can sell all my toys, Papa. How much do you think they're worth?"

Gretl's Help

"*Nein*, Gretl. *Nein*. I'd better not—certainly not at Demel's. They're sure to watch the best coffee house in Vienna." Mama was on the telephone, pacing back and forth as far as the telephone cord would reach. "Why don't you come here? I have some leftover Nuss Torte."

"Tell her to bring Hans when she comes," I said. I liked playing with Gretl's seven-year-old son, especially after he lost his two front teeth and whistled with every word he spoke.

"*Nein*, Illy, not today. Some other time," Mama said.

Nein. Nein. Nein. That's all I ever hear these days. No one has time for me.

Mama and Gretl were best friends and told each other all their problems. They were nothing alike. Gretl had an almond-shaped face with shiny, golden hair and was as good-looking as any actress in Vienna. She went to her Catholic Church every day, cried about not having enough money, and complained that her husband, Leo, was seeing other women. Papa said she was just imagining things, and Mama said she wasn't.

Mama, with her olive complexion and mousy hair, was not good-looking at all. Everyone said she looked Jewish. I didn't know what that meant, because I didn't look anything like Mama, and I was Jewish just like her. Mama never went to synagogue, and Gretl didn't think that was right. After she gave up trying to make Mama a Catholic, she tried to make Mama a better Jew. She'd say, "If you won't come to church with me, you should go to your own synagogue." But that didn't work either. Mama wasn't interested in going to either one.

Mama and Gretl had become friends when neither one of them had had any money. It began when they'd walk all the way to the other side of the city to save a few *Groshen* to buy soup meat from a cheaper butcher. But even after their husbands made enough money to buy food near us, they stayed friends. They'd take Hans and me to the park to play while they sat on a bench and complained to each another—Gretl about Leo seeing other women, and Mama about Papa being nasty to her. I didn't understand why Gretl was so upset about Leo seeing other women. Papa saw other women in his office every day. Only Mama didn't call them *other women*—she called them *patients*.

Mama spread a white tablecloth with cross-stitched red and pink roses over the round table in our living room for Gretl's visit. She put down the cups, saucers, and plates, and placed the Nuss Torte on a Rosenthal cake plate decorated with tiny roses. The table looked like a picture in one of Mama's magazines. On the couch, Betti's sheets, towels, blankets, and goose down comforter were stacked next to Mama's crocheted tablecloths. On top of all the linens, Mama placed three petit point miniatures. They were of village scenes and sailboats gliding along blue lakes, their reflections upside down in the water. I liked them even more than the pictures on the pages of my pre-school primer.

The bell rang and I ran to the door. "Wait, Illy. Don't open the door. Let me do that." Mama grabbed my arm and held me back. "Who is it?" she asked, not opening the door until she was sure it was Gretl.

"*Servus,* Gretl. Come in."

When Gretl saw Mama's linens and handiwork piled on the couch, she said, "Jenny, what's this? What's going on here?"

"We're going to try to sell those things." Mama looked at the floor.

"But why?" Gretl faced Mama, her eyebrows raised.

"The Nazis froze all Jewish bank accounts. We can't withdraw our money. That's why."

"Terrible! Terrible!" Gretl sat down at the table, her face twisted. "But you'll get nothing for them here in Vienna. The market is flooded with Jewish furnishings."

"I know."

"Jenny, I'll take your belongings to Pitten and sell them for you there. It's my hometown, and everyone knows me. Out in the country, you'll get a better price."

"*Nein!* I won't let you do that. It's really nice of you ... really ... but that's too much to ask of anyone." Mama shook her head a few times.

"Why not, Mama? I said. "Why don't we all go to Pitten, all of us ... and Hans, too." I pulled on her arm, remembering the summers our two families spent together in the mountains in Semmering.

"Will you please stop!" Mama's voice was two tones louder than normal. I was not used to being yelled at. My eyes filled with tears.

"Jenny, leave the child alone. All this trouble is not her fault. I'll take care of selling your things, and I won't hear otherwise." Gretl was on her feet and halfway to the door. "Now be nice to Illy."

Before Mama could say another word, Gretl was gone. She hadn't taken one bite of cake, or even a sip of coffee.

Where's Papa?

Mama and Papa ignored me all week. They even passed each other in the apartment without saying a word. Sometimes I'd hear them speaking so low in the kitchen, they sounded as if they were a block away. If I came into the room, they'd stop talking in a flash, fast as someone turning off a radio. Then Mama would say, "Do you want some cookies or a slice of cake?" and I'd forget all about asking them what they were talking about.

When it was finally Sunday, I thought I'd have a good chance to get someone in the apartment to pay attention to me. Papa didn't see patients any longer and Fredi didn't go to school. Of course, Fredi would have to be forced into playing with me, but I didn't care—as long as he'd play. I went to work on him first. I ran into his bedroom and jumped on his sleeping body, curled up like a cat.

"Why do you do that? Can't you see I'm still sleeping?" he said. He tucked in his shoulders, buried his face into the pillow, and lay still.

I straddled him like a horse. "Get up!"

"Go away!" He burrowed his head deeper into the pillow.

"No. Get up already."

"Pest!" Fredi rolled over. Knowing he'd get no more sleep, he swung his feet over the edge and sat on the side of the bed, his eyes half-open and crusty.

"Come," I said, pulling him into the kitchen. Mama sat at the table—her chin rested on her chest—her fingers were hooked through the handle of her coffee cup.

"Mama, what's wrong? Where's Papa?" I asked.

"Papa's gone, Illy. Papa's gone." She looked like she was sick.

"When's he coming back?"

"He's not coming back," Mama said, her eyes teary.

"What do you mean, 'He's not coming back?'" Fredi asked with a face white as a platter.

"Papa had to get out of Vienna fast. We got the bad news last night—they're going to start arresting all the Jewish doctors and dentists in Vienna today." Mama looked straight at Fredi, as if he were all grown up.

"But how could he go anywhere? We hardly have enough money to buy food, let alone a train ticket."

12

"Gretl's husband helped us. Leo went to the bank and told them Papa owed him all the money in our account, and he wanted his loan paid back. They believed him. They allowed Leo to withdraw our money. They had no idea that Leo would hand it over to Papa the minute they got home. Can you just imagine it?" Mama's eyes were round as buttons.

"What luck!" Fredi slapped his forehead.

"Where did Papa go?" I said. My hand pushed her leg for attention. "When will he be back?"

"He went to Memel, Illy. He won't be back."

"Where's that, Mama? Why can't we go to him?"

"It's far from here—in another country far away from this terrible place." Mama took a sip of her coffee.

"How'd he get to Memel? Why couldn't we go with him?" Fredi's words shot out fast.

"*Warte … warte eine Minute.*" Mama pulled me onto her lap. She took a deep breath and said, "Papa went with his cousin, Gustav. He'd gotten two visas to Memel, saying he and his partner needed to go there to buy goose feathers for his business. He told them Papa was his partner." Mama stopped talking. With a half-smile on her face and a shake of the head as if she didn't believe it herself, a sound like, "Hhmmp!" escaped from her lips. "Thank God the Viennese love their goose down comforters."

"So why can't we say we're going to buy goose feathers and get some visas for ourselves?" I said.

"You dummy!" Fredi said. "Do the three of us look like businessmen?"

"We were lucky to get Papa out in time," Mama said. "Lucky that Gustav needed goose feathers, and lucky that Gustav's marriage is not so good so that he took Papa instead of his own wife. Now it's up to Papa to get visas for the rest of us …" Mama held me tight and rocked back and forth in her seat, her chin resting on top of my head. "… if he can."

"What are visas, anyway?" I said.

"They're papers, dummy, papers that say we can get into a country. Don't ask so many questions."

I hated the way Fredi talked to me, treating me like a baby just because he was fourteen. I wanted to be with Papa, but as long as I had Mama and Fredi around, I felt safe. And I thought Papa could do anything—even get visas when nobody else could.

I pulled on Fredi's hand as if we were playing a game of tug of war and said, "Fredi, come play with me."

13

The Other Slipper

Having Papa gone was hard on all of us, especially Mama. He wasn't there to make all our decisions and take care of everything. The first thing Mama did after he left was to get sick. She ran around with a face as red as an apple, and kept taking aspirin around the clock. She didn't even get dressed in the morning, staying in her nightgown and flannel housecoat all day. Her feet slid across the floor as if they were too heavy to lift. At first, Fredi and I didn't worry much because, whenever we got sick, we were well again in no time.

But Mama didn't get any better—she even got worse. She stopped swishing her slippers along the floor like a dust mop, and lay on our couch all day. Oma and Opa called a doctor for her, but when I saw the pudgy-faced man with a handlebar mustache who came to take care of her, I knew right away he wasn't as smart as Papa. He told Mama whatever was wrong with her would make itself known sooner or later. He said to take aspirin and drink lots of hot tea with honey. Oma could have told her that.

Mama did what the doctor said, but she still felt hot as a poker. Fredi tried to help by putting ice cold, wet washcloths on her forehead. Oma and Opa took care of all of us, which made me happy. I hoped Opa would play chess with me, but he always said, "*Nein*, Illy, not now."

No matter how bad Mama felt, Papa's letters made her feel worse. Papa couldn't get any visas for the five of us, and Mama wouldn't leave Oma and Opa behind in Vienna. She said, "How can I leave you here all by yourselves? You'd have no one to look after you."

Opa shook his head, his smile showing more jaw than teeth. When he spoke, crinkled lines appeared around his kind eyes, filled with love. "You and the children must leave. Don't worry about us. We're old already. We've lived most of our lives. But you—you must go."

Days went by and Mama still didn't get any better, and Papa still couldn't get visas for us. Mama had to call the doctor back, and this time, he said she had a huge infection in her foot. He drained the pus out and told her she'd be all right.

"Are you better now, Mama?" I asked.

"*Nein*, Illy. Not yet—I still have a fever."

14

"I know this doctor isn't as good as Papa. You'd be well by now if Papa took care of you. And his gold chain is not nearly as nice as Papa's, either."

Fredi had a really hard time with Papa being gone, Mama being sick, and me being no help whatsoever. He wasn't wearing his normal half-sad, half-mad face anymore. Now, his face was always ashen, and his eyebrows sat high on his forehead as if he was looking at a ghost. More days went by until finally, he came into Mama's room with a letter from Papa. "Mama, open it. Hurry!"

Mama was too weak to do anything in a hurry. When she was through reading, she looked up at us with red eyes. "They granted us three visas." But instead of looking happy, she lifted the letter over her head and said, "But how can I go anywhere *now* with such a high fever, and two children to take care of? And how can I leave Oma and Opa here alone in Vienna without anyone to look after them? I can't leave now."

"I'll take care of you, Mama," I said. I looked at Fredi. "We'll take care of you. Maybe Oma and Opa can come later. Let's go see Papa."

The next day Mama found out the Nazis were stopping Jewish women on the street and making them scrub the sidewalk with their bare hands, without any soap. When Oma heard that, she told all her five grown children to get out of Vienna as fast as they could, to run to any place that would take them, so that they would be safe from the Nazis. She said not to worry about her and Opa. They'd stay in Vienna with Mama's cousin, Regina, who'd decided not to leave because what was happening would surely blow over soon.

Mama thought hard about all of it and then announced, "Illy, Fredi, we're going. We have no choice. If we don't go now, it may be too late."

As soon as Mama bought our train tickets, Gretl came over with two furniture movers and a truck. They took everything in the apartment, except Mama's linens and dishes and handiwork. That was left for Oma and Opa, and Regina, to sell when they needed money. Within a few days, Gretl had sold our furniture in Pitten and gotten a good price for it.

Even though Mama was still sick with a foot as big as soccer ball, she was out of bed, deciding what to put into our suitcases. We took only as much as we could carry. Two days later, I sat between Fredi and Mama on a train bound for Memel, my fingers wrapped around the edge of the seat. It had been six weeks since Papa had left Vienna in the middle of the night.

"This is fun!" I squealed. I'd never been on a train before.

Fredi sat beside me. He leaned against the back of his seat, arms folded at his waist, and stared straight ahead. I could see that he was scared. But I wasn't—I didn't know what to be scared of. I had Mama and Fredi to take care of me. I bounced up and down on my seat.

"Sit still!" Mama's firm grip on my arm stopped me.

"Can I take my coat off now?" I pleaded. Even though it was August and as hot as it had ever been in Vienna, Mama made us wear our winter coats. We couldn't pack them in our suitcases because if we'd done so, there wouldn't have been room for any other clothes. Mama told us we could always take our coats off in the summer, but what would we do in winter without our coats?

Mama looked terrible. She still had a fever, and her infected foot was so swollen she couldn't put a shoe on. She wore a regular shoe on one foot and a soft brown slipper on the other. With each step that she took, we heard *clump ... swish ... clump ... swish ... clump.*

Our train first lurched forward, then back, before sliding out of the station. I jumped out of my seat onto the floor and looked out the window. While I was constantly in and out of my seat, Fredi sat as motionless as a statue. The rhythmic grind of the train's wheels made all of us feel happy. We were going to be with Papa again. Mama pulled the hatpin out of her fedora and wove it back into its rim before placing it into her lap. Her head fell against the back of her seat and with a deep sigh, she shut her eyes and dozed off. The train chugged along, one kilometer after another, and stopped in one unfamiliar train station after another.

At every station, I pressed my nose against the window and watched the commotion outside, or leaned back and looked at my reflection in the glass. I no longer had yellow spirals bouncing up and down my back—my hair was now in two thick braids. Mama said she had neither the time, nor the patience, to use the curling iron on my long hair—braids were easier. At one of our station stops, I was engrossed in watching the conductor collect tickets when I heard the loudspeaker, "*Jenny Fell ... Jenny Fell. Report to the stationmaster immediately! Jenny Fell.*"

"Mama, Mama!" I shook her awake. "They're calling your name."

Mama shot forward in her seat and listened. "*Jenny Fell ... Jenny Fell ...*" She jumped to her feet.

"Wait here!" Mama was breathing fast. "Fredi, watch your sister. And don't move." She grabbed her purse and ran down the aisle of the coach. *Clump ... swish ... clump ... swish.*

What little color Fredi had left in his face was now gone. I wasn't at all sure Fredi could take care of me, but I slid my hand under his arm and wrapped my fingers around it. He put his free hand over my fingers, and we held onto each other for what seemed like hours. Mama didn't return. The train gave its now familiar lurch forward, then back. The slow glide followed.

"Where's Mama?" I asked in a panic. I looked at Fredi—my hold on his arm, tight—my stomach, hard as a rock.

"I ... I don't ..." His voice cracked. "... know."

The train began to pull slowly out of the station when we heard BANG! BANG! on our window. It was Mama ... running along with the train ... a frantic look on her face ... pounding on our window ... arms waving ... motioning us to get off ... her face all knotted up ... shouting something we couldn't hear over the roar of the engines. Fredi grabbed my hand. We bolted out of our seats, down the aisle of the coach, and down the two steep steps to the platform, just as the train picked up its pace and sped off down the tracks.

"What happened?" Fredi shouted, breathless.

"They've closed the border." Mama stood on the platform, looking like a whipped dog. "Papa found out about it and telegraphed every station we passed since we left Vienna. If we'd stayed on that train and tried to cross the border with our passports stamped with their red *J*'s, they'd have known we were Jewish. We'd have been arrested then and there. That would have been the end of us." Mama's face was a mesh of lines. "We have to re-route, take a train to the Baltic Sea, then a boat to Lithuania."

"*Gott im Himmel!*" Fredi's eyes were round circles, his mouth wide open.

I stood on the platform and watched the train roll out of the station. "Mama, Mama, we might be off the train, but our clothes aren't. What are we going to wear?" We all turned to watch the train pick up speed and pass us by when, off in the distance, we saw a suitcase fly out of a window.

Mama said, "The other passengers must have figured out we weren't able to stay on the train. How nice of them to help us like this."

"Sure," Fredi snapped. "'Nice' because they haven't seen the *J* on our passports."

"Never mind," Mama said. "Here comes another suitcase."

After picking up all three of our suitcases, we saw what looked like a sparrow fly out of the window.

"*Ach, mein Gott!*" Mama said. "That's my other shoe."

I looked in the direction of Mama's shoe and shouted, "Look! Look!" I pulled on her sleeve and pointed to a speck in the horizon. "And here comes your other slipper!"

The Border Crossing

We took a bus to a port on the Baltic Sea and boarded a boat to Memel. The whole time we were at sea, Mama was mad at me. Whenever anyone would speak to me and remark how cute I was, or ask me questions, she'd grab my arm and yank me away, saying that I shouldn't talk to strangers and tell them things. I didn't know which of the things I knew were so dangerous that I needed to keep them secret. I'd learned in Vienna that it wasn't good to be Jewish and now, on the way to Memel, I'd learned it was better to keep my mouth shut.

When our boat arrived in Memel, Papa was waiting for us at the dock. The three of us walked down the gangplank wearing our coats, the ones that wouldn't have fit into our suitcases. I wanted to be the first one to get to Papa, but my suitcase was so heavy that I couldn't get to him fast enough. Besides, Papa went straight for Mama and put his arms around her. Mama kissed him, and then her head fell against his chest, as if it were too heavy to hold up. Her fedora slid up on her forehead as she dug her face into his chest and started to cry. I didn't know why she was crying, when I was happy to see Papa. He just held her, crying, for a long time without saying anything. I stood beside them, wishing he was holding me instead of Mama.

"At last we're together," Papa said, looking down into Mama's face. "Whatever happens now, at least we're together."

Papa picked me up and kissed me. He kissed Fredi too, even though Fredi was almost as tall as Papa and too old to be kissed. The whole time we were hugging and kissing and crying, a tall, thin man with a bend in his back like the top of a walking cane, watched us.

"This is Herr Lehman," Papa finally said, moving us toward him. "Herr Lehman helped me get your visas to Lithuania. He's made arrangements for our stay here and I hope he'll be able to help us move on as well." Papa gave Herr Lehman a look, and then turned to us. "You see, the visas I was able to get for you are only good for a month."

We shook hands with Herr Lehman, whose face was as long and thin as his body. Then he walked us toward a car which, to me, was a large moving toy—a shiny, black box with four doors and four white tires. I was excited to ride in it since I'd never been in a car before. Only rich people had cars in Vienna, and we weren't rich. After putting our suitcases into the trunk, Papa got into the front seat with Herr Lehman and rest of us got into the back.

Herr Lehman started the motor with a grinding roar, moved the stick in the middle of the floorboard into place, and threw us all back against our seats as the car shot down the street. This ride, however, was different from any I'd had before. It wasn't slow and smooth like the miniature train at the Prater. It didn't roll gently from side to side, like the trolley on Austellungstrasse. This black box threw us around in every direction like dice in a cup.

After driving a few blocks, my stomach clamped down on itself. I felt as if I'd eaten too many of Mama's sweet butterhorns. A hot layer of sweat covered my skin. The car screeched to a stop and, as my head was thrust forward, I emptied the contents of my stomach onto my lap.

"*Ach, mein Gott!* She's sick," Mama shouted. Herr Lehman pulled over to the side of the road and Mama took a handkerchief out of her purse and cleaned me up.

When she was done, Papa said, "The apartment isn't far from here. I'll walk home with Illy." The instant I stepped out of the car, I felt better. At the apartment, we followed Herr Lehman's curved back up two flights of stairs to the third floor, walked a short distance down a dark, carpeted hallway, and rang the doorbell. A short, plump woman with puffy cheeks the color of peaches answered the door. I didn't know what this round-faced person was doing in Papa's apartment, but it didn't take long before I learned the apartment wasn't Papa's—it belonged to Frau Schiff.

We carried our suitcases into a small room with two narrow beds, two cots, and not much else, other than two small end tables. There was no space for anything else. We shoved our suitcases under the beds, sat down, and told Papa about our trip. He laughed when we told him about Mama's shoe and slipper flying out the train window.

But he didn't think it was funny when Mama told him how bad I'd behaved on the boat—never sitting still, talking to complete strangers, and wandering off so that she didn't know where I was. Fredi said I acted like that because of all the terrible things that were happening to us. Then he called me a baby and I got mad, so I pushed him down on the bed.

"See?" Fredi said. And then Papa yelled at him.

We spent most of our time in Frau Schiff's living room, which was as dark as everyone's mood. A black leather couch and two forest-green stuffed chairs hugged two walls, facing one another. A set of chocolate-stained, wooden chairs circled the dining table. That's where I sat, turning the pages of a picture book, just like I had done in our living room in Vienna. Papa sat in one of the chairs next to Frau Schiff's radio, a dark brown, wooden box with curtained cutouts and a curved top.

"Hitler's taken the Sudetenland!" he said, his face pale. We'd been in Lithuania only a few days.

"It won't be long before he'll take the rest of Czechoslovakia," Frau Schiff said, her puffy cheeks quivering.

"Of course. He won't be satisfied with only Austria and Czechoslovakia. He wants all of Europe," Papa said. "Who knows where he'll go next."

"Is he coming here, Mama?" I asked, turning a page of my picture book.

"God forbid!" Mama said.

"He'll be here sooner or later, and we'd better be gone before then." Papa started pacing, his hands clasped behind his back.

"What are we going to do?" Mama's voice was high.

"We can't do anything without Herr Lehman. We're completely dependent on the Jewish community. We'll have to wait until he can help us," Papa said.

I couldn't understand anyone telling Papa what to do. It was supposed to be Papa telling everyone else what to do, how to act, what to think. Ever since those Nazi soldiers marched down my street in Vienna, nothing was the same. Herr Lehman came to the apartment the next day, and everyone sat in their same chairs—Papa next to the radio in shirt sleeves rolled up to the elbow, Mama in the stuffed chair with a forehead lined with worry, and Fredi and me at the table.

"You heard the news about Sudetenland?" Herr Lehman sat down on a wooden dining chair facing us. He leaned forward with his elbows resting on his knees, his fingers interlaced between his legs.

"Of course," Papa said. "We should get out of Memel as soon as possible." Papa's hands grasped his knees. I saw his knuckles turn white.

"I know that. We all have to get out." Herr Lehman sat up and rested his rounded back against the chair.

"Can I go with Papa this time?" I asked.

"Will you keep this child quiet?" Papa looked at Mama as if she were the one who'd spoken. Mama took my hand and led me to our room, the dormitory with four beds.

"Stay here and be quiet!" she said, squinting. "Your toys and books are under the bed." She left me alone in the room, shutting the door behind her. I didn't know why she was angry again.

Herr Lehman came back every day after that, but I always had to stay in our bedroom when he came. When I complained, Mama made Fredi stay with me. Then Fredi got mad because he wanted to know what Herr Lehman had to say. Poor Fredi. He was old enough to be able to keep his mouth shut, but he was saddled with taking care of me.

One time when Fredi opened the door to go to the toilet, I heard Mama say, "It's impossible. We can't take her in a car for such a long time. She gets terribly carsick." The door slammed shut and I couldn't hear anymore. I went back to writing the letters of the alphabet on a tablet. Fredi had been trying to teach me to read and write, which he liked doing better than playing with me and getting into a fight.

We hadn't been with Frau Schiff very many days when Mama woke me in the middle of the night and, in a hushed voice, said, "Get up, Illy. Get dressed."

"But ... it's nighttime," I said, blinking sleep from my eyes.

"We know that already, dummy." Fredi said, buttoning his shirt. "We're leaving." Mama pulled my nightgown over my head and slipped my arms into a dress. Our suitcases were on the beds, packed and ready to be closed. Papa was tying his shoes.

"Where are we going?" I said.

"You ask too many questions. Just get dressed." Papa replied, in a voice that frightened me.

We met Frau Schiff in the living room. She held Mama's hands and pumped them up and down and kept saying, "Good luck, Frau Fell, good luck." Then she handed Mama six big white towels, neatly folded into a stack. I didn't dare say, "What are those towels for?" We made our way down the two flights of stairs as if we'd robbed the apartment, wearing our coats and carrying our suitcases. Herr Lehman was waiting for us next to his car. Papa got into the seat next to him, and the rest of us climbed into the back, with me in the middle seat.

"Where are we going?" I whispered to Fredi, hoping Papa wouldn't hear.

"Shush!" Mama jerked my arm. "Keep your mouth shut."

"Not a sound out of you—do you hear?" Papa looked at me, his eyes like daggers. This time, both Mama and Papa were angry with me, and I was scared.

We drove down the street, and the car started to bounce and lurch. It wasn't long before I felt as if I'd eaten too much again. Mama was ready this time. When she heard my first burp, she draped a towel over her arms and held it under my chin. I obliged her with my first offering of slimy, greenish vomit. A foul odor filled the car. Several bumps and lurches later, my stomach emptied again. My face felt hot; sweat covered my forehead. After my stomach was empty, I kept on retching, my body in uncontrollable spasms. While Mama was busy keeping towels under my chin, everyone remained silent. Herr Lehman finally stopped the car and turned around to face us.

"Put the children down on the floor. We're almost at the border. It'll be easier if they only see two of us. And don't make a sound! Not … a … sound."

Mama bent over so that her head was below the back of Papa's seat. Fredi slid off the seat onto the floor, leaned against the door, clasped his knees with his arms, and dropped his head forward so that it would be below the window. I sat on the other side by Mama's feet, mimicking Fredi's position. The smelly wet towels, full of my sickness, lay on the floor between us.

The car stopped and Herr Lehman got out, slamming the door shut. We were engulfed in silence, in darkness, in stench, and in fear. Time passed, and passed, and passed. Herr Lehman did not return. It was as if we'd been frozen stiff in our places. More time passed. My legs began to ache, but I was too scared to say a word.

After what seemed like forever, we heard footsteps. Herr Lehman opened the car door, sat down behind the steering wheel, and drove off. Still, no one moved or said a word. He drove a short while before saying, "You can sit up now. We've just crossed the border into Latvia. It won't be long before we'll be in Riga."

"*Gott sei Dank!*" Mama said, placing a clean towel under my chin.

Herr Lehman said, "It took a little longer this time to get the guards drunk. Luckily, there's no shortage of slivovitz in this country. The trouble is, they raise their price every time we try to smuggle anyone across the border. It not only takes more money, but more time to bargain out the price before they agree to let us pass into Latvia." Herr Lehman looked at Papa and smiled. "But I was prepared. We've learned how to do business with these people."

"We can't thank you enough." Papa said, breathing deeply, as if he'd been running for fifty kilometers. "I only wish that I could repay you in some way for all you've done for us."

"I know that's impossible," Herr Lehman said. "All the payment I need would be to know that at least some of us will survive this terrible threat."

Our car sped on in the blackness of night and I began to feel like I'd eaten too much again. Whispering to Mama, I said, "How much further is it to Riga?"

What Happened to Opa?

Our apartment in Riga was nothing like the one in Memel. The living room walls were painted the color of green pea soup, and not a single picture hung on the walls. A scratchy beige couch sat on a floor covered with brown linoleum squares, inlaid with yellow flowers. A table and several spindly wooden chairs added to the boring, dark feeling of the room. The only halfway bright objects to be seen were the many green glass ash trays. But the apartment had two bedrooms, so we wouldn't all be squashed together in one room, and it was *our* apartment—with no Frau Schiff.

Tante Dora and Onkel Max were in Riga with us. I didn't know how they got there or why my other aunts and uncles weren't there. A letter from Oma and Opa told us that the others had run out of Vienna in all different directions. Onkel Ignatz walked through the Alps into Switzerland. Onkel David and his family did the same thing, except for my ten year old cousin who'd been placed in an orphanage in France to save his life. And Onkel Jacob managed to cross the border into Belgium and then into England, where he joined the RAF(Royal Air Force) to fight the Nazis. We were stuck with Tante Dora and Onkel Max in Riga.

I heard Mama say, "Why couldn't it have been David or Jack that made it here instead of Max and Dora?" I wished it could have been Onkel Jacob—he wasn't married and treated me like I was his own child. He'd lift me up and swing me around, until I got dizzy and begged him to stop.

Onkel Max may not have been our favorite, but Mama was happy to have at least one of her brothers with her. And since he was married to Papa's sister Dora, Papa had one of his two sisters with him, too … the wrong one. He wished it could have been Tante Nelly, who was the most beautiful person in our whole family, with hair the color of buttercups and ink blue eyes. Everyone liked her—even Tante Dora, who didn't like anybody.

And no one liked Tante Dora. Her head was as round as a ball and her body looked like a stuffed sausage. She and Papa fought like cats and dogs from the moment they were born. When they got into trouble with their parents, Tante Dora would blame Papa for everything, and then he'd catch it for both of them.

Papa said she might be grown up now, but she hadn't changed a bit. "She still lies and cheats and fights like a tiger. She's just plain crazy." Mama just shook her head and said, "Poor Max."

When they came to our apartment to visit, Onkel Max would puff away on his cigarettes, squinting against the gray cloud of smoke that curled past his eyes, and then burst into a fit of coughing. Papa said he shouldn't be smoking, because of the asthma he got in Siberia when he was taken prisoner in the First World War. Tante Dora stuck her nose in the air as if she were the Empress Maria Theresa and said, "What's the use telling him anything. He doesn't listen to any-one."

Herr Berman looked after us in Riga. He was a short man with ears that stuck out like an elephant's. Every time he came to the apartment, Mama made coffee, and then asked if he'd gotten our visas yet.

"No," he answered, "not yet. I'm doing everything I can. I'm trying to get people to Palestine. And there may be a possibility to get some visas for Buenos Aires."

"Any place," Papa said. "Any place. Terrible things are happening to Jews in Europe. People are disappearing left and right. It won't be long before Hitler takes Latvia."

"I know," Herr Berman said, looking at the floor and shaking his head. "But there is nothing I can do."

Most of the time, Papa sat at the end of the scratchy couch next to the radio, his elbow on the doily armrest and a fist under his chin, listening to the news.

"Papa, aren't you going to be a doctor here in Riga?" I asked.

"No, Suzi." He went back to listening to the radio.

"Why not?"

He glanced at me for a second. "They won't let me."

"Is Onkel Max going to work?"

"No." Papa kept listening.

"Why not?"

"He can't work here either." Papa turned his face to me, looking annoyed. "None of us can work here. Now don't ask so many questions."

I walked to the window, pushed the lace curtain aside, and looked down. On the sidewalk below, streetlights that looked like giant black candles lined the street. Summer had ended and fall had started, so that everyone already wore winter coats with scarves around their necks. I turned to Fredi and said, "Let's go outside. Let's go to the park."

Fredi was reading a book at our table, and before I could get another word out, he looked up and said, "I don't want to go to the park. Go play by yourself." He ducked his head into his book again. I went into the kitchen and found Mama with tears streaming down her cheeks from chopping onions for goulash. "Can we go to the park?"

Mama stopped working, her hands red from the onions' biting juices. She stuck her head into the living room and said, "Fredi, take her to the park for a little while."

"Do I have to, Mama?" Fredi looked at me as if I were a rotten apple.

"Please Fredi—do it for me. Don't you want to make your Mama happy?"

Papa turned to look at Mama and ground his teeth back and forth, as if to control the words on his tongue. He said nothing as he watched Fredi take me for our walk.

I liked being outside, either in the park or on the streets where the buildings were decorated in all sorts of different ways. Statues of people stood on columns and straddled the sides of doorways. Sometimes, leaves on vines hung over the arched tops of windows. My favorite was the building with beige-colored squares and rectangles—they reminded me of the building blocks I had as a baby. I wished Fredi had as much fun as I did being outside.

When we returned, Tante Dora and Onkel Max were in the living room having coffee. Even though we were no longer in Vienna, we still had a *youse* every afternoon at four o'clock. Tante Dora brought a *Kugelhupf* with powdered sugar that looked like a dusting of snow.

Mama passed slices of cake to everyone but when she came to Onkel Max, he shook his head and lit another cigarette. Papa didn't eat his cake either, putting the plate down on the table. The room was quiet, the rest of us eating. Then Papa got up and walked to the window, clasped his hands behind his back, and said, "Max, tell her. We have to tell her sometime."

Onkel Max leaned forward in his chair, his elbows on his knees, and drew deeply on his cigarette. He sat up, leaned against the back of his chair, and blew a long funnel of smoke into the room. It hung in the air like a heavy fog. We all looked at Onkel Max, but he didn't say anything. Then he looked at Mama and said, "You heard what happened? You heard about *Kristallnacht?*"

"Of course," Mama said. "Our radio's on all the time. Such terrible things are happening—the Nazis breaking windows of Jewish stores and synagogues, vandalizing our homes, burning our books." She hung her head forward, shaking it from side to side. "It's just as bad as the pogroms in Poland were—maybe worse."

It was silent in the room before I whispered to Fredi, "Why are the Nazis doing that?"

"Shut up!" Fredi whispered back. But it was too late. Papa heard us and looked at me with cold eyes. I froze in my chair, mute. Papa turned to Onkel Max and said, "Tell her."

"It's our father, Jenny." Onkel Max looked at Mama. "They picked him up on *Kristallnacht*."

"What?" Mama shouted, her face stiff. She stood up, walked over to Onkel Max, and bent over him with her hands between her legs. "What?"

"They've killed him." Onkel Max choked before repeating, "They've killed our father."

"How do you know? Maybe they just picked him up. Maybe they've just taken him somewhere. Maybe he's in jail. How do you know they've killed him?" Mama's face was as lined as a prune. Her voice grew louder with each thing she said, her arms pumping up and down.

"Our mother knows for sure, Jenny. When he disappeared, she went to their offices and asked about him. They turned her away each time she went until they finally told her that if she wanted him so badly, she could buy his ashes. They even told her how much she'd have to pay to get the ashes." Onkel Max looked up at Mama, his face full of pain.

"*Nei-ei-ei-ein!*" Mama stood in the middle of the room, her hand on her forehead, and screamed, "*Nei-ei-ei-ein!*" Papa left his place by the window, wrapped his arms around her shoulders, and held her while she wailed.

I felt a stone in my throat and turned to Fredi, whispering, "What happened to Opa? Does that mean we won't ever see him again?"

"Get that child out of here!" Papa shouted. "Both of you—out!"

Fredi grabbed my arm and pulled me into our bedroom and sat me down on my bed. Fredi's eyes looked like puddles. He said, "None of us are ever going to see Opa again."

Opa! Opa coming to our apartment in Vienna every day ... Opa playing chess with me and letting me win every time ... Opa with his pushed out jaw and short gray whiskers ... Opa with the corners of his mouth turned up, pushing lines around his chocolate-ball eyes ... Opa, who'd lift me onto his lap and tell me it's time to pee and go to bed. Opa was gone. I hung my head, my eyes a waterfall of tears.

Bye, Fredi

After Opa's death, winter came to Riga. It was nothing like any of us had ever been through before. Winds cold as steel swept in from the Baltic Sea and stormed into the city. When we were outside, our cheeks felt like they were being bombarded by sharp needles. We bundled up in layers, using almost all the clothes we brought with us from Vienna.

Except for the swishing sound of Mama's slippers sliding along the floor, our apartment was as quiet as a cemetery. She hardly spoke, just did her cooking and baking and cleaning like a machine. Sometimes she sent Fredi and me to the store for food. That's where I learned to speak Latvian and soon understood more than anyone else in my family. Mama or Papa would smile and call me *Gescheite*. For them, being smart was just as good as being pretty and well behaved, maybe even better.

The cold in Riga was not only outside our apartment—it was freezing inside as well. Mama was right about having taken our winter coats with us in August when it was so hot. We were glad to have them in Riga and often wore them inside our apartment. On one such day, Papa sat on our prickly couch with his head bent over like a wilting flower, his ear next to the radio. He looked up at us and shouted, "The Nazis have taken Memel."

Mama dropped her knitting needles and grabbed her armrests. "They could be Riga in a few hours."

"I know," Papa said, before walking over to the window with his hands clasped behind his back—a sure sign that he was at his highest level of nervousness.

I went to his side, took hold of his and, looking at him, said, "Maybe they'll get as sick as me coming here, and they'll have to go back to Memel."

Mama and Papa smiled. I didn't know what was so funny.

The icy, dark days of winter gradually gave up their hold on us—stuck in Riga—needing to run—and having no place to go. Mounds of snow, pushed to the side of the streets, turned into grayish slush full of dirt and soot. The winds lost their punch, and we no longer had to walk down the street, slanting forward against the winds. We came out of our apartments, like sleeping bears coming out of their dens in spring.

My favorite place in Riga was the city park with its green lawns and trees. I couldn't wait until the trees spread their canopy of leaves overhead, and the bronze cherubs in the fountains splashed water from their smiling faces. It was March 1939, and Fredi and I went to watch the gardeners in their ink blue coveralls get the flower-beds ready for spring planting. It would not be long before they'd be ablaze with yellow marigolds and red tulips. The park was much more fun than our apartment, where Mama and Papa wore sad faces, and the radio brought only bad news.

"We'd better get home," Fredi said. "It's almost time for dinner." He started walking ahead of me.

"Wait! Can't we stay a little longer?" I yelled at his back, without taking another step.

"*Nein*, we can't." Fredi walked back and grabbed my hand. "Why can't you do what I say?" He yanked me forward, and I stumbled along, being pulled as if I were a puppy on a leash.

"Good night! When are you going to grow up?" Fredi mumbled under his breath, shaking his head.

When we got home, we found Papa standing by a lamp, reading a letter under its light. Mama stood behind him with her fists on her hips—her arms forming a perfect triangle.

"It's a letter from Gretl," she said. "Sit down and be quiet."

Papa read, "She says it isn't safe for any Jew to be in Vienna now. We'd be in great danger if the Nazis came to Riga. She knows about Opa." Papa read a bit more. "She says we must get out of Riga." Papa swung the letter to his side and said, "How stupid—as if we didn't know that already."

"Don't get so excited," Mama said. Two creases appeared between her eyebrows. "Just read the rest of the letter. What else does she say?"

"She says she has an aunt in America."

"I know. Actually, it's Leo's aunt. I met her once when she visited them in Vienna. I think her name is Lotte. But what's that got to do with us?"

"She says she's written a letter to her, asking her to help us."

"What good does that do us? She's only a maid, she has no money. How can she afford to sign an affidavit saying she'd support us for five years, in case we couldn't support ourselves—a family of four yet? It's ridiculous. She's barely supporting herself." Mama paced back and forth, just like Papa did when he was nervous. "Gretl means well, but she's wasting her time."

"Gretl's a good-hearted person—but she's also a little crazy," Papa said. "You know how she'd always have aches and pains for no reason at all. And how about the time she couldn't walk—the time she sat in a chair for a month, as if she was paralyzed?"

"*Ja,* but she really couldn't walk," Mama said.

"But there was nothing wrong with her. It was all in her head. She's like those crazy people who're in a wheelchair and go to some religious shrine. All of a sudden, they can walk again. Those people are crazy. Doctors know about them. They're hysterics. We don't pay any attention to their complaints."

"I don't care what she is, Papa. I like her, and look how she's trying to help us. Anyway, we don't need Lotte's money. We can work and support ourselves," Fredi said.

"We can all work, Papa," I said. "I can bake cookies just as good as Betti, and we could sell them."

"I know, Fredi," Papa said, ignoring me, "but the law says Lotte would have to support us in case we couldn't support ourselves."

"She's just a maid, Fredi," Mama said, raising her shoulders to her ears, her palms facing the ceiling.

Papa folded the letter and put it back into the envelope, as if to close the door on hope.

We continued our routine—Papa parked by the radio, Mama silently cooking in the kitchen or knitting in her chair, and Fredi and I going for walks in the park or shopping for groceries. At home, Fredi tried to teach me to read and write, happy to call me "dummy" every chance he got.

"You are so dumb. How many times do I have to tell you that you write a 'd' like a backward 'b'?" he said, writing the letters down for me yet again.

"I wish I could go to school," I said. My elbows were on the table, the heels of my hands under my chin holding my head up. "If we were in Vienna, I'd be in the first grade already." I tried to print a "d" on my lined tablet.

"But you're not in Vienna. You're in Riga and the kids here don't start school until they're eight. And you're still a baby, nowhere near eight." Fredi rocked his yellow pencil between two fingers, tapping the table like a woodpecker.

"I don't know why you think you're so smart. You're not going to school either."

"That's because none of us refugees are allowed to go to school, dummy. The Latvians don't want to spend one *Groshen* on us." Fredi put the pencil down, as if to tell me our lesson was over. "It's the same reason they won't let Papa work. They don't want him to take any work away from their own doctors."

"But Papa still takes care of sick people. I heard him tell Frau Schneider what to take for her stomach flu." I dropped my hands from my chin and sat up straight.

"Will you be quiet?" Fredi shouted, glaring at me. "Papa only takes care of other refugees. And you're not supposed to say anything, in case somebody hears you. How many times do we have to tell you to keep your mouth shut?"

"I only said it to you, Fredi. I didn't say it to anybody else. Nobody could hear." I felt my chin quiver as I thought about how dumb I'd been to say anything, even to Fredi. Then I remembered, "Don't tell Papa."

"So don't do it again."

Papa had his ear next to the radio, a cup of coffee, almost white with cream, in his hand. Mama came in the room carrying a plate of warm *Palatschinken*.

"Yum! Mama, can I have some?" I said, coming to look at the thin crepes filled with strawberry jam, dusted with powdered sugar. I liked licking the white mustache off my lip after I'd taken a bite.

"Quiet!" Papa shouted from his place on the couch, waving his hand up and down to silence us. "Hitler's taken Czechoslovakia!"

"And here we sit. Waiting, and waiting, and waiting, for God-only-knows what." Mama sank into her chair, as if she'd lost the strength to stand. "We're finished."

"I don't know what more we can do," Papa said. "The only thing I can do is call Herr Berman again." He stood up, clasped his hands behind his back, and stood by the window. He didn't say another word. None of us ate any of Mama's *Palatschinken*.

Two weeks later Papa came into the apartment carrying a letter from Gretl. It was morning, and Mama hadn't gotten dressed yet. She was in her pink housecoat, dusting the furniture with a soft, gold dustcloth, leaning over to get at the green glass ashtray on Papa's end table. When she saw Papa with the letter, she stood straight up, whirled around to face him, and said, "Open it. Hurry. Open it already. What does she say?"

Papa opened the letter with his thumb and read silently.

"Well?" Mama said.

"What does she say, Papa?" I said. "Does Hans know how to read yet?"

"She writes that she received a letter from her Aunt Lotte telling her the same thing we said all along, 'she has no money'."

"What else does she say?" Mama said, stretching her hand out to look at the letter.

Papa pulled it away from her and said, "*Wart' eine Minute.*" Then, "She writes that Lotte will ask her boss, Mr. Elfenbein, to sign the papers for us. He's Jewish, like us. And he has money. He should do something to help his own people."

"*Ach ja,* but why should he?" Mama said. "He doesn't even know us. How does he know that we wouldn't be a stone around his neck for five years?"

"We wouldn't do that, Mama. We're not bums," Fredi said.

After that, one day followed another with all of us forced to go on waiting. The flower beds in the park blossomed and looked like fields of lemons and oranges. When they began to look like potatoes, Fredi and I watched the blue-clad gardeners replace them with a new rainbow of colors—red, pink, and white begonias.

That summer our apartment was as hot as the inside of Mama's oven. Even though our windows were open all day and all night, not a single breeze passed through. The heat helped to get us out of our apartment, so that we could discover the beach. The feel of powdery sand between my toes made me tingle all over. The roar of the sea was like a song that went up and down the scale, as wave after wave crashed onto the shore. I sat on the warm sand at the water's edge and waited for the bubbles to catch my toes, grab my ankles, and encircle my waist. When I walked into the welcoming sea as far as I could, Mama, Papa, and Fredi looked like small toy dolls back on the beach. This calm and peaceful place knew nothing about the war raging so close to us, or how frightened we all were.

We'd been in Riga a year when Herr Berman made one of his regular visits. Mama served iced coffee with a huge glob of whipped cream on top. They talked about the weather and how beastly hot it was, but I could tell by the way Papa's heels bounced up and down, and by the way Mama wrung her hands, that they wanted him to get around to talking about getting us out of Riga.

"I have good news today," he said. "We were able to get three visas to America—but they're only good for youngsters under eighteen years of age. I thought you would want one for your son, Alfred."

Mama and Papa's eyes locked onto one another, then onto Herr Berman. "But what about the rest of us?" Papa said.

"I don't have anything more. It was a miracle that we were able to get these three visas."

"But he's only fifteen-years-old. How can we send him off by himself like that?" Mama said.

"I'll go with him, Mama," I said. "I'm under eighteen, just like Fredi."

"*Ach*, be quiet now, will you?" Mama's face was pinched again.

"We don't know anyone in America. He'd be all by himself. And who knows if we'll ever be able to follow him," Papa said.

"He's only fifteen," Mama said again, trying to remind Herr Berman fifteen wasn't old enough to take care of oneself.

"I can't tell you what to do, but I'm sure you know Hitler has taken Poland, and sits in Memel deciding when to march into Latvia. It's dangerous for all of us here. If you get him out, at least you'll have saved one life," Herr Berman said.

Mama and Papa locked eyes again and said nothing. Mama's face looked like it did when she'd burned her hand on our kitchen stove. "Mama?" I said, going over to her side and taking hold of her hand. "If we don't go with Fredi, does that mean the rest of us are going to die, like Opa?"

"*Ach mein Gott*, Illy." Mama hoisted me onto her lap, brushed a few stray hairs off my face, and kissed my forehead. "*Nein*, Illy. *Nein*. Don't worry." She wrapped her arms around me and rocked from side to side.

"When do we have to give you our decision?" Papa said.

"I have to know by tomorrow morning," Herr Berman answered. "I only wish I had visas for all of you."

Fredi was scared to death to go off to America all by himself, without knowing a single soul, without speaking English, and not knowing if he'd ever see any of us again. Mama and Papa made him go. The day he boarded the ship, he was all dressed up in a navy blue, double-breasted suit, a white shirt, and gray sweater. He looked like someone who was going to a wedding, instead of a boy who was running for his life. He stood on deck and leaned over the railing, holding onto the rail so tight, that I imagined his knuckles must have turned white. A weak smile made its way across his face as he waved down to us standing on the dock.

There were about twelve of us refugees that came to see Fredi off. Everyone was dressed in their best clothes, even suits and hats, despite the August heat. Our blouses and shirts stuck to our skin, and shiny beads of water collected on our foreheads. Papa took off his jacket and hung it over his shoulders as if they were a coat hanger. When the boat pulled away, everyone smiled and waved, even Mama. She didn't cry. She said she didn't want Fredi to see how bad she felt. He'd have to be brave from now on.

"Be sure and write to us often." Mama shouted up to him, her hand at the side of her mouth.

"I will," Fredi said, without a smile.

"Be careful. Take good care of yourself," Papa shouted.

The boat started to pull away from the dock, and we all walked alongside as far as we could. I ran ahead and waved and screamed, "Bye, Fredi!"

When we couldn't see him anymore, we all stopped smiling and waving at the same time.

Mama took a handkerchief out of her purse and wiped away the tears that were now pouring out of her eyes. Papa took a long puff from his cigarette, looked down on the ground, and cleared his throat. I wondered who would play with me now, who would try to teach me the alphabet, who would call me dummy.

Mr. Elfenbein—A Stranger

My eighth birthday fell on a cloudless day in the middle of April, 1940. Papa was at his usual place by the radio. Mama, in a black dress patterned with yellow peonies, walked around the house with a long face filled with trouble. She always wore slippers inside—her bunions, big and red as cherries, hurt in every shoe she owned. Besides, she didn't need to get dressed up for the company coming to dinner this day—it was only Tante Dora and Onkel Max.

Mama came out of the kitchen carrying plain white plates, cups, and saucers. They were thick and heavy and chipped on the edges, not anything like the delicate, thin, almost see-through china we'd left behind in Vienna. She stacked them at the end of the table and said, "Bobi, why don't you go downstairs and see if there's any mail?"

"I'll go." I said. "Can I go?" I asked.

"Sure," Papa said. "Come right back."

I returned, waving a letter in my hand, and shouted, "We have mail. Who's it from?"

"It's from Gretl," Papa said, tearing into the envelope.

"Read it out loud." Mama sat down on the edge of a dining chair as Papa read:

My dear friends,

I received a letter from Lotte in America and she has spoken to her boss, a certain Mr. Louis Elfenbein, about you. She wrote that he is a rich Jewish banker, an older man with four grown sons. He told her he would consult with his sons. Unfortunately, after speaking to them, he decided against signing the affidavits for you. He even reproached Lotte for coming to him with such an unreasonable request. He asked her how she could even imagine that he would take on the financial responsibility of an entire family for five years, a family completely unknown to him. Lotte wrote that he was quite indignant and she hopes she won't lose her job over this.

My dear friends, I know that you would never be a burden to anyone. But I also know how much danger you are in. So I have already written a letter back to

Lotte telling her that she must find someone, anyone, to sign for you, or she will have to answer to Our Maker for the loss of your lives.

I hope you are all well and that I will have better news for you next time.

Alles Gute,

Gretl

"Of course," Mama said, raising her shoulders. "I didn't expect anything else." She returned to the kitchen.

"Are we going to America or not?" I asked Mama's back.

"I don't know, Illy," Mama said over her shoulder. "We don't know from one day to the next what's going to happen."

"I'll go see Mr. Berman again," Papa said. "The only visas he had the last time I saw him were to Buenos Aires." He took a deep breath and picked up his German newspaper.

"I won't go there," Mama said, turning back into the room and facing Papa. "I'll only go to America. How can we leave Fredi there all by himself and go anywhere else?"

The doorbell rang and I shouted, "They're here! Can we have cake now?"

Mama opened the door to see Tante Dora standing on the landing by herself. "Where's Max?" Mama asked.

"I don't know and I don't care. I'm getting a divorce." Tante Dora marched into the room and took off her hat and coat.

"What are you talking about?" Papa said. "You're talking crazy again."

"*Nein*—not this time. I have proof this time. I saw them together myself." She folded her arms at her waist.

"You saw who together?" Mama said.

"Max and Inga Kaplan. They're having an affair." Tante Dora arched her back and tucked in her chin into her chest. "I have proof. I saw them myself."

"Mama, what's an affair?" I tilted my face up to hers.

"It's nothing, Illy, nothing. Just two people who are—good friends." Mama faced Tante Dora and said, "Max would never have an affair. Max—of all people—Max!" She shook her head back and forth, looking like she was trying to stop laughing. "He can hardly breathe after all those years in Siberia, let alone have an affair."

35

The doorbell rang, and Onkel Max came in holding a lit cigarette cupped in his hand. He lifted his hat off his bald head and tossed it into a chair. "She's gone crazy again. You wouldn't believe what she's done this time."

"I'm not crazy," Tante Dora shouted. "I saw you myself."

"Stop it, you two." Papa jumped to his feet and stood in the middle of the room. "Here we sit in Riga, with Hitler at our heels, and you two do nothing but fight. Who knows if we'll be able to come out of this alive, and you have nothing else on your mind, except affairs!" Papa paced back and forth, thrusting his right hand up in the air.

"It's not on *my* mind," Onkel Max said, pointing a thumb at himself. "It's on *hers*." His hand flipped over to point to Tante Dora. "And to top it all off, she embarrasses me by letting the whole world know just how crazy she is."

"Why? What did she do?" Mama said.

"I'll tell you what she did. I was coming home from the store when I saw Inga Kaplan in front of our apartment, coming from the opposite direction. We greeted each other and stopped to chat. All of a sudden, Dora opens the window upstairs, sticks her head out, and yells down to us that she knows what's going on between us. Can you imagine? I was so embarrassed."

"What was going on between them, Mama?" I said.

"Nothing, Illy, nothing." Mama said. Then she looked at Tante Dora and said, "How can you think such a thing … about Max … of all people … Max …" Mama shook her head. Papa laughed out loud.

"What's so funny, Mama?"

"Nothing, Illy," Mama said, and then started laughing with Papa.

"I don't want to hear another word about all this nonsense," Papa said. "Now, how about having some coffee and cake? After all, it's Illy's birthday, and there must be a present around here somewhere."

Mama and Papa had no money for presents. The Jewish community charity gave us money only for essentials. Mama bought fabric to sew larger clothes for me. I was outgrowing everything we'd brought from Vienna. Papa bought me picture books, including one in English, about two white rabbits. I didn't know how to read and didn't understand English, but Papa said he'd translate for me. He'd bought a German-English dictionary and had started to teach himself the language. In case we ever made it to America, he said, he'd be ready, and not have to go through what poor Fredi had to do when he landed in New York—learn English overnight.

Fredi had written us several times. The HIAS (Hebrew Immigrant Aid Society) moved him to Poughkeepsie, where he lived with a Jewish farmer. He wrote that the farmer's family ignored him and treated him like a hired hand working for room and board. He did learn English, however, and was going to high school—where his classmates made fun of him just as they'd done in Vienna.

I wanted Papa to take over Fredi's job of teaching me to read and write, but his heart wasn't in it. Not that Fredi's had been either. Papa thought I could learn to read later, like Mama had done when she left Poland and came to Vienna as a twelve-year-old. They thought I could do the same thing when we got to wherever we were going.

After my birthday, it was Papa who took me on walks to the park instead of Fredi. It would have been like old times in Vienna, except there were no squirrels to feed, no waltz music to hear, and no Ferris wheel to ride. In June we saw barren tree branches push out their first tender yellow green leaves. And we watched the gardeners, looking like a flock of blue jays, plant a new spray of color—this time pink, purple, and red petunias.

One day Papa and I heard a roar in the distance and felt the ground tremble under our feet. Papa groped for my hand and said, "Let's get home!" He walked so fast that I had to run at his side to keep up with him. We reached the big iron arch at the entry to the park and Papa looked down the street to see what was causing the roar, loud as thunder.

"It's the Russians!" Papa said, taking a deep breath. "Thank God it's the Russians and not the Germans." Papa held my hand as soldiers in baggy, olive green uniforms passed by. Others joined us along the sidewalk, but there was no waving or cheering.

"Papa, shouldn't we run home and stay inside now, like we did when Hitler came to Vienna?" I asked.

"No, Illy, the Russians don't mean to kill us. They're too busy fighting Hitler to have time for killing Jews," Papa said.

Nothing changed for us after the Russians came. Mama and Papa were still sick about not being able to go to America. Papa kept going to an office inside one of those decorated buildings—but nothing changed. I liked having the Russians there. Even though they wore drab uniforms, they sang catchy, melodic songs at the park's outdoor theater. And they danced, stomping their feet and clapping their hands. Lots of townspeople came to watch and clap along with the music. The dance I liked best was called the Koro Boushka. When I tried to do it myself—hands on my waist, bouncing down on one heel while kicking the other foot straight out—everyone laughed.

Papa and I came home from the park one day and found Mama at the door, wide-eyed. "You won't believe it!" She waved a letter in the air. "It's from Gretl. Mr. Elfenbein signed the affidavits."

"What?" Papa's jaw dropped. "I don't believe it. Show me the letter." Papa snatched the letter out of Mama's hand. He bent his head over the page, eyes flying over the script, hands shaking, the letter trembling like a leaf. "Can you imagine … she says Lotte wouldn't leave his house until he signed the affidavit. She told him a Jew should be the first one to understand what danger we're in." Papa placed his hand on his forehead. "I still can't believe it's true!" Papa fell into a chair by the table and looked at Mama. "Now all we need is for the Russians to grant us visas."

"They have to give us visas, don't they?" Mama's face was pinched again.

"They don't have to do anything. They're in control—they can do whatever they want. I know they need doctors to take care of their troops. I hope they'll let me go."

"So are we going to America or not, Papa?" I asked.

"We'll see." Papa said, reading the letter again. "We have all the right papers now, but in times like these, who knows?"

Waiting at the Train Station

We were the only ones on the platform. Even though it was only eleven o'clock in the morning, it was already steamy hot on that day in August. I wore one of my old dirndl dresses from Vienna, one that still fit, though I was already eight. Mama had a habit of making clothes too big for me so that I could grow into them. It turned out to be a good idea.

Three months had passed since the Russians marched into Riga and all that time, Papa had tried to get them to sign our papers, giving us permission to leave for America. Papa had spent half the night before at the Russian military head-quarters trying to get our visas. He'd argued and reasoned and even begged, tell-ing them about Fredi in America all by himself. But he went home empty-handed. They told him, "Just go to the train station and wait. That's all. Dis-missed!"

We arrived at the station two hours before our train was due to be there—without our papers. The three of us stood next to our scuffed, brown leather suitcases, each belted with two straps. Mama sat on her suitcase, a silent figure of gloom. I couldn't remember the last time she'd smiled or laughed. She only cried these days, and cried often. When I saw how much she missed Fredi, I could see how much she loved him. I wondered if she loved me half as much. No—I knew she loved him more. Lucky for me, I had Papa, who I knew was more mine than Fredi's.

Now Mama sat with her arms folded at her waist, her eyes locked onto some spot on the dusty cement in front of her. She seemed to see nothing, as if her mind was someplace else. She'd lost so much weight, her dark print dress hung loose from her shoulders like a window drape. She wore no makeup except for a little lipstick, a thin red hyphen across her face below two gray half-circles under her eyes.

Papa paced back and forth, his hands clasped behind his back, his eyes sweep-ing from left to right like searchlights at a prison. He was looking, hunting, searching for anyone in uniform who might have our passports. Sometimes, he stopped by Mama, shoved his brown fedora back on his forehead, rocked up and down on his toes, and then went back to pacing.

I walked a crack in the cement, one foot in front of the other, heel to toe, my blue dirndl skirt tented out with every gust of wind that swept by. Bored with that game, I sat down on my suitcase and played with its straps, unbuckling, buckling, unbuckling.

Mama pulled my hands away from the belt and barked, "Will you please leave that alone!" I stopped, bent over with my elbows on my knees, pulled a pigtail over my shoulder, and sucked its tip. "*Ach,* Illy, don't do that. *Im Gottes Willen,* can't you sit still?" she yanked the hair out of my mouth.

I sighed. After a few minutes, I said, "I'm thirsty."

"Will you stop it? Can't you see there's no water here? You just have to wait!"

I knew I'd have to wait, as we all had to wait. I had to wait to go to school. I had to wait to play with others ... wait to have friends ... wait to see Fredi. Mama waited to have a home, waited to care for her family. Papa waited to work and earn money, waited to support his family. Wait. Wait. Wait. We'd been waiting in Riga for two years.

The platform began to fill with people—couples, families, singles—all holding onto as many suitcases, string bags, and brown paper boxes as they could carry. Soldiers appeared in pairs, their dull green uniforms decorated with bright red stripes. With high cheekbones and eyes tilted up at the corners, they looked like playful elves—except for the missing smiles on their faces. They paraded back and forth, in step with each another. As each pair came near us, Papa stopped pacing, his arms rigid at his sides, like a soldier at attention. I ran to his side and stood next to him, waiting for one of them to approach us. Each time they passed by, I heard a frustrated, "Damn!"

"Papa, what'll we do if they never come?" I asked.

"They have to come, or ..." He didn't finish his thought. He looked worried—it frightened me. I went to Mama's side, sat down next to her, and took her hand.

We heard a long, sharp blow from the train's horn in the distance, then a rhythmic *shrump ... shrump ... shrump* from its wheels. A monstrous gray engine pulled into the station, its broad windows like huge black eyes. A headlight in the center of the engine's face lit the way ahead, while the protruding sweep of an iron grate above the tracks seemed like the devouring teeth of a beastly mouth. It was a frightening sight, but we welcomed it, wanting to be swallowed up by its mouth. We wanted to be safely inside the belly of that monster train headed for Moscow.

A long line of coaches followed, sliding into the station with a cloud of smoke shooting out from under their wheels. The train stopped with a sputter, a scrape, and a final lurch. The waiting throng, papers in hand, lined up quickly. A pair of soldiers studied their documents before allowing any one of them to climb aboard.

"Come on. Let's go," I said, knowing we'd have to be on that train or we'd never see Fredi again.

"Illy, you don't understand. We can't get on unless we have our passports and visas. We don't have them yet. Now will you please sit down and be quiet?"

Papa stood next to us by the suitcases and lit another cigarette. The platform had emptied out of its horde of passengers, except for the soldiers manning the doors of the coaches. We were alone, standing next to our luggage, alone and left behind. There was no other sound except for the muffled remarks between the soldiers. Mama and Papa gave each other a look that said we'd lost our fight to join Fredi. My eyes welled up and I choked.

A cool breeze swept through the station, kicking up a few fallen leaves. The quiet was shattered as a uniformed military policeman threw open the door of the station building. His heavy boots stomped toward us, his face a cold, blank mask. With a gruff thrust of his hand, he flung an envelope at Papa and said, "Here are your papers. You can go."

Mischief on the Trans-Siberian Railway

We settled into our seats on the train and every stiff muscle in Mama's and Papa's bodies seemed to melt with relief. Papa stopped smoking, and the lines on Mama's face faded away.

I hopped onto my seat, my short legs hanging down like two clubs. I was so excited to be riding on the train, I bounced up and down on my cushion. Across the aisle, a small girl in a red-and-white plaid dress joined me in my bouncing game. She looked like a mischievous pixie with a smile as wide as her face. Her name was Trudi, and her parents were part of our group of twenty-four Jewish refugees running from Hitler.

Trudi was four years younger than me, and my exact opposite in every feature. I was big and plump with a puffy round face, blue eyes, and curly blond hair wanting to escape from the two braids down my back. Trudi was thin and small, with shoulder-length, wavy dark hair, and shiny black eyes. We fell into the same rhythm, bouncing up and down on our seats. By the time we arrived in Moscow and transferred to the Trans-Siberian Railway to Vladivostok, we were friends. For us, the train ride was more fun than being at the Prater. We liked being jiggled and jerked around like two eggs in a pot of boiling water.

"*Ach* Illy, now look what you're doing," Mama's face was no longer at peace. She grabbed my arm to make me sit still. "What's the matter with you? You were never like this at home."

Of course, I wasn't anything like this in Vienna, or Memel, or Riga. Mama wasn't anything like she was at home. Papa wasn't anything like he was at home. We had no home.

The sleeping car was a new adventure with its upper and lower bunks—wooden shelves covered by thin pads that were to be our beds. A narrow aisle crowded with people going to the toilet at the end of the car separated the two sides. Climbing up the short ladder to the upper bunk and lying down was just like crawling into a coffin. But what fun it was to go up and down the ladder, which Trudi and I did as often as possible, pretending to go to the toilet. It didn't take Papa long to figure out what we were doing. On my last climb up the ladder, he grabbed my arm to stop me.

"Next time you come down, young lady, you won't be allowed to go back up. You may have to sleep in the toilet." His nostrils flared. Our ladder game was finished.

I thought Mama and Papa were always grouchy, maybe because they didn't get much sleep. The thin pad on our bunks was full of fleas, and the flimsy privacy curtain that hung across our sleepers was so dirty that Mama said they must have used it as a dust cloth. Besides, it didn't block any of the noise in the coach. During the night, we heard snoring, coughing, clanking on the ladders and footsteps in the aisle. But Trudi and I didn't mind—we could sleep through any noise. We were having fun.

Like a pair of puppies sniffing around for something to do, we discovered a troop of Russian soldiers in the adjoining coach. They looked like the military police at the train station in Riga, only these young men weren't stiff wooden sticks with faces blank as platters. They looked relaxed with their caps pushed off their foreheads. Their light hair stuck straight out like bundles of straw under their visors.

Some of them slept in their seats, slouched back as if they were resting in feather beds. Others sat in a circle on the floor playing cards. Their shirts were open at the collar; they talked in deep voices. A bottle of water was passed from one soldier to another. Every time they took a drink, they scrunched their faces as if they had bitten into a bitter apple. One soldier offered me a drink and when I shook my head to say no, they burst out laughing. *Why would I drink something that tasted so bad?* A few of them stood up to watch the card game. Every so often, someone put a card down and swooped up the pile of money in the middle of the floor to booming laughter. At the back of the car, someone pumped a concertina to a lively tune. A small group of soldiers sang along, tapping their feet in time to the music.

Trudi and I thought we'd walked through a magical mirror and ended up in a fairyland. One of the soldiers, looking no older than Fredi, spotted us. He picked Trudi up in his arms, took me by the hand, and put each of us on his knees at the back of the car. We sang with them, mimicking their sounds. It made them slap their knees and roar with laughter. We had no idea what the words meant.

Back in our own coach Trudi and I sang those very songs for Papa. His eyes narrowed down to slits and he said, "What do you think you're doing, singing Russian military songs?" He clenched his teeth. "Stop it! I bet we're not allowed to hear those songs—let alone sing them. Who knows what they'll do if they know we heard their songs? What if they throw us off the train? Why can't you just sit quiet in your seat?" I sat down, mum. I needed to get used to being yelled at.

When our train passed through Siberia, two soldiers entered our coach, lowered the shades on our windows, and then stood at each end of our coach with their guns strapped across their shoulders. The cabin was dimly lit, with only a couple of yellow electric bulbs in the ceiling. I sat by the window next to Mama. It wasn't long before my curiosity made me pull the shade away just a crack to look outside. A slice of bright, glaring sunshine flashed into our cabin. Miles of flat land of nothing stretched as far as I could see—no fields, no crops, no houses—nothing. In an instant, a soldier stood in the aisle next to us, his rifle in hand, shouting Russian words at us as fast as bullets shooting from a machine gun. His hand pointed to the shade again and again. It was clear that I shouldn't have moved it, let alone touched it. Mama and I could do nothing but remain silent and wait for the barrage to end. With us whipped into silence, he left.

Then Mama said, "*Ach* Illy, look what you've done now. Don't you know we're not supposed to look out the window? Why do you think they've pulled the shades down? What do you think they've got those soldiers watching us for? They're here to make sure we don't see what's out there!"

"But there's nothing out there. What are they afraid we're going to see?"

"I don't know—military bases—tanks—I don't know. Just sit still, *im Gottes Willen*, and don't do anything before asking me first."

Mama looked so tired, as if she were about to fall asleep. Some of her wavy dark hair had escaped from the tight roll at the back of her neck and hung limp against her skin. She dropped her head against the back of the seat and closed her eyes, but I knew she wasn't asleep. I took hold of her hand and said, "Mama, don't tell Papa." I didn't know why I always got into trouble.

The train sped on, and Mama and I sat holding hands in that darkened capsule, without saying another word. Some time later, the train slowed down, and we heard the sputter and screech of its wheels braking, followed by a final lurch backward as it came to a complete stop. The shades were pulled up. We were allowed to get out and walk about the station.

Papa said we were in Manchuria. I didn't know how he could tell where we were. The writing at the station didn't have any letters like I'd seen before. The "h's" and "m's" were upside down, the "r's" and "e's" were backwards, and some letters had arches and boxes and didn't look like letters at all.

The big shock was that someone actually met us at the station in Manchuria. He was a tiny, bird-like man, with a beak for a nose and dark eyes like two roasted coffee beans. A rumpled cotton cap with a black visor covered his shoulder-length, steel gray hair. He found Trudi's papa, who was the head of our little group of refugees, and took him inside the station building to talk to him. When they came out, we learned his name was Moishe. The HIAS had told him we were passing through and he brought hot chicken soup for all of us. It was the best food we'd had since leaving Riga. It tasted just as good as the matzo ball soup Oma used to make for Passover.

Papa called Manchuria "the end of the earth" and he didn't know what a Jew was doing there. Nobody else knew either, but all of us were happy he was there. I hoped the place called America was not "the end of the earth," but I wouldn't have minded if someone like Moishe lived there.

Wonderment in Kobe

Our two-week train ride ended and we traveled on to Kobe, Japan, where we had to wait two weeks for a boat to take us to Seattle. When I saw the room assigned to us in Kobe, I felt like a bird sprung from its cage. I wanted to fly. It was as large as a handball court and without any tables or chairs. Woven grass mats the color of hay covered the floor. Trudi and I were bursting to run from one end to another, to play tag and have races. We didn't want to sit still and be quiet another minute.

"Race you to the other wall," I said, getting into a crouching position.

"What are you doing?" Mama yelled. Then louder, "Get off those mats. Don't walk on them—they're our beds."

"Those are our beds?" My jaw dropped.

Trudi and I thought the room belonged to us, to our two families. It did belong to us, but also to the other twenty-four refugees who were traveling with us. The grass mats, each one with a square, mahogany brown wood block, were to be our beds and pillows. Trudi and I saw them as building blocks, construction pieces for a playhouse, a place for us to have fun.

That night we lay down to sleep, one person next to another, like sardines in a can. We placed our heads on our blocks and tried to sleep. Before long, the edges of our blocks felt razor-sharp. I heard Mama ask Papa, "How do they do it? How in the world can they sleep?"

Papa said, "I don't know. They must be used to it."

"Maybe it's because they have so much hair. Have you seen those enormous hairdos? It must cushion the wood block," Mama said.

"You're crazy," Papa said, shaking his head and turning over on his side.

Two minutes later, I said, "I can't sleep, Mama."

"I know," she said. All twenty-four of us were in constant motion, turning from one side to the other, flapping around like a flock of birds, trying to find a position that would bring us sleep.

"Wait a minute. I have an idea," Mama said. "Let's take some of our clothes and make a pillow out of them." She took some underpants out of her suitcase, placed them in the center of an open blouse, and folded it into a fake pillow. She made a second one out of a wool sweater and Papa's jacket was the third. We placed the clothes on our blocks and settled down.

All was quiet until I said, "But the bed is so hard. My hips hurt."

"I know it is. But don't complain. Just remember how lucky we are to be here," Mama said.

The others in our group often talked about how terrible it was for people back in Vienna who'd been taken away. I didn't know where they went, why those places were so bad. I just wanted to go to America where I could be with Fredi.

When I was out on the street in Kobe, I was fascinated by how different people looked and dressed from the way we did. I couldn't stop staring. Grown men and women were not much taller than me. Their round faces and black eyes, peeking out through slanted slits, made them look like porcelain dolls. I wanted to touch their enormous, shiny hairdos, to pull out the black lacquered sticks stuck into them, and make the baubles hanging from their ends tinkle like bells. I wanted to wear their shiny kimonos in all the colors of the rainbow, and slide my fingers across the slick fabric. I mimicked their tiny steps as they walked down the street. I copied the writing on the street signs that looked like trees and houses and stick people. I wanted to be outside all the time with Trudi, but Papa said, "Stay inside. We shouldn't be noticed."

A couple of days into our stay, Papa was asleep on his mat, and Mama was braiding my hair, when I poked Papa to wake up. He sprang up into a sitting position, looking like he was ready to confront an enemy. When he realized I was the culprit who'd startled him, he said, "Don't do that! That's not funny." Then he dropped his chin to his chest and remained motionless, steadying himself with his hands, flat on the mat. He stayed like that without moving or saying anything for such a long time that Mama jumped to her feet and ran to his side.

"What's the matter with you? Are you all right?" She clasped her hands together between her knees and bent over him, her skirt a circular drape above her ankles.

"I'm dizzy. The whole room is spinning around me. I don't think I can stand up." Papa just sat on his mat, without moving his head, holding onto the floor, trying to focus his eyes.

"Are you sick?" Mama's voice was a tone higher. "You can't get sick now! What'll I do? I'll call for a doctor."

"No! No, you won't. No doctor," he said. "I'll just take care of myself. Let's see what's going to happen. It's not so bad when I lie down."

But every time Papa sat up, he got so dizzy that he had to steady himself by placing his hands flat of the floor. Mama helped him to the toilet, and often I

47

could hear him throw up. She wanted to call a doctor, but each time she mentioned it to Papa, he said no and got angry. "I know what I have. I have Meniere's! Now leave me alone."

"Meniere's? What is that?" Mama pleaded, almost crying. "What'll we do?"

"There's nothing you can do. Something is wrong with my inner ear. The dizzy spells go away after a while. We just can't know how long it will take."

Papa lay on that hard, stiff grass mat the entire two weeks we were in Kobe. I'd never seen Papa sick before. My stomach was in knots, and I didn't want to go outside or play with Trudi. Papa was the one who took care of everyone. He was the doctor. He was the strong one, the healthy one, the smart one. I was afraid all the time. *What'll we do if he doesn't get better and can't take care of us?*

Surviving a Typhoon

Our group of twenty-four refugees left Kobe on a sweltering day in September 1940. We gathered with our suitcases and formed a circle on the dock, a bull's eye of white people surrounded by dark-haired locals. The men hung their jackets over their shoulders like capes, leaving the empty arms of their coats hanging limp like laundry. Most of them smoked, holding their cigarettes backwards, the glowing embers cupped inside their palms. The ladies whispered among themselves, trying to imagine what sailing on the old Japanese freighter, the *Hikawa Maru,* would be like.

Trudi stood next to her parents, as I did. She looked like her mother, Mitzi, even having her fun-loving giggle, which brought a bit of relief to our forever-worried group. Mitzi always wore gathered skirts, which no one noticed, except Papa. "Of course she wears full skirts. She's trying to hide her scoliosis."

"What's that, Papa?" I asked.

"Her spine is curved. Can't you see how one shoulder is higher than the other, and how she walks a little funny?"

"No," I said, trying to see what Papa was talking about. "Anyway, I don't care about how she walks—I like her."

Trudi's Papa was named Ernst, but Mitzi called him Pepi, and so did everybody else. He was a full head shorter than Mitzi, with eyes as blue as the clearest, breeziest day of fall. His black hair was combed straight back on his head and shone like hot tar. The only thing Trudi got from Pepi was the deep dimple in the middle of her chin just like his. I liked all three of them.

Pepi had been "in business" in Vienna. We didn't know what kind of business that was. I thought it might have been buying goose feathers for down comforters like Papa's cousin, or selling suits and coats like Mama's brothers had done. Papa shrugged his shoulders, lifted his hands palms up, and said, "It doesn't matter what he did for a living. When you marry a girl as rich as Mitzi, you don't have to make any money." Papa never said anything nice about anyone.

While we waited on the dock to board the ship, I overheard Papa tell Pepi, "If we make it to America, it'll be a miracle. Look how old this tub is. They should have junked it long ago. I hope it makes it across the Pacific one more time."

Papa shook his head and put his hand on Mama's shoulder to steady himself. Even though his dizzy spells were no longer as bad as they had been, they still were a problem.

Pepi eyed the ship and said, "Even if the ship makes it to America, I wonder if we will. I found out in Kobe that the Japanese are planning to go to war with America. What does that tell you about how they feel about white people? If they attack while we're still at sea, we'll be the first ones they go after." No one said anything more. We had no choice but to board the ship.

We climbed up the steep gangplank like a line of ants. Once on board we climbed down one set of steps after another until we reached the bottom of the boat. Our dormitory was dark and damp, like the dungeon in the fairy tale where the evil witch used to lock the beautiful princess. But no one in our group complained—we knew how lucky we were to be sailing for America.

We were up on deck when we set sail. Our spirits lifted as a cool breeze swept off the ocean, stroking our cheeks, sending our hair flying, inflating our blouses and skirts. We watched the setting sun paint the waves a golden glow, before it disappeared into a smooth, quiet pool of sea green. Once again, Trudi and I had fun. We squealed as if we were on a seesaw each time the boat lifted or dipped. We made a game of choosing the biggest wave on the horizon, then seeing how high we could count before it disappeared.

A few hours out to sea, the numbers we counted became higher and higher. The gentle gusts of wind that had stroked our faces when we set sail, turned into blasts of air that felt like sandpaper. Slow, lazy, rolling waves grew larger, until they were like huge commas over our heads. When they came crashing onto the deck, we hurried down to our dormitory.

Our freighter bounced up and down and rolled from side to side. Trudi and I shrieked—for us it was like being on a ride in an amusement park—while the others got seasick. On top of being dizzy, Papa was now as seasick as the others. The aisle to the toilet was as congested as a street in Vienna during rush hour. Many had black and blue marks on their bodies from being thrown against the bunks as the boat rolled from side to side. But no one complained.

Mama sat on her bunk, holding onto its edge, her eyes fixed. "I worried about Hitler catching us and killing us. I worried the Russians wouldn't let us leave Riga because they needed Norbert to take care of their troops. I worried that the Japanese would go to war and kill us before we left Kobe. But I never thought we might die in a typhoon."

Eventually the wind died down, the waves became lower, and the boat's rocking eased. We were allowed to go on deck, but Mama and Papa were still too sick to do anything but lie in their bunks. It was Pepi who was well enough to take Trudi and me outside. "Come on, Trudi," I said. "Let's go to the front of the boat."

"I don't feel like it," Trudi said, holding onto Pepi's hand. Her eyes were like dark glass as she added, "Pepi, wipe my nose."

She retreated to her bunk with a beet red face and began to cough nonstop, except to occasionally plead, "Pepi, wipe my nose."

Two days later, I joined Trudi with a dry, barking cough of my own. I'd caught the whooping cough from her. From then on, the sounds within steerage on the *Hikawa Maru* were the footsteps of grownups running to the toilet with their seasickness, along with Trudi and I barking like a beach full of seals, only to be interrupted by an occasional, "Pepi, wipe my nose."

PART II

Seattle's Magic

After two weeks on our old Japanese freighter, we landed in Seattle. We were driven to a three-story building and herded into a huge room with tall, green plants which were everywhere, in corners, by windows, next to couches. I sat between Mama and Papa and felt as if I were in an enclosed garden. Groups of two or three people walked by us speaking a language we didn't understand. The room sounded like an auditorium before the curtain rises.

I was used to hearing language I didn't understand after being in Riga, in Russia, and in Japan. But now, in this large room, in this strange, foreign garden, with different new sounds flying all around me, I was struck dumb again. My head rolled from side to side like a buoy in the ocean as I heard sounds like *yu, mi,* and *hu,* wondering what they meant.

"Papa," I said, "What are they saying?"

"I don't know, Suzinka. When they talk so fast, I can't understand them any better than you."

I knew Mama was nervous. She held my hand so tight, my fingers started to tingle. Her fears traveled straight down her arm, through our hands, to me. I released my grip to lean against her warm body.

We heard the sharp click of high heels coming toward us. A plump woman named Gisela, dressed in a flimsy peach-colored dress, told us in German to go into a small square room with metal walls. It had no furniture, no windows, and no light except for one small lamp in the center of the ceiling. We stood shoulder to shoulder facing the door, and when no more could fit in, its doors clamped shut with a bang. I felt like I was inside a giant box and groped for Mama's hand again. Then the entire room rose straight up like a hot air balloon. I didn't know whether I should be frightened, or whether to enjoy the ride.

I was busy trying to understand the young man standing next to me. With an open-collared cotton shirt showing a tangle of dark hair, he was eating something. *What a strange place to be eating.* We weren't in a kitchen or dining room or restaurant. *Why is he eating here?* I wondered if he'd started eating something elsewhere and was finishing it here in this strange place. I stared at him, forgetting my fear in this rising box, waiting for him to swallow. *Why doesn't he swallow?*

Was it tough like the chewy squid we ate on the Japanese freighter? My stomach cramped as I thought of the foul smell of fish. My companion must have felt my staring eyes, because he looked down and said, "Want some gum?"

I flicked my eyes away from his face as fast as I could, just as our rising giant hatbox came to a stop. Gisela then led us to a hotel room where I asked Papa, "What was that thing we were in?

He looked at Mama and, after they both got through laughing at me, he said, "That was an elevator. You've never been in one before. In Vienna, only the most expensive apartment houses had elevators."

"And what was that man eating inside that elevator—that needed so much chewing?" I asked.

"I don't know myself?" Papa said. "He said something that sounded like 'gum'? Hand me that dictionary, Suzi."

From then on, the red dictionary was with Papa wherever he went.

Second Street Apartment

Papa wanted to move to New York to be with Fredi, and to study for the exam that would license him to practice medicine in that state. Since we spoke no English and had no money, we needed help from the HIAS. But they wouldn't give us any if we'd stayed in New York, saying there were too many Jews there already, especially doctors. They'd only help us if we moved to Portland, Oregon. Fredi couldn't make enough money working as a shipping clerk to support all four of us, so Mama and Papa had no choice but to say okay, we'd settle in Portland—and we'd send for Fredi to join us. And that's what happened. Lucky for me, the Feldmans were settled in Portland as well, and I could keep Trudi for my friend. As soon as we were moved into our apartment, I asked, "Can I go play with Trudi?"

"No, she lives far away from us, too far to walk."

"So let's take the bus."

"And where's the money for the bus fare supposed to come from?"

I had no answer.

Our apartment on Southwest Second Street was supposed to be in the "Jewish neighborhood." I didn't know what that meant, because our street didn't look different from any other street. Besides, there weren't any Jews living there. Mama said anybody who had a few dollars in their pocket would find someplace better to live. Then we discovered a city block of stores that brought Jews from the entire city to shop. A delicatessen selling corned beef and pastrami and dill pickles was the most inviting, but Mama said we couldn't afford to buy anything there. It was Mosler's Bakery, with its smell of fresh baked bagels, challa, and rye bread wafting through the front door, for which we had enough money. And a good thing it was, because we couldn't eat the American white bread that tasted like a glob of dough in our mouths.

There was another store at the end of the block, but it didn't have any aromas pulling you inside. The front door and window facing the street were as cloudy as a shower door, and painted with circles, squiggles, dots, and lines. Sometimes, a few men in dark suits and hats shuffled around on the sidewalk, their hands clasped behind their backs. Most of them were older, with gray hair like Opa's, and wiry beards that looked like bird's nests. I asked Papa what they were selling inside that store.

"They're not selling anything—that's a synagogue and those are Orthodox Jews," Papa said. "Don't they look ridiculous? They should cut their beards and not make such a spectacle of themselves. Imagine what the Gentiles must think when they see these clowns."

"What do they think?"

"They think all of us are like that. No wonder they don't trust us when they see strange looking creatures like that." One side of Papa's full lip lifted up into a sneer. I was glad we weren't Orthodox Jews.

The HIAS lent us money to rent a furnished apartment in a building so old, that its hallway smelled like wet wool or spoiled milk—we couldn't tell which. Mama said that no matter how much she cleaned, she couldn't get rid of the stench. What I didn't understand was that after we were inside our apartment for a while, we didn't notice it anymore. We didn't care—we were safe in America and going to be together with Fredi. Never mind the smell.

I was so excited the day he came—a rainy day like all the others had been since we arrived. Mama, Papa, and I took the bus to the train station to meet him, and stood on the platform under our umbrellas. Fredi stepped out of his coach, after having traveled for three days and three nights, carrying the same suitcase he'd taken to America with him. Even though he was sixteen now—he hadn't changed a bit, except for being thinner and having dark circles around his eyes.

Mama screamed, "Fredi," dropped her umbrella upside down on the platform, and clamped her arms around his neck. Then she took his face into her hands and kept kissing it, while fat teardrops ran down her cheeks.

Papa and I stood right behind Mama, but I only got to hold his hand because Mama wouldn't let go of Fredi. And Papa just stood waiting, smiling and clearing his throat. It wasn't until Papa had a chance to get a hug, and I stopped jumping up and down, calling, "Fredi, Fredi," that Papa finally said, "Let's go home."

Fredi had learned English, finished high school, and seemed different in many ways. One minute he'd be teaching me how to play chess and laughing at my mistakes. The next minute, he'd be sitting in a chair, silent, his coffee-bean eyes looking at the fluttering green leaves of the walnut tree outside our window, listening to a voice that none of us could hear. Mama felt sorry for him, but his going off into his own world like that made Papa mad.

"What's the matter with you? Don't you have anything better to do than just look out the window?"

Fredi moved his stare from the leaves onto Papa, and said nothing.

"Leave him alone, why don't you," Mama said. "He did enough already, all by himself on that farm, having to take care of himself as if he were a man. Imagine him staying alone in that big house without enough food to eat. What do you want from him?"

"He could read the newspaper. He could read a book. What can he learn by looking out the window?"

"Maybe he doesn't want to read a book right now. I don't care what he does. It's just good to have him home." Mama shuffled across the room on her flat feet and sat down on the arm of Fredi's chair. She put her arm around his shoulders and said, "For me, he's good just as he is."

A short, small-boned, hawk-nosed man named Mr. Katz owned our apartment building. He could be found in front of our building's front door morning, noon, and night, strolling back and forth in a drab green raincoat and crumpled safari hat.

"When does he eat and sleep?" I asked.

"Or take a bath and get dressed." Fredi had a rare smile on his face.

"Maybe he's afraid somebody is going to steal his apartment house," Papa said.

"Maybe he's being paid as a detective to see if any of the ladies inside has a lover," Fredi said.

"Stop it, you two." Mama giggled. "He's just an ugly little man who doesn't have anything else to do."

"But the ugly little man likes you well enough," Fredi said. "I saw how he looked at you."

"What are you talking about?" Mama pulled herself up, square shouldered, smiling.

"Remember when you and I came back from the store and he asked me if you were my sister?"

"Stupid man!" Mama said. "I told him right away, 'Zat's not my brazza—I'm his mazza.'"

Papa and Fredi burst out laughing. When Papa caught his breath, he said, "He probably didn't understand a word you said."

Every time we passed Mr. Katz coming and going he'd say, "Goood mornyink" or "How arrr yooo?" We may not have spoken English right ourselves, but we knew Mr. Katz didn't speak right either. Papa said he had a Russian accent.

Mr. Katz may have known everything about everyone in his building, but he didn't know we all laughed at him.

Mama and Papa hated having to take money from the HIAS. They wanted to be able to support themselves, but they couldn't do it without their help. What Papa didn't know was that the state of Oregon wouldn't allow him to take the exam licensing him to be a doctor. They'd taken that privilege away from any doctor who wasn't American after having given the license to a foreign doctor that Papa said turned out to be a "quack." So Papa and Mama needed to find some other way to make a living. Every day, they'd take a bus to the Jewish Community Center and talk to the lady from the HIAS. After one such visit, Mama sank into her favorite mustard-colored chair and dropped her hands into her lap. "I don't know why I told her I could knit and sew and embroider."

"You told her the truth," Papa said, blowing a plume of smoke from his cigarette into the room.

"She asked me what my hobbies were," Mama said. "I didn't know what she meant. I told her I was just a housewife who did a little sewing and needlepoint and took care of my children." I followed her fingers as they coasted along one of the lines in the patterned blanket on her chair.

"She asked me the same thing, but I didn't want her to know that I didn't understand her," Papa said. "I told her I didn't have any hobbies." Papa got out of his chair and picked up his red dictionary. "Let me read you what hobbies are: 'An activity or interest pursued for pleasure or relaxation and not as a main occupation. Example: *His hobbies include stamp collecting, gardening, and woodcarving.*' Ridiculous! Who had time for relaxation working fourteen, fifteen hours a day at the hospital and in the office? Who had time for stamp collecting? How could I garden when we lived in an apartment? Or woodcarving! Do you know one person in all of Vienna who did woodcarving? Stupid woman!" Papa was mad. Whenever Papa got mad, somebody would be called stupid—this time it was the HIAS lady.

Mama leaned forward in her chair. "But look what trouble I'm in now. She got me a job in a factory making uniforms. How can I do such work when I don't know how to use a power sewing machine? How could I tell her I can't take that job? She might think I don't want to work, that I just want them to support us." It upset me to see Mama like that. I sat down next to her and put my hand on her knee.

"Well, you'll have to try it," Papa said. "You can't say no to the HIAS."

Mama went to work at the factory and it didn't take but two days and five ruined uniforms before she was fired. Still, the HIAS didn't give up on Mama's sewing ability. The HIAS lady bought Mama a used Singer sewing machine so she could do alterations at home.

So Mama sat with the Singer in one corner of our living room, whirring away at her own speed. A standing lamp sprayed a beam of light onto her hands as she fed fabric under a pounding needle. She took dresses in at the waist when ladies lost weight; she let them out when they gained it back. She shortened hems; she lengthened hems. She took collars off the neckline; she put them on when the fashion demanded it. She was paid five dollars no matter how much time she spent on the alteration, whether it was one hour or three.

"Why don't you charge more for the three-hour collars than the one-hour hem?" I asked.

"Never mind 'why,'" she said. "I'm happy with anything I can get, and five dollars keeps the customers coming back." Her shoulders hunched over, her back a perfect half-dome, Mama tilted her head forward as she watched the needle race to close a seam.

At home, no one had time to play with me. Mama always said "*spater*," but I knew she didn't mean "later." She really meant "I'm too busy." Mama sat at her Singer all day long with the rhythmic whirr of her machine a constant sound in the room. Fredi was no longer around. He'd found a job as a shipping clerk in a factory making ski clothes.

It was Papa who couldn't find work. I thought I'd have him all to myself, but he spent all his time with his ear glued to the radio. I'd tug on his hand, look straight into his eyes, and pull out all my cute-little-girl tricks that had always worked before. But he'd only say, "*Spater*, Suzinka. I'll play with you *spater*." I'd watch him pace up and down the living room floor smoking cigarettes, clouds of smoke trailing behind him, and I knew he meant, "I'm too nervous to play with you."

One day Papa returned from the Center, went straight to the window with his hands clasped behind his back and said, "They offered me a job."

"That's wonderful, Bobi." Mama used his nickname only when she was happy.

"But you don't know what kind of a job it is." He spun around and faced her sitting at her Singer, resting her fabric-feeding fingers in her lap. "They want me to work at a men's social club."

"What's wrong with that? You can't practice medicine here, so don't be fussy about what kind of work you do. I don't have to tell you how bad we need the money."

"But you don't know the whole deal. I'd be a sort of caretaker for the club. I'd have to make sure the club is cleaned up and all set for their parties. I'd have to greet the men when they come in, take their hats and coats, hang them up, get their drinks, call their taxis for them, and make phone calls for them—things like that."

"So what's wrong with that? A job is a job. You can't be the big 'Herr Doktor' anymore."

Papa walked over to Mama's chair by the machine, bent over her, and wagged his finger in front of her eyes. "Who are you to tell me what I am and what I'm not? Why do you talk when you don't even know what it's all about? What makes you such an authority about what's right and what's wrong?" He turned his back to her and walked back to the window. "The job would require all of us to move into the quarters behind the club."

Mama sat mute for a while, studying her hands in her lap. "We have to live somewhere, after all. If we get free rent, why not live there?"

I sat on the couch feeling my muscles harden. Whenever Mama and Papa fought, I worried about how nasty it would get and tried to decide which side to be on. Papa walked back to face Mama again, his hands safely tucked into his pockets. "You don't understand. These men would come to the club to have a good time. They'd eat and drink—have women there. They may be drunk. Is that any place for a young girl like Illy? How would you like her to see all that? And maybe it wouldn't be such a safe place for you either."

Mama didn't say anything, her head bent forward.

"I won't take a job like that and that's final!"

After that, Papa spent most of his time studying *The Oregonian* and listening to the radio. It was November 1940, and he'd heard that Romania and Hungary had allied themselves with Hitler. That alone would have put Papa in a bad mood, but Mama's working when he wasn't, upset him even more.

Mama's hard work at the Singer all day long, making five dollars a clip, had paid off. She'd built her business up to the point where she could pay our rent. One afternoon I heard her hum a tune from a Strauss operetta while she was sewing. Papa lifted his head from reading his newspaper and, with a frown on his face, said, "I don't know what you're so happy about. You might be paying the rent, but you're not earning enough to keep us from taking money from the HIAS."

Adventures in the Store

The leaves fluttering outside the living room window dotted the room with shadows. Papa came through the door, sending the curtains flying, and put his hat and suit jacket on the wall rack. A pair of button-down suspenders held his pants up over his paunchy stomach, like clothespins hanging onto sagging laundry.

Mama stopped pumping the grate under her feet and turned away from her Singer to face him. "So, what did she say?"

Papa had been to see if the HIAS had found work for him. "This time she proposed setting us up in a small business." He dropped into his chair and rolled his eyes to the ceiling as if they'd asked him to wrestle a bear. "They would buy a small grocery store for both of us to run. We'd pay them back when we could, as we earned the money." Papa stood up and started pacing from one wall to another with his eyes on the rug in front of him. "But what do I know about running a business? I'm a doctor—a professional man. I don't know how to run a store."

Mama moved from her Singer to the stuffed chair and sank into it. "Let's just think about that a little bit. You can't practice medicine here—you don't have a license. They can't find you a job. And I don't know how much longer I can keep working these long hours. Maybe we can learn to be grocers."

Papa stopped in front of Mama. "There you go again—talking about something you know nothing about." His hands were on his hips and he leaned forward as he spoke. "What if we take the store and don't make any money at it? Then we'd owe the HIAS all the money they've already spent on us, plus the cost of the store." He walked away from her as if she were a stupid child.

"But we have no choice. You can't turn down everything they offer you. If you do, they might give up on us altogether. And without them, what would we do in this country ... not knowing the language ... not knowing anyone who might help us ... not having training in any other kind of work. We must take their advice." Mama was sitting forward in her chair now, her arms pumping up and down as if to hammer home every point.

"They did say the owner would stay on to teach us the business."

"Then we must accept the offer. We'll learn how to run that business—somehow."

I went to Papa's side, and pulled his hand. "Let's do it, Papa. Let's buy the store."

Papa looked at me and smiled. I could get a smile out of him better than anyone in our family. "Not so fast, Suzinka," he said. "Let's have a look at the store first before we make any decisions. We should go over and meet the owner and see what we're getting into."

I was excited about the store, thinking it would be like those in our neighborhood with their mouth-watering aromas. But the store wasn't in our neighborhood or anywhere near us. It was on the other side of the city—the southeast side. We had to take the Hawthorne Bridge over the Willamette River, a muddy brown waterway that cut Portland in half, to get there. I wanted to take the bus but Papa said, "What? Spend ten cents a person bus fare? That's thirty cents—too much—we'll walk."

We took our raincoats and umbrellas—the first things we bought in Portland after finding out it rained nine months out of the year—and started off for the store. I was excited to be on the bridge, listening to the low muffled wail of the tugboat foghorns and watching the V of the rippling waves as the tugboats sliced their way through the cocoa-colored water. Rubber tires that looked like giant black lifesavers hung from the tugboat sides to protect them. One of them pulled a barge filled with barrels so heavy, it looked like it wasn't even moving in the water. From a distance, the boats looked like toys in a bathtub. I lagged behind to watch, not noticing that Mama and Papa were a long distance ahead of me.

"*Ach*, Illy, come on already. Mr. Wirth is waiting for us." Mama came back for me, yanked my fingers off the rail, and pulled me after her. When we got to the middle of the bridge, a metal gate clanked down to stop the traffic. Cables screeched as the middle section of the bridge lifted up to allow a freighter to pass.

For me it was like watching a huge mechanical toy—but not for Papa. He paced back and forth, smoking furiously, finally stopping in front of Mama. "See, I told you we should have left earlier. But no, you couldn't get ready. You always have your own ideas."

"How could I know that the bridge would open up? I didn't know it was a drawbridge." Mama stood flatfooted in front of him, her arms hanging loose at her sides, her palms turned forward.

"You never know anything. You should just listen to me and we'd all be better off." Papa lit another cigarette and threw the match into the river. Mama said nothing.

I didn't want to hear anymore. Mama usually let Papa have the last word. Every time she said anything to explain herself, Papa would find some way to make her look bad. Once she stopped talking, Papa would stop, too. I just kept watching the bridge and the river and the boats, and wished we were at the store already.

Once we were off the bridge and a few blocks into the southeast side of the city, we turned down a street lined with two-story, square-shaped apartment houses lined up next to one another. With two windows upstairs and two windows downstairs, they looked like a row of dice, the number four facing the street. There were no trees, shrubs, grass, or flowers anywhere around them.

Ahead of us on the left side of the street, an entire city block was bare of anything but low-growing weeds and grasses. A brown dirt path cut diagonally from one corner to the other. Broad dandelion leaves covered the field, each one sending up a stalk to hold a ping-pong-ball-shaped collection of fuzzy seeds. An occasional breeze would send their tiny soft feathers flying, inviting me to come chase them, to catch them, to make a wish, and send them off into the wind. I fell behind Mama and Papa again.

"Illy … Illy, *im Gottes Willen*, can't you hurry? We're late enough as it is."

The store was on the corner directly across the street from the empty block. In the front window, several cardboard cutouts of canned peaches, green peas, and yellow corn, hung from the ceiling and flipped from side to side. Papa entered to the sound of reindeer bells attached to a leather strap on the front door.

We heard, "Howdy-doody." It came from behind a meat case filled with chicken parts, hamburger, pork chops, and ground sausage lying neatly on trays. We didn't understand what we heard—not even Papa, who'd learned more English than any of us.

Papa said, "Hello?"

A round-faced man with thinning gray hair that came to a V on the top of his head stepped out from behind the meat case. He approached us, wiping his hands in the skirt of his soiled butcher apron, and thrust five sausage-shaped fingers at Papa to invite a handshake.

"You must be Dr. Fell. I'm Mr. Wirth," he said, making his thick broom of a moustache twitch.

Mr. Wirth walked us around his rectangular-shaped store. As one entered the store, they'd see the meat case was on the left. The checkout counter stood next to it and held a brass cash register that shone as bright as the sun. Mr. Wirth pushed one of its round alabaster buttons, and a smile sprang onto my face as its sharp ring filled the room, and two numbered tabs popped up in the window at its top. The entire wall of the right side of the store was filled with shelves of canned goods. At one end, a metal coffee grinder, painted deep red, sat on an island that it shared with packaged baked goods. Boxes of apples, oranges, lettuce, tomatoes, and vegetables were displayed in the front window under the flapping cardboard signs.

A green-and-white striped cloth, hung on rings like a shower curtain, separated the front and back rooms. The stock room held cardboard boxes of canned goods stacked on top of each other, forming passageways throughout the room. Along the back wall, burlap sacks filled with brown potatoes, white onions, red kidney beans, and yellow macaroni invited me to dig my hands into them. A black potbellied stove took up one corner, its smoke carried up and out through the ceiling by a long black pipe.

"You wouldn't believe it, but this little fellow heats up the whole store," Mr. Wirth said, smacking the pipe twice as if it were a favorite pet.

Mr. Wirth led us to an open rolltop oak desk, papers strewn helter-skelter across its top. It looked like a windstorm had passed over it. "This is where I keep all my receipts, my bills, and my order forms." His fat hand pointed to the mess.

Papa would never have had a desk like that. He'd have the receipts, order forms, and bills stacked in neat piles. I knew Papa was wondering how Mr. Wirth ever managed to make money in that store.

Mr. Wirth smiled and invited me to sit down in the desk chair. I lifted myself into the seat to the sound of a grinding screech that put goose bumps on my arm. My weight had pushed the black coil under me down while the base, on four rotating coasters, slid away from the desk. What fun! I felt like I was back on a ride at the Prater.

For me, the store was filled with playthings. I liked the sound of the brass register with its grinding ring and pop-up numbers, the feel of waxy red-and-white kidney beans slipping through my fingers, the big oak desk with its secret papers hiding in dark cubbyholes, and the ride in the squeaky desk chair. I liked old Mr. Wirth, with his friendly smile and his unexpected bursts of laughter. I wanted Mama and Papa to buy what I thought was a giant fun house.

Mr. Wirth sat down in his chair to show Papa his accounting. After he got through pushing his papers this way and that, a proud, self-satisfied grin spread across his face He folded his arms across his chest and, with a smile, said, "So there you have it. You can see plain enough that I make money here."

Papa kept looking at the papers, then bowed his head a bit, smiled a little too wide, and said, "Mr. Wirth—if you would be so kind—would you show me your sales receipts one more time?"

While Papa was shuffling through the papers all over again, Mr. Wirth said, "I'm only selling the store because I have to help my wife out at home with our retarded son. She's not too well, and she can't handle him herself anymore." He stuffed his hands in behind the bib of his apron and lost the smile on his face.

"I see." Papa put the receipts back on the desk. "Mr. Wirth, this is such a big decision for us. Please give us a little time to think about it."

Walking back to our Second Street apartment, Mama and Papa didn't stop talking about Mr. Wirth and the store. This time I didn't lag behind watching tugboats and freighters. "Papa … Papa, are we going to buy the store? Are we going to be grocers?" I held his hand and looked up at him. I knew Papa thought being a doctor was better than being a grocer, but I wanted that store to be ours.

"I don't know, Suzinka. I don't know yet." He kept walking.

"But don't you like Mr. Wirth?"

"Sure, I like Mr. Wirth."

"But don't you believe Mr. Wirth?"

"Sure, I believe Mr. Wirth. Why would anyone lie about a thing like having a retarded son?"

"But don't you think he's making money in the store?"

"*Ach,* Suzinka, everything looks good so far, but sometimes things are not as they seem. You'll learn that when you're older. You can't always believe what other people tell you."

"But Mr. Wirth wouldn't lie to you about the store making money, Papa. I like Mr. Wirth. And I like the store. Papa, let's buy the store." Mama and Papa looked at each other and laughed. I didn't know what was so funny.

In the end, Papa had no choice but to take a chance on Mr. Wirth. He couldn't turn the HIAS down again. They bought the store for us and we'd pay them back when we could. I wasn't sure that Papa actually believed Mr. Wirth was honest, but he couldn't see where he was cheating, either. We were going to be grocers.

The next time we walked across the Hawthorne Bridge, we all walked fast without speaking to one another. We were going to spend the whole day at the store. Mama wore flat-heeled shoes and a navy sweater to guard against the cold draft that blew in each time the front door opened. Papa wore the only clothes he had, a brown suit, a light blue shirt, and a patterned tie—"doctor" clothes that he brought from Vienna. And he carried his red German-English Dictionary with him, which went everywhere with us. To me, he looked more like a professor, or lawyer, or doctor going to work, than a grocer. He always would.

Papa and Mama walked fast, so fast that I had to take two steps to every one of theirs. We were in step with one another, like a marching band, and I could almost hear the words Mama had said, "We must make it work. We must make it work. We must make it work."

A Foreigner at Abernethy School

Mr. Wirth greeted us with another "Howdy" and a wide toothy smile. He told Mama she would learn the grocery business just by watching him. Mama's eyes were open as wide as a cat's. I knew she didn't think it would be all that simple. He told Papa to stay at the desk in the back room. In between waiting on customers, he'd show him how to make out order forms, pay bills, and keep books. It would be Mama's job to cut meat, clean produce, and wait on customers while Papa would do the bookkeeping, which he considered to be more important.

I started to explore the back room on my own. Boxes of canned goods, stacked one upon another as high as I was tall, formed several aisles. I moved through them, as if I were in a mysterious maze. I ran my fingers through the beans in the burlap bags, picking up a handful and dropping one bean at a time to hear it ping on impact. I transported myself into an imaginary land that had secret passageways and hiding places behind boxes and bags. The grimy black potbelly stove became the pursuing evil witch, the encircling oak chair the safety of home base. I could have stayed in this small amusement park indefinitely, but Mama and Papa had other plans for me.

I was playing one of my imaginary games when Papa called me to his side. "Suzinka, come here." I appeared at his desk. "We're settled now—we're not going to leave Portland. It's time for you to go to school. Tomorrow, you'll enroll in Abernethy School."

My jaw dropped—my mouth became a silent open space. "Papa, I don't want to go to school. I want to stay here with you and Mama."

"Suzinka, you have to go to school." Papa put his hands under my armpits and lifted me onto his lap. "All kids have to go to school. You don't want to grow up being stupid, do you?"

I wouldn't have minded being stupid as long as I didn't have to go to school. But being stupid was the worst thing a person could be in Papa's eyes, except maybe being a liar or a thief.

"I don't want to go to school, I'm afraid to go to school." My spine was as stiff as a stick.

Mr. Wirth pushed aside the green-and-white striped curtain to the back room in time to hear what I'd said. He tucked his chin into his chest and laughed out loud, his round stomach bouncing up and down like a rubber ball. He stood inside the doorway looking at me, as if I were a cute puppy. I just wanted him to go away. He couldn't possibly know how scared I was.

"I won't understand one word they say at school. What will I do if I need help? They wouldn't understand anything I say, either." Some internal faucet filled my mouth with water, making me swallow hard before I croaked the words, "Papa, will you go with me?"

Mama came into the back room wearing her usual frown and placed her fists on her hips. "What's going on here?" she asked.

"We're talking about school," Papa said. "She wants me to go to school with her."

Mama bent her knees, crouched down next to me, and took my hand into hers. "We can't do that. We have to work." Her eyes were dark and warm like chocolate sauce.

Papa said, "No, Suzinka, you already know we can't go with you. You'll be all right. We'll tell them at school that you don't speak English—that you've never been to school before. They'll understand. You're a smart girl. You'll learn English fast." He kissed my forehead. My poker spine softened and I sank back into his chest.

A lady from the HIAS came to help Papa enroll me at Abernethy School. We went down a long hallway on a slick, brown linoleum floor, waxed to shine like a mirror, and entered a door marked "OFFICE." Mr. Winters, the principal, was waiting for us. He had not a single hair on the top of his head, and only a hint of a jawbone—it made his head look like a giant light bulb. He knew I'd never been to school before, that I'd spent two years in Riga, and that I didn't speak a word of English. He looked at me with hooded eyes; the straight line that was his mouth didn't move. He had no idea what to do with me. I needed to start in kindergarten, but I was at least a foot taller than any five-year-old and even a bit chubby at that. He could put me into the third grade class, but not knowing how to read or write or speak English was like putting a retarded, deaf-mute into a normal school. Mr. Winters put me into the third grade.

I wore my best clothes that first day at Abernethy School—a gray sweater with pewter buttons and navy blue skirt held up at my waist by cloth, suspender-like straps, both handmade by Mama. A short piece across my chest, meant to keep the long straps from slipping over my shoulders, formed a perfect H under my chin. It could have stood for the wail of HELP that I heard inside my head.

Mr. Winters took me by the hand, led me into the third grade classroom, and left me standing in the corner just inside the door. Behind me, a wall-to-wall green chalkboard was marked with words I couldn't read or understand. Four tall windows took up another wall, their tan shades pulled up halfway from the bottom, leaving a view of the tops of the pine trees planted outside the building. Five rows of children sitting at their desks had their eyes on me, my pigtails, my old-world sweater, and my long, beige-ribbed stockings. It didn't take long for me to see that I was not like any one of them. I felt my cheeks flush and warm. I swallowed, and knew all of them were silently laughing at me.

The teacher, a young woman in a soft blue print dress, left her desk and met Mr. Winters in front of the chalkboard. They turned their backs to the class and whispered to one another. I stood like a statue with my hands at my sides, feeling sick to my stomach. Mr. Winters finished talking with the teacher and left the classroom. She then took my hand, said something I couldn't understand, and with her high heels clicking, led me down an aisle to a seat at the back of the room.

Safe at last and away from everyone's puzzled stares, the tense muscles in my arms softened. I began to pay attention to the symphony of sounds in the room. None of them made any sense. I darted a glance at some of the kids around me, but didn't fix my gaze until I was sure they weren't looking at me. I noticed most of the girls' hair was cut short in a bob or held back in a rubber band. They wore shirts and skirts, and bobby socks—no pigtails, no bumpy sweaters, and definitely no dreadful, long beige stockings. I wished I looked like them.

A bell rang, loud and sharp. The kids slammed their books shut, started jabbering loudly, and clamored to get out the door. I didn't know what had frightened them. I didn't know what to do. *Should I run out with them? Is there some danger here? Where were they going? Perhaps there is some danger outside?* I stayed in the classroom. The teacher stayed behind at her desk, marking papers and ignoring me.

I wanted to tell her, "*Ich bin noch immer da.*" But I didn't know how to say, "I'm still here," in English.

When she finally saw me, she said something that sounded like, "Oh, I forgot about you." She smiled, showing me a mouthful of white teeth lined up like a string of pearls, and I felt better. She walked down the aisle to my seat, took my hand, and led me outside to the play yard. She kept repeating something that sounded like *re-ses*.

71

At the end of the school day, Papa came to walk me home. He said that from then on, I'd have to go to school by myself. I knew I would. Mama couldn't leave the store, and, when he wasn't managing the store's accounting, he was still trying to find work as a doctor.

"How was school today?" he said, taking my hand.

"I don't know. I didn't understand one word ... except *re-ses*. That means I have to get out of my seat as fast as I can and run outside."

I wasn't afraid to go to school by myself. After all, I had survived my first day. I knew my way to school. And if I could only make it to the safety of my seat at the back of the classroom, away from all those staring eyes, I'd be all right. Besides, I now knew about *re-ses*. I just didn't know how to avoid that sea of staring, blinking eyes in the play yard.

The next day after school, I found Mama by Mr. Wirth's side, watching him cut a pork rib roast into chops. "Mama, you've got to make me some new clothes."

"What are you talking about? Why should I do that? Your clothes are still good." For Mama, clothes were still good if they didn't have holes in them or I hadn't outgrown them.

"Mama, I hate my clothes. They look funny."

Mr. Wirth handed the cleaver to Mama, and she stepped up to the butcher block. Its top had been worn down from constant use, so that its surface was wavy instead of flat. She placed a pork loin along its edge, moving it around to find the block's flattest part. The cleaver in her hand sent a flash of light across the room.

"And what's wrong with the clothes you have?" Mama had one hand on the pork loin and the other ready to hack at the meat, as she looked me straight in my eye. "They're not worn out, they still fit, and we don't have money to spend because—all of a sudden—you don't like them." She thrust the cleaver down past the flesh of pork, through the rib bone. The moist, pink, chop fell limp on the butcher block.

"Mama, I know the clothes are still good, but nobody at school is dressed like this. This bumpy sweater looks terrible. None of the girls at school have a sweater like this."

"Of course they don't." Her eyes were on me again, her brows bunched together. "How many kids have mothers who knit a complicated stitch like that? You have a beautiful sweater. You don't know how lucky you are!"

I went back to school the next day in my hateful old clothes. My sweater felt like sandpaper on my skin. My stockings made me hot and sweaty. The sidewalk filled with more and more children the closer I got to school—all of them staring at me. My cheeks felt as if they were aflame. I wished I could tear the clothes off my body.

I passed a cone-shaped pine tree on the front lawn of a small, wood-shingled house. Its branches hung low to the ground around its base like ostrich plumes. White camellia bushes bloomed by the front door steps, their yellow centers like tiny lemon lollipops. I darted behind the pine tree, unfastened my garters, and rolled down my drab, clammy long stockings until they reached my shoe tops. I wanted them to look like bobby socks.

Back on the sidewalk I found out that what I had done didn't stop any kids from staring. My ribbed beige stockings that I thought looked like tree trunks now rested at my ankles like two big fat sausages. I fought the urge to cry.

Inside my classroom at last, I slid into my seat as fast as I could. A chubby girl on my left looked at me, all of me, head to toe, including the sausages, and smiled. A boy with eyeglasses to the right of me looked over his shoulder, then turned away. I was sure they were laughing at me. Not until our teacher entered the room and all eyes went up front, did the heat leave my cheeks.

Somewhat more relaxed, I turned my attention to the symphony of sounds in the classroom. They were nothing like those I'd heard in Latvia, or Russia, or Manchuria, or Japan, and I felt lost all over again. But when I began to notice certain combinations more than once—*pay-per, pen-sil, oh-pen*—I was able to figure out what they meant. The thrill of understanding each new word made me forget all those staring eyes. When the school's final bell rang, I went into the bathroom, rolled my stockings back up, and hooked them onto my garters. *Maybe tree trunks look better than sausages, after all.* I walked home feeling miserable.

At the store, Mama was helping Mr. Wirth wait on a tall, heavy-boned woman with dark wiry hair. Mama looked like a real grocer now. She wore flat shoes, a flower-patterned dress with a sweater over it for the cold draft, and a white butcher apron over the lot. She looked like she belonged there, working next to Mr. Wirth. I wished I looked like I belonged in my classroom.

Mr. Wirth said what sounded like, "What else, Mrs. Fabrocini?" He leaned on the counter with his weight on his hands.

"And Wonder Bread," she said.

Mr. Wirth picked up a loaf of bread from the bakery island and said, "See, Jenny, this is Wonder Bread." He held it up before placing it on the counter. Mama nodded.

Mama had seen me come into the store. After learning about "Wonder Bread" she said, "*Gehe nach hinten. Ich komm schon.*"

I did as I was told and went into the back room. I heard Mr. Wirth say, "Anything else for you today, Mrs. Fabrocini?"

"The last thing I need is a bottle of milk."

Mama said, "I know. I know. I know 'milk.'" I heard footsteps going to the refrigerator, then the door slammed shut.

"Good, Jenny. Good." Mr. Wirth said. "Mrs. Fabrocini, that'll be five dollars and twenty-three cents." The brass cash register rang, followed by the jingle of the reindeer bells. "You're doing fine, just fine."

Mama learned English fast and called Mr. Wirth a good-hearted man. I could tell he liked her, too. He looked at her like Papa looked at me when he'd call me *Gescheite.*

Mama came into the back room and placed her stocky, square body next to me. She pulled a stray lock of hair back from my forehead, tucked it behind my ear, and said, "Do you want some cookies, some milk?"

"*Ja,*" I said. "But I also want you to cut my hair. I want you to cut my braids off. Nobody at school … not one girl … has braids. You have to cut my braids off." I knew there was no money for bobby socks or new clothes, but cutting my braids wouldn't cost anything.

Mama sat down on two boxes of canned goods. "Illy," she said, as she placed her hands together in the dent above her knees. "I can't cut your hair. I don't have time to take care of it, to curl and fix it, and make it look nice. This way, with your hair in braids, it's one, two, three, and I'm done. You can see for yourself that I don't have time. You're a smart girl. We'll just keep your hair in braids." She put a plate of cookies and a glass of milk down on the desk in front of me and said, "Here, take some. They're really good," and went back to help Mr. Wirth.

Saying anything more would mean I wasn't a smart girl. At Abernethy School, I had to remain the strange foreigner with two long pigtails and funny-looking clothes.

The Fell family at Semmering

Gretl and Mama-1937

Opa before Kristallnacht-1937

Fredi and Illy in Riga-1938

Mama in Riga-1938

Papa in Riga-1938

The Feldman family in Riga

Fredi sails for America-1939

The send-off party

Mr. Wirth

"Elsie" at Abernethy school-1940

Senti Sitay

The HIAS had set Trudi's parents up in a Texaco station on the other side of town. Mitzi and Pepi knew as much about running a service station, as Mama and Papa knew about running a grocery store. And that was nothing. But like all of us, the Feldmans needed to make a living. So Mitzi, who used to have servants to do her cooking and cleaning, was now pumping gas. And Pepi, who used to spend his time doing business in Vienna's café houses dressed in expensive tailored suits, was now doing oil changes in greasy coveralls.

One Sunday morning, I followed a sizzling sound into the kitchen to see Mama slipping her spatula under two eggs in the frying pan. "Get dressed into something nice. We're going to visit the Feldmans today," she said.

"Really?" I ran over to her side and pulled on her hand. "Really?" I was so excited to see Trudi that I forgot to ask where the money for the bus fare was coming from.

"Fredi, we're going to the Feldmans," I said, putting my hand through his bent elbow at the kitchen table. "We're supposed to wear something nice. What are you going to wear?"

"I'm not going," he said, never looking up from his plate. "And don't call me Fredi anymore. Call me Fred. Just … Fred."

"Why aren't you going? It'll be fun." I wanted to be with Fredi all the time now that he was living with us again.

"I'd rather take the bus to my friend's house, that's all. I don't even know the Feldmans." His cinnamon eyes told me not to ask any more questions.

"Where are you going?" Papa peered over the top of his newspaper.

"I'm going to a friend's house. You don't know him." The muscles around Fredi's mouth tightened.

"I'll bet your friend is a girl, isn't she? That's why you won't tell me who your friend is, isn't it?" Papa put the newspaper down on the table, covering his ever-present red dictionary, and narrowed his eyes.

"Why don't you leave him alone?" Mama said, turning around from the stove. A drop of grease from her spatula landed on the gas flame with a sharp *sssst*. "What difference does it make if his friend is a girl or a boy? Leave him alone."

"Because he's always chasing girls … that's why. And that's why he never has time to help out in the store. Girls … girls!" Papa's hand flew up over his open newspaper. "That's all he ever thinks about."

"Why shouldn't he be thinking about girls?" Mama said. "After all, he's seventeen. Have you forgotten how you were when you were seventeen?"

"I wasn't like him. I was in the army … I was an officer … I was fighting in a war like a man. I wasn't like him, chasing girls," Papa said, one corner of his lip rising.

Fredi clenched his teeth so hard that the flesh in his cheeks rippled. But he didn't answer. He did what Mama had taught us to do, and that was to never talk back to Papa. "Remember, he's your father," she would say. We didn't know if our silence was to be out of respect or fear. For Fredi and me, it was fear.

"I'm going," Fredi said, looking at Mama, his cheeks red. "I'll be back for dinner."

Mama sat down to eat her breakfast. "Finish up now, Illy. We've much to do before we go to the Feldmans."

It took half an hour on the bus to get to the Feldmans' house, a square building of gray wood siding surrounded by scrubby evergreen bushes that grew no higher than the windowsills. Three steps led to the front porch, where a two-seat swing hung on chains from the ceiling. I ran past Mama and Papa and rang the doorbell.

"*Servus*, Jenny." Mitzi reached for Mama's hands, pulled her close, and placed her cheek on Mama's, first the left side, then the right. Papa and Pepi shook hands, smiling. From then on everyone spoke German, with Mitzi beginning by saying lunch was ready, and why didn't we all sit down?

A handmade crocheted tablecloth covered a small table in the living room. Mitzi had dared to take some of her fine Viennese linens with her. She'd also brought some jewelry and a few pieces of silver. Mama and Papa said they never would have taken a chance. If they'd have been caught with those things crossing any of those borders, it would have been the end of them. They always wondered just how the Feldmans smuggled those things to America—in the false bottoms of suitcases or on their persons somehow.

Mitzi made *Wiener Schnitzel* for lunch along with fried potatoes, green peas, and a green salad. Even though all of us had our big meal in the evening after work—American style—we'd have our big meal at noon on weekends, as we'd done in Vienna. One question followed another: "So, how are you?" "How is the business doing?" "How is the English coming?"

"People are very nice to us at the station," Mitzi said. "They help us a lot, teaching us how to change oil and clean carburetors. Pepi didn't know what a carburetor was before we came here. We never owned a car. He told the HIAS he was an engineer, so she came up with the idea of putting us into a gas station." Mitzi giggled, her chin bobbing up and down.

"Now I know how to change oil, rotate tires, and put in a new battery," Pepi said. "I have so much grease under my fingernails that I can't get it all out no matter how hard I scrub." He showed us the dark crescents under his nails. "The biggest surprise is I learned everything from my customers."

"The same happened to me," Mama said. "The customers saw I couldn't speak English, so this young woman ... her name is Mrs. Amato ... offered to come two afternoons a week to teach me. She stands at my side and when a customer comes in to ask for—let's say a jar of mustard, she takes me by the hand to the shelf holding the mustard and says, 'See, Jenny—mustard.' Can you imagine that? It's hard to believe how kindhearted these Italian people are."

After lunch, Trudi led me to her bedroom. We started to play a board game on the floor, which followed a set pattern that suited us both—I always won and she always lost. Trudi didn't mind, since she was four years younger.

Mitzi served *Kipferl* for dessert, another one of my favorites. I'd loved watching Betti roll out the butter dough on the kitchen table in Vienna, cut it into little triangles, fill them with sweetened nuts, and roll them into crescents. After they were baked and dusted with powdered sugar, they melted in your mouth. What a treat! Papa sat on the couch with a cup of Viennese coffee in his hands, a mound of whipped cream floating on top like an iceberg. Sometimes he'd let me have a swallow—by the time I was eight, I'd fallen in love with this famous, aromatic Viennese specialty. There was no place else in the world I'd have rather been right then, than at the Feldmans.

"So, how is it going for you two at school?" Papa asked, stirring the sugar in his cup.

"*Gut*," Trudi said. "I don't understand anything they say to me, so I just stand there and laugh. The kids must think I'm funny because pretty soon, they laugh with me." She tucked her chin into her chest and giggled, sounding exactly like Mitzi. I didn't say anything. I wouldn't have liked anyone to laugh at me.

"... and for you, Illy? How is it for you?" Papa looked at me with eyes that I thought could see right inside my head.

"I learned a few words of English," I said. I sat on my hands at the edge of my chair.

"What have you learned?" Pepi asked from his place across the room. A spray of laugh lines danced around his eyes.

"I learned a song," Trudi said. "They sing it every day at school." I was glad Trudi answered for me.

"A song? Come stand next to me and sing it," Mitzi said.

Trudi stood right up and walked over to her mama's side. Mitzi kissed her and said she ought to stand in the middle of the room and sing. She was neither shy, like me, nor ashamed of her European clothes. I wished I was more like her.

"I want Illy to sing with me," Trudi said. "She knows the song, too."

"*Gott im Himmel,* I thought, *how can I get out of this?*" I wanted to be back in Trudi's bedroom where I'd be a sure winner.

"Go ahead, Illy," Papa said. "Sing with Trudi."

I stood in the middle of the room next to Trudi with my hands clasped behind my back and my stomach pushed out. The hem of my skirt made a half-circle over my knees. We sang, "Gott bles Amerika, land zat I luf ..." and on, until we got to, "senti sitay, and gitay ..."

"Wait a minute," Papa said. "What is this, 'senti sitay, and gitay?' What does that mean?"

"I don't know." Trudi said, giggling. "I don't know what it means. I just sing what the others sing." She laughed. Then all of us laughed, except for Papa.

"There are no such words. You're singing it wrong," Papa said ... no smile ... serious.

"We're singing it right, Papa. Trudi's right," I said. Trudi stopped giggling and everybody stopped laughing.

"Maybe they're right, Norbert, maybe there are words like that but we just don't know them," Mama said. "After all, we don't know English so good."

"What do you know?" Papa jumped out of his chair, his voice loud. "I'll show you in the dictionary—there are no such words."

Trudi's face went limp and her eyes filled with tears. "They *do* sing those words," she said. A few small wet spots appeared on her blouse. Mitzi pulled Trudi onto her lap and whispered, "*Shshshsh,* it's all right."

I walked over to Mama and sat down on the arm of her chair. I didn't cry. I'd seen Papa yell at Fredi and Mama often enough that I'd gotten used to it, but I'd never seen him do it in front of anyone else. I was ashamed of what the Feldmans would think of Papa. I wished he were like Pepi, with his twinkling eyes and constant smile.

Mama thrust both hands up high and said, "Now look what you've done. Look how you've upset these children. How can you be like that? You've even made Trudi cry." She dropped her hands on her lap, shaking her head.

"But there are no such words as 'senti, sitay and gitay.'" He picked up his red dictionary and threw it into Mama's lap. "Here, just show me where you see those words?"

Mama looked at the book in her lap and back up at him. "I'm not going to do that. If you can't find them, how can I?"

The party was ruined. Trudi was in tears. Mitzi and Pepi started to clean up the dessert dishes. Mama said we'd better go home. Papa insisted all the way home that we were wrong and he was right. Of course, he was. We didn't know until a few weeks later that what Trudi and I heard as "senti, sitay and gitay," stood for "stand beside her and guide her."

Answering to Four Names

The harder Mama and Papa worked, the longer the walk across the Hawthorne Bridge seemed to be. They decided to rent a furnished apartment three blocks away from the store, in one of those square boxes that looked like a giant dice. We moved into an upstairs unit, painted sky blue. It had a living room, kitchen, two bedrooms, and a bathroom. Venetian blinds hung on all the windows, cutting down what little light could be found in the forever-cloudy skies of Portland. A sofa and stuffed chairs were upholstered in a variety of fabrics—plaids, chevrons, and floral chintz, all out of focus from wear.

My favorite was the plaid couch. No two springs under the cushions were the same height; sitting down meant being pushed to one side or another. A large woven grass mat covered the floor of the living room, reminding me of our beds in Japan. What our apartment was like mattered to none of us—we hardly spent any time there. Mama was at the store all day, Fredi worked at his shipping clerk job, and Papa was out trying to find a job as a doctor that didn't require a license. I didn't like being home alone, and the neighborhood kids who played baseball never said "Hi," or, "What's your name?" or, "Want to play?" when I passed by. Of course, I didn't say anything either.

In time I became somewhat more comfortable at school. The kids got used to seeing me in my strange clothes and stopped staring. During recess, I separated myself from the rest and leaned against the school wall, my body weight resting on my hands, flat against the building. I watched them running around doing playground stuff, bouncing balls, chasing each other, playing hopscotch. Every so often someone shot a glance at me. I looked down at the tops of my shoes as fast as I could, afraid to meet anyone's eyes.

During one recess, I was at my usual spot when a boy with a soccer ball tucked under his arm approached me. I thought he looked good in his crumpled, long-sleeved white shirt open at the collar, loose navy blue pants, white socks, and black Oxford shoes polished to a high shine. They matched the shine of his straight black hair and doll-button eyes.

"What's your name?" he said.

I was stunned. I stopped leaning on the building and stood straight up.

"What's your name?" he pointed at me with his right hand. I shifted my weight from one foot to another. "My name's August. What's yours?"

"Ilse."

"Isse?"

"Ilse!"

"Elsie?"

"Ill … zeh!" I said, louder.

"Elsie! I'll just call you Elsie," he announced. He bounced his ball up and down twice. "Wanna' play?"

"*Ja*."

He bounced his ball toward me and I bounced it back to him. A chubby boy with corn silk hair and skin like cold cream walked by and asked, "Can I play?"

"Sure, Johnny. This is Elsie. She's playing with us."

When I got back to the store after school, I wanted to tell Mama that I actually played with some kids. But she was busy waiting on Mrs. Carbone, a short woman in black with her hair in a bun, who was saying, "Gimmi burrr."

Mama bent forward as if she hadn't heard. "Please?"

"Gimmi burr," Mrs. Carbone shouted.

Mama stood straight up, her hands flat on the counter top. She turned her head toward the back room and shouted, "Mr. Wirth!"

He pushed the striped curtain aside and said, "What can we get for you, Mrs. Carbone?"

"Gimmi burrr," she said in a low voice, showing her yellow teeth.

"She wants butter, Jenny … a pound of butter. She's saying, 'give me butter.'" Mr. Wirth slipped back through the striped curtain.

When Mama finished with Mrs. Carbone, she came into the back room carrying a pound cake for my snack. Shaking her head back and forth, she said, "Now I'm supposed to learn English *mit* an Italian accent. I have enough trouble learning English *mit* an American accent, let alone an Italian one." Mr. Wirth laughed. Mama blew a *pfff* through her teeth.

I took a bite of pound cake, leaving some crumbs around my mouth, and said, "Mama, they call me Elsie at school. That's not my name. They should call me Ilse. I tried to tell them how to say my name, but every time they try, it comes out as Elsie. I don't want to be called Elsie. It makes me think about Elsie the Cow on our cans of Borden's milk."

"Let zem call you Elsie if zey want to."

"But that's not my name."

"I don't think there's a thing you can do about it. Zey can't say Ilse right, anymore than Mrs. Carbone can say "butter" right. Just let zem call you Elsie."

"But …" Before I could finish what I was going to say, Mama passed through the striped curtain saying, "Now go outside and play."

I looked at the empty lot across the street. It was deserted. I sauntered onto the field's razor-edged crabgrass, my head hanging like a wilted rose. A gentle breeze blew some dandelion seedlings into the air, where they stayed a brief moment before floating back down to earth. I sat down cross-legged on a patch of clover and looked for the lucky one, the four-leaf clover. I needed it to make my wish come true, my wish to be like the kids at school. But I knew in my heart that even if I found one, or a rabbit's foot, or a spotted red ladybug, I still would be different.

I had no one to play with, nothing to do except go back to the store to stock shelves or help Mama fetch items for her customer. I looked up at the fire station next to our store. A shiny red truck, its hoses neatly folded and its brass fixtures shining like liquid gold, was on the driveway ready to be washed and waxed. It was a daily ritual. Papa said the firemen's enthusiasm for cleaning was due to the fact that they had nothing else to do. We never heard a fire alarm. "What a great job, getting paid for doing nothing."

"But they do keep a 'Victory Garden,'" I said, referring to the small plot of land between their station and our store where they grew vegetables to help with our wartime shortages.

In winter, the corn stock leaves dried up and crumbled like burnt paper. The tomato plants hung limp on their stakes, their juicy red fruit no longer on the vine. Beetles, mealy bugs, and snails crocheted holes in the remaining lettuce leaves, so that they looked like handmade doilies on the ground. The firemen retreated to their station and played cards all day long.

The garden was abandoned now, and I crossed the street to explore. A few stringy rhubarb stalks, overripe in a deep maroon color, remained standing. I broke one off at its roots for a taste. The moment it cracked free in my hand, the side door of the fire station opened and a uniformed firemen yelled, "Hey, Sally, come here."

I stood up holding a red, stringy stalk in my hand, slack-jawed, my heart banging, with legs like columns of concrete. He laughed and said, "Come on over here, Sally. We want to talk to you."

Like a thief who'd been caught in the act, I dropped the rhubarb and ran in the opposite direction to the safety of the store, my pigtails bouncing on my back. I hurried past Mr. Wirth behind the meat case, past Mama restocking cans, and stopped, breathless, next to Papa at his desk in the back room.

"What's the matter with you?" Papa said. "You're all out of breath."

"Nothing."

"What do you mean 'nothing'? You look like you saw a ghost."

"Nothing—I'm all right."

"Come here." Papa swiveled his chair around to face me and pulled me onto his lap. I felt warm and safe in his arms. "Now—tell me what happened."

"It's the fireman. I was standing in their garden and … and …" *I can't tell him about stealing the rhubarb.* "He said, 'Come here, Sally.' That's not my name. He doesn't even know my name. Why does he call me Sally?" I picked up the gold chain to Papa's watch and wound it around my finger.

"I don't know why he calls you Sally." Papa kissed my forehead. "Maybe it's the English way of calling you Sara."

"Why would he call me Sara?" I asked.

"Because he's probably an anti-Semite—just like the Nazis were when they put Sara on your passport. It wasn't enough for them to just put a big, red *J* on it. They had to add an extra 'Sara' to make sure that no one would mistake us for being anything but Jewish."

We all considered the firemen anti-Semites, until one day when Mama stepped out onto the sidewalk in front of the store and called me to come in. I was across the street still looking for that lucky four-leaf clover, when she shouted, "Illy." I realized then that it sounded much like "Sally" from a distance, especially with her German accent. We never did know whether or not the firemen were anti-Semites, but we did figure out why they called me "Sally."

The name "Sally" was yet another name added to the others: "Ilse" on formal documents, "Elsie" at school, "Illy" at home and by friends, "Suzinka" by Mama and Papa when they were especially affectionate, and "Sally" by the firemen next door.

Delivering Spuds

I was in the back room after school one day, fixing myself a snack. I'd taken a slice of Wonder Bread, spread lots of Best Foods Mayonnaise on it, and topped it with a slice of bologna. I wished it was rye bread, like the bread we could buy at Mosler's Bakery in our old neighborhood, but that was too far away. Anyway, I'd gotten used to the soft chew of American bread, and it was at least one way that I was like other kids. However, I still couldn't bear the taste of peanut butter and jelly sandwiches or cereal for breakfast.

I poured a little 7-Up into a small glass that had been a Velveeta Cheese jar. Mama never threw anything away. Decorated with yellow Marguerite daisies, standing tall on straight stalks dotted with tea-green leaves, it became a drinking glass when the cheese was used up. I liked watching the soda bubbles attach themselves to the side of the glass, and then rise like see-through balloons to explode on top with a fizz. When I finished, I slid through the striped curtain and leaned against the doorjamb.

Mama was weighing macaroni into half and full pound portions and packaging them in brown paper bags. The reindeer bells jangled and Mrs. Amato came in to teach Mama English. "Hi, Jenny. Hi, Mr. Wirth. How are you today?" she said.

"Oh ... so, so, la, la," Mr. Wirth answered, while stuffing beef into the meat grinder.

"Goot ahfterrnoon, Mrs. Amato," Mama said.

Why doesn't she just say hi?

"Mr. Wirth, what happened to you? What a nasty-looking black eye."

"Oh, that. It's nothing really." He turned to face her, wiping his hands in his apron.

"How in the world did you get so banged up?" she asked.

"Well ..." Mr. Wirth hesitated. "I'm just a clumsy stumble bum, I guess. I was in a hurry, and I walked into the edge of a door." He laughed at himself, as if he'd acted like Charlie Chaplin, and went back to grinding beef.

But that's not what Papa said about Mr. Wirth's black eye. He said Mr. Wirth's retarded son probably socked him. Mr. Wirth didn't want anyone to know about it, so he made up a silly excuse. I wondered how Papa could know that. I wished I was as smart as Papa.

Right after Mrs. Amato came to help Mama, a short woman built like a round peg waddled in, shifting her weight from side to side like a duck. It was Mrs. Riveti with a long shopping list. Mama chased all over the store, fetching a bunch of items that made a huge pile on the checkout counter. I knew Mama was happy—the more she sold, the more money she'd make.

"And I'll have fifty pounds of spuds." Mrs. Riveti folded her grocery list and stuffed it back into her purse. "You'll have to deliver them, of course."

"Spuds?" Mama asked.

"Yes, a fifty-pound sack."

"Spuds?" Mama blinked and kept looking at Mrs. Riveti before she lifted her chin over her shoulder and shouted, "Mrs. Amato!"

"Potatoes, Jenny. Spuds are potatoes," Mrs. Amato said. "And someone will have to deliver them."

"I'll tell *mein* husband to do zat," Mama said.

After Mrs. Riveti jangled her departure, Mama turned to me and said, "*Komm,* Illy, you can do me a big favor if you'd just go through that big box of MacIntosh apples in the back room. Pick out the bruised ones *und* throw zem in the garbage. Save the good apples for the display counter. Can you do zat for me?" She put her hands on my shoulders and steered me through the striped curtain to a box of apples that smelled rotten. My stomach cramped. "*Hier,* I'll show you." Mama picked up a damaged apple. "See zis dent? It's brown and mushy underneath, so throw it away. I know you can do zis for me. You're a big girl."

Before I could tell her I didn't like that job, she twirled away from me and went back to weighing macaroni. It seemed that when I was forced to do something I didn't like, I was either a smart girl or a big girl.

Papa came into the store a little later and sat down at his desk to look at a couple of bills. He was dressed in his suit—he was going out to look for work as a doctor again. Mama slid her feet along the floor as if they were too heavy to lift, sat down on two cardboard boxes next to him, and let out a tired sigh. She'd been on them since early morning.

"Bobi, you have to bring a sack of potatoes to Mrs. Riveti's apartment."

"What?" Papa's whole body jerked as he faced Mama.

Mama knew he'd heard her all right, because she said, "She lives two blocks *von* here, in an upstairs apartment."

"Have you gone crazy?" Papa jumped up to his feet. "You expect me to deliver potatoes?"

"I told her you'd be there *bevor* dinner."

"You stupid cow," Papa shouted. He bent forward, his face close to Mama's, his bushy eyebrows standing on end. "Did you forget who I am? Why did I struggle so hard to become a doctor—so that you'd turn me into a delivery boy? How dare you ask me to do such work? You don't deserve to be married to someone like me."

My attention was fixed on their fight as I reached for an apple inside the box. I felt something soft and squishy in my hand. I'd picked up a shrunken brown ball surrounded by white fuzz. A shudder passed through my body. My fingers snapped apart like a fan, and the apple dropped with a thud. I wanted to yell for Mama—but not while she was going at it with Papa.

"I know who you are." Mama's palms lifted, her forehead creased into ridges. "I *know. Aber* what could I do? She needed the potatoes *und* I don't have anybody else to deliver zem. I couldn't ask Mr. Wirth. He's too old. What could I do? If we don't deliver the potatoes, we'll lose the customer. *Und* I don't have to tell you how much money she leaves here every week, *mit* her big family." Mama dropped her hands into her lap, her eyes on the floor.

"So you decided to ask me to be the delivery boy … dressed in my suit ready to go to the hospital … to be the delivery boy … to carry a dirty fifty-pound burlap sack of potatoes … on my shoulders … on my good suit … to Mrs. Riveti. Brilliant!" Papa walked away from Mama toward the black potbellied stove. He turned his head to the side and said over his shoulder, "I know you don't have any education, but I didn't know you were this stupid."

"What do you want me to do now? I can't carry fifty pounds up a flight of stairs. Who else can I get to bring those potatoes now?"

"Why don't you get Fredi to bring them—a strong young kid like that? Why can't he do a little work around here? Why do you treat him like he's some kind of prince?" Papa was pacing again, down one aisle to the back wall, and back up to face Mama.

"Fredi's not home *von* work yet." Mama stayed hunched over her hands.

Papa pulled his watch out of his pants pocket and said, "Fredi's through with work at three and it's five now. Why isn't he home?"

"I don't know."

"He's probably spending his time with girls again. That's all he ever thinks about. He never thinks that maybe Mama could use some help. He only thinks about himself—himself and girls. He's good for nothing." Papa walked away from Mama.

"Leave him alone. I don't know where he is, *oder* what he's doing. Just leave him alone."

Papa could call Mama stupid all day long, and she never answered him back. But when it came to Fredi, she'd always stand up for him.

I wonder if she'd do that for me.

Mama didn't say another word. The room was quiet except for Papa's footsteps pacing back and forth. Mama just sat there on those two cardboard boxes with her head bent over like a question mark. I went back to sorting apples. I didn't want to bother her with my disgusting hand. I wiped it on one of the thin, crinkled paper wrappers inside the crate and picked up another apple. It had a punched-in dent as big as a quarter and I threw it into the trash barrel. In that silent room, it sounded like a bomb landing.

Papa walked toward the striped curtain and, as he passed Mama, a hiss escaped from his lips. From the front of the store we heard, "Mr. Wirth, can I borrow your Pendleton jacket? I'm going to deliver Mrs. Riveti's potatoes."

Now English

On a sparkling clear Sunday, the apartment was perfumed with an inviting aroma of hot butter. I imagined bubbles hopping over a frying pan filled with two golden mounds, quivering on a shiny, white base. I swung my legs over the side of the bed, slid my feet into my fake-fur slippers, and skated into the kitchen just as Mama plopped two fried eggs onto Fredi's plate. Papa was bent over the front page of *The Oregonian*. He looked up with wide-open eyes and announced, "Hitler crossed the Russian border with three million men and 3,300 tanks."

"*Mein Gott,*" Mama said. "He means to rule the world."

"*Ja,* but he doesn't know what he's done taking on the Russians. They're willing to lose ten men for every German."

"Still …" Mama said. "*Gott sei Dank,* we're in America."

After that, we ate our breakfast in silence. Papa kept turning the pages of his newspaper, and Mama finally got on her feet and cleared the dirty dishes. I said, "Are we going to work in the store again today?" I dreaded the thought of spending another Sunday restocking the shelves.

"*Nein, aber* I have to do the laundry *und* get this place cleaned up." There were dark circles under her eyes. Mama never had a day off. On Sundays, she cleaned the apartment and did the washing and ironing.

"What are you doing today?" I asked, walking over to Fredi, dressed to go out in a gray V—necked pullover.

"I'm going to meet a friend," Fredi said, without moving a muscle in his pasty face.

"What friend?" I asked. "I thought you didn't have any friends."

"Another girl, I suppose," Papa said.

"No, not a girl," Fredi said, without looking at Papa. "It's a guy."

"What's his name? Where'd you meet him?" I asked, wishing I had a friend.

"At work," Fredi said. "His name is Hans and you don't know him and don't ask so many questions."

"Hans?" Papa took his head out of the newspaper. "Hans is a German name. He couldn't be American with a name like that. How'd you meet him?"

"He's not American, Papa," Fredi said. "I met him at work. He's a refugee just like me. Of course he's not American."

"Where's his family from?" Mama said. She stood up, pulled a bobby pin out from one of the patch pockets on her duster, and pushed it into the roll of hair at the nape of her neck. I wished she wouldn't wear her hair like that. I wished she'd wear her hair loose and bouncy around her neck like all the other American women.

I knew all the next questions that would follow, questions like, "When did they come to America?" and, "What does his father do for a living?" and, "Did they get any of their money out of Germany when they came?" Poor Fredi. I could tell that he didn't want to tell Mama and Papa anymore by the way his answers got shorter and shorter. At seventeen, he didn't want them to know anything about what he did.

"Illy," Mama turned to me. "Go get dressed. We're going to the Feldmans today."

"Really?" I was thrilled.

Sometimes we met other refugees at the Feldmans, like the Cohens and the Scheins. The Feldmans had lots more friends than we did, which was pretty easy to do since we didn't have any. I wished we could have made friends with some of the people we met at the Feldmans, especially the Scheins, who had a daughter only one year older than me. Mama liked all the refugees she met there, but Papa didn't like any of them. He said Herr Schein walked around like he was smarter than everybody else, and Frau Cohen slept around with other men.

I wondered how Papa knew whom Frau Cohen slept with. I wondered what kind of a walk Herr Schein had that made him look smart. I looked to see if Papa walked the same way as Herr Schein because Papa, for sure, thought he was smarter than everybody else. Lucky for us, he didn't think Pepi walked that way. As long as Papa could be smarter than Pepi, we could be friends with the Feldmans.

On this Sunday, we were the only family invited to the Feldmans. We were finishing lunch when Mitzi said, "How about going for a little walk? It's not raining for a change—it would be a sin to stay inside on such a beautiful day. We can do that the other ten months of the year." Mitzi's tight curls bounced as she talked.

We strolled down the sidewalk in two's, Trudi and I in the lead, Mama and Mitzi behind us with their arms hooked together, and Papa and Pepi in the rear in their shirt sleeves, their suit jackets draped across their shoulders. After two blocks of houses and apartments, we passed a small white church surrounded by rhododendron bushes twice as tall as Papa, loaded with balls of lipstick red blossoms that were as big as melons. The grownups stopped and admired the plants as if they were in a garden. In the next block a row of stores invited us to window-shop.

"Look, Mama, look. It's a grocery just like ours," I said, pointing to the corner store.

"Maybe I can find out how much they charge for oranges," she said.

She led Mitzi inside while Trudi and I walked on past a barbershop's candy cane pole and a dress shop displaying mannequins in long pants. We stared at the sight. We'd never seen a woman wear a pair of pants. When Mama and Mitzi caught up with us, they were shocked, agreeing they'd never wear such an outfit, saying it would make them look like men. We moved on to a movie house whose billboard displayed a picture of a dimpled girl about my age, looking like a porcelain doll. She was crowned with golden curls and dressed in ruffles and frills and Mary Jane shoes. The smile on her face made all of us smile back at her. Mitzi said it was Shirley Temple and wasn't she beautiful?

"Mama, can we go inside? Can we see this movie?" I asked.

"Not now," Mama answered. "But let me see how much the tickets cost." Mama walked up to the box office and peered at the board inside. "They're twenty-five cents." Mama's face turned serious. "Maybe we'll go … some other time." I knew that meant going to the movies was too expensive.

In the distance we heard a faint jangling tune that sounded like an organ grinder's box. As it grew louder, a small white truck with a "Good Humor" sign on its side, came into view and stopped next to us. A red-haired, freckle-faced young man stuck his head out the window and said, "Ice cream?"

"Can we have some?" Trudi jumped up and down in front of Mitzi, her red polka-dot skirt flaring out like an umbrella.

"How much *ist es*?" Mitzi asked.

"*Funf* cents," Pepi said.

"Vee'll take srree," Mama said as Papa took his wallet out.

"Excuse me?" the Good Humor man said.

"Vee'll take srree!" Mama said, holding up three fingers.

"Three?"

"*Ja* … srree."

"Vee'll take vun," Mitzi said.

We strolled on eating our cones. Mitzi's skirt waved sideways with each step. She said, "I know they can tell we're not Americans as soon as we open our

mouths, *aber* what I don't understand is how they know just by looking at us."
She giggled, then added, "Trudi, *komm her*. Let me have a bite."

Trudi stopped, then slowly held it up to Mitzi's mouth. Pepi caught up with
them and said, "Let me have one, too."

"Leave some for me," Trudi squealed. "There's hardly any left."

"*Ja*, there is," Mitzi said, as she handed the cone back to Trudi. She looked at
Mama and laughed, as if Pepi had just told the funniest joke.

Mitzi slipped her hand through Mama's arm and continued walking. "They
can just smell that we're not American. You know what happened to me?" Mitzi
pulled Mama so close that their shoulders and hips touched. "I was on a train *von*
Portland to Seattle *und* sat next to some woman. I didn't say a word ... no hello
... no nothing. This woman looked over at me and said, 'Where are you from?'
Can you imagine? How could she know I'm from Vienna? But I wouldn't give
her the satisfaction. I just said, 'I'm *von* Porrtlant, Ohrregon!'"

We reached the end of the block and Trudi and I ran ahead to put our foreheads against a windowpane that read, "Hot Dogs." Mitzi stopped behind us and
said, "*Was ist den das?*"

"I don't know," Pepi said. "Norbert, do you know what that is?"

"I don't know either," Papa said. "I'll look it up." He pulled his red pocket
dictionary out of his pocket and read, "Dog, a domesticated carnivore, bred in a
great many varieties. Any animal belonging to the same family, including wolves,
jackals, foxes, etc." His forehead was furrowed as he said, "*Ein Hund!*"

"*Ein Hund?*" We all spoke in unison.

"That can't be," Mama said. "Bobi, look up what "hot" means."

"I don't have to look it up. 'Hot' means '*heiss*,'" Papa said.

"*Ein heisser Hund? Nein, das kann nicht sein!*" Mitzi said. We all burst out
laughing.

Trudi and I went back to the window and looked inside just as a clerk handed
a customer a sausage wrapped inside a bun.

"Mama ... Mama," I shouted. "*Es ist ein Frankfurter!*"

We laughed all the way back to the Feldman's house. Trudi and I wasted no
time going to her bedroom and pulling out a board game. Through our open
door we could hear our parents talking in the living room. Papa told everybody
they ought to talk in English to learn the language quicker. We'd hear a few
words labored in English, then many more quickly spoken German words. Those
were followed by, "*Nein—nein*, now English!"

An American Friend

Mama ran a knife around the top of a cardboard box of Heinz Baked Beans and told me to stock the shelf. The front door bells jangled and a girl a bit taller than me came into the store. I knew immediately who she was ... she was a carbon copy of her mother. Her coal black hair was crinkled like electric wire, her nose already too long for her face. She could be nobody else but Mrs. Fabrocini's daughter, Dolores.

"Hi, Mr. Wirth." She glanced at him with eyes as brown as raisins and walked to the checkout counter. "Mom sent me to get these things on her grocery list," she said, holding up a scrap of paper, her hair vibrating with every word.

Mama and I filled her order and bagged it in three large brown paper sacks. It was more than she could carry and Mama told me to help her carry them home.

Is she going to stare at me like the kids at school do? I didn't need to worry. She didn't look any better than me, being the homeliest girl I'd ever seen. I picked up a large brown paper bag and said, "Sure, Mama, I'll help her."

Dolores and I turned down the street bordering our store and passed a narrow dirt alleyway filled with empty beer bottles, Popsicle sticks, ripped cardboard boxes, a grayish car tire, and chewing gun wrappers. It was like the city dump. A few hollyhock stalks and grasses struggled through the pile of trash toward daylight.

Dolores's house bordered this alley but looked like it belonged in a much better neighborhood. With wood siding the color of sand and snow-white trim, it looked as if it had just been painted. A black Model T Ford shone like patent leather in front of her house.

As we climbed up four steps to a landing and passed through the front door, Dolores said, "My name's Dolores ... what's yours?"

"Elsie," I said.

"I'm ten. How old are you?"

"Almost nine."

"Want to play some time?"

"*Ja.* Sure I do." I smiled.

Dolores was the first kid—other than Trudi—who wanted to play with me. August didn't really count. After that first time at school, when he asked me my name, he didn't pay any attention to me. Maybe he didn't like me. Maybe it was because I was a girl. Maybe it was because I looked weird. I pretended it was because I was a girl.

Two days later, Dolores was outside the front door of our store shaking the extra water off her umbrella. Once inside, she asked if I could come over to her house to play. Mama thought about that for a while, looking for a reason to say no. Finding none, she said okay.

Dolores led me into a living room like none I'd ever seen. A large couch covered in forest green velvet hugged one wall. It was set into a chocolate brown wood frame that was carved with chunky grapes and zigzag-edged leaves. Two claw-footed end tables held etched glass lamps with spiked crystal droplets. As we walked by, red and yellow and green rays of light flashed across the room.

An upright piano was pushed against another wall, its top covered by a long crocheted cloth. Lined up across its top were a series of silver picture frames in all sizes. I was looking at the photos of dark curly-haired people—surely Dolores' family—when I noticed a painting of a blue-eyed man dressed in a white robe on the wall above the piano. A crown floated above his smiling face and he held his hand up as if to greet us. I didn't know who he was. He didn't look like any of the Fabrocinis.

Before I could ask Dolores, a high-pitched voice from the kitchen called, "Girls, come and have a snack." Mrs. Fabrocini leaned against the sink, arms folded at her waist. Mr. Fabrocini sat at a rectangular table in the middle of the room, drinking a bottle of Budweiser. He was in a sleeveless undershirt that showed us he had more hair on his chest than on his head.

We were in a room of white—white cabinets, white oven, and a white refrigerator. The floor was black-and-white squares, laid down like a giant checkerboard. Three blooming African violet plants on a speckled green linoleum counter gave the kitchen its only color. I thought this was the most beautiful house I'd ever seen.

"Hi, girls, have a chocolate cupcake." Mr. Fabrocini smiled, showing us two teeth were missing from his lower jaw.

"Hi, Dad." Dolores went to his side and leaned against his shoulder. He wound his arm around her waist and kissed her cheek. "This is Elsie—you know—Elsie from the store."

"Hello, Elsie from the store," he said, with a playful lilt in his voice. "So what are you two up to today?"

"I don't know." Dolores looked at me. "Want to play Monopoly?"

"Sure," I said. I was so happy to have a friend in the neighborhood that I wouldn't have cared if I won or lost our game.

At dinner that night Papa asked me if I liked playing with Dolores.

"*Ja.* We had fun."

"What about her Mama and Papa?"

"I like them. They're really nice."

"What's their house like?" Mama said.

"It's really beautiful. They have crocheted cloths covering almost everything. Their couch is inside a wood frame carved with grapes and leaves. And there's a picture of a man in a white robe with a gold crown floating over his head. I don't know who he is. He doesn't look like any of the Fabrocinis."

Mama looked at Papa before they both burst out laughing. "That's a picture of Jesus," Mama said. "Mrs. Fabrocini is very religious. Mr. Wirth tells me she goes to church every morning."

"Every morning—just like brushing your teeth," Papa said, making fun of them.

"Who's Jesus?" I said.

"That's their God," Papa said. "Not ours."

I didn't care if her God was Jesus and not mine. I didn't even know my God, so none of that mattered to me. I hoped it didn't make any difference to Papa, either, because I just wanted to keep playing with Dolores.

"Mr. Wirth says that Mr. Fabrocini never goes to church with her," Mama said, taking a bite out of her roll. "She's tried all her life to get him to go, *aber* so far she's gotten nowhere."

"I like him already," Papa said.

"You should see those lamps they have in their house," I said. "They sparkle like anything. You can see all the colors of the rainbow when you walk by."

Mama laughed again and said, "Illy, you silly one, they're crystal." She looked at Papa and said, "I wonder how they can afford such beautiful things."

Papa said, "What does this Mr. Fabrocini do for a living?"

"I don't know."

"Probably works in a factory," Mama said.

"I don't know, Papa, but he's really nice."

"I didn't say he wasn't nice," Papa said. "Isn't it amazing that he makes out so well working in a factory? But then, in wartime, any idiot with two hands and two feet can make money."

I knew that for Papa, being a factory worker wasn't as good as being a doctor. For Papa, anybody that worked with their hands wasn't as good as somebody who worked with their brain. I was worried he'd think a Fabrocini wasn't good enough to play with a Fell.

"Papa, I like Dolores. She's really nice."

"I didn't say she wasn't," Papa said. "At least you have somebody to play with."

Dolores and I played together often after that day. She needed someone to play with as much as I did. Perhaps Mr. and Mrs. Fabrocini thought playing with a Jewish girl was not the best of choices either. We didn't care what our parents thought.

In spring, the alley between our houses came to life. A patch of hollyhock stalks grew as tall as Dolores and me, with white petals thin as crepe paper. Their yellow centers were magnets for the neighborhood bees. A constant hum filled the alley with black-and-yellow buzzers flitting from one flower to another. Dolores and I scrambled through the litter on the ground to make a game of catching them. We snuck up behind the flowers and snapped the petals shut the second a bee stopped to gather its nectar. The petals trembled as the bee tried to escape, tickling our palms. We squealed and hopped around until we could stand it no more. Then we'd let it fly free. I had such fun with Dolores!

But with Papa, I always had to be on guard—like the time I came into the store after having played with her and found Papa at his desk. He swung his chair around to face me, placed his hand over his lips so that it looked like lined paper, and casually asked, "Is Dolores in your class at school?"

"No." I sat down on a cardboard box next to the stove.

"What grade is she in?"

"I don't know."

"Didn't you ever ask her?"

"Fifth, I think."

"Is she a good student?"

"I don't know."

Nobody said anything for a while. "Why?" I asked.

"I just wondered."

I was glad that we'd never talked about school. I hadn't thought about whether or not she was smart. It didn't matter to me, but I learned fast enough that it mattered to Papa. Not knowing one way or another, I didn't have to tell him she was a bad student, in case she was. Some time later when we did talk about school, I found out that Dolores was in the fifth grade at a Catholic school. But Papa already knew the Fabrocinis were Catholic, and he still let me play with her. It was hard to figure Papa out.

Two weeks later on one of those rare days in Portland when the sun shone, Dolores and I sat on the scratchy grass covering the empty lot across the street looking for four-leaf clovers. "Maybe there's no such thing as a four-leaf clover," I said.

"Yes, there is," Dolores said. "Just keep looking."

Our heads were tilted forward, intent on finding this good luck charm, when a yellowish green insect sprang into our view. Its long legs were bent, and its round head bobbed up and down. I screamed, jumped up, and hopped backwards. Dolores laughed. She said it was a grasshopper and we should catch it.

"Not me," I said.

"Why not?"

"I'm not touching that thing."

"Okay, I'll get it."

"No, don't."

"Don't be scared. It won't hurt you."

She got up on her feet and put her hand out to grab it. It hopped off and away.

"Stop!" I shouted.

"Scaredy-cat!"

She tried to catch it again and again. On the last try, she managed to grab one leg, which promptly broke off when the grasshopper tried to get away. I screamed. She laughed, threw down the amputated leg, and trapped the three-legged cripple with her hands. I wanted to get away from the maimed creature. And at the same time, I was fascinated by it and couldn't stop watching.

"Let me see it," I said. She lifted the caged grasshopper off the grass into her cupped hands and held it up for me to see. Moving her thumb a little, I peeked inside and felt a pang in my stomach. I squealed, "Oooh! What are you going to do with him?"

"I don't know." Dolores put him back down on the grass. He didn't move.

"You can't just leave him here. He'll die."

"I know. Let's take it to the store and get an empty jar. We'll put him inside and get him something to eat. Come on."

"No!" I shrieked, thinking how mad Mama and Papa would be if they thought I'd hurt this poor creature. "You take it. I don't want him. What are you going to do with him?"

"I don't know. I'll take him home and ask my Dad."

Ask my Dad? I could never do that. Papa would have gotten as mad at me for maiming a grasshopper as he'd done when Mama asked him to deliver potatoes. Papa loved animals. He wouldn't have done anything to hurt them. He was always talking about how the horses would follow him around on the farm in Poland when he was a boy. He would have thought I was stupid and cruel and bad. He'd say, "What kind of a person are you anyway? How can you do such a thing?" And if he knew that it was Dolores who'd hurt the grasshopper, I'd never be able to play with her again.

"Take him then," I said. "And don't ever tell my Mom and Dad about it. Okay?"

That night we had dinner at the store. That happened every day except Sunday. Mama cooked dinner on the wood-burning potbellied stove in the back while she worked. In between waiting on customers, she'd run back and stir the soup, or chop onions, or check the frying chicken. Sometimes she'd send me back to do all that. What I liked best, though, was putting wood inside our little, round-bellied pot stove.

During dinner, Mama asked what Dolores and I had done that day.

"We went out on the empty lot."

"What did you do there?" Papa said.

"Nothing much—just looked for four-leafed clovers." I dunked a chunk of sourdough bread into the spicy reddish brown goulash gravy.

"Dolores is such a nice girl," Mama said. "I'm so glad you have a friend."

Mama pushed her shoes off her feet under the table and smiled. Papa picked up the front page of *The Oregonian.*

There was no need to tell them about the grasshopper.

Boredom and Playtime

Sunday was the worst day of the week for me. No school ... no store ... no Dolores ... nothing to do. Our apartment was abuzz with noise—the drone of splashing rain on the sidewalk, the bell-shaped wood radio spitting out bad news about the war, and Mama pushing a whirring vacuum cleaner over our hemp rug.

Fredi was hardly ever home anymore, and even when he was, he wouldn't pay any attention to me. Maybe he thought he was too old for me ... maybe he thought he was a big shot now that he was earning money as a shipping clerk ... maybe he didn't want to have Papa find fault with him all the time.

This Sunday was different. All of us were home. It was the Sunday before my ninth birthday, and Mama made not only my favorite meal—spareribs and sauerkraut—but a *Sacher Torte* as well. Over the radio we heard, "This is Edward R. Murrow reporting from London." Papa leapt into his seat and waved his arm at us to be quiet. The broadcaster continued, "Hitler's taken Greece."

"*Mein Gott!*" Mama gasped, and stopped pushing the vacuum cleaner.

"And Yugoslavia, he's going for Yugoslavia as well!" Papa moved his ear even closer to the radio.

Mama's face went limp. "*Ach, mein Gott! Und Oma ist noch immer in Wien.*"

"I know Oma's still in Vienna." Papa got to his feet, walked to the window, and looked out at the rain, his hands clasped behind his back. "And here we sit in Portland, unable to help her."

Mama sat down, wove her fingers into a ball in her lap, and fixed her eyes onto a spot on the floor. "We shouldn't have left her behind."

"What are you saying?" Papa said. "You know very well that I could barely get visas for you and the children. Where would I have found a visa for an old woman? Besides, she wouldn't have gone anyway."

"Does that mean Oma is going to die—just like Opa?" I asked about Oma without feeling anything. It had been two and a half years since I'd seen her and I didn't remember her.

"We don't know, Suzinka. We don't know." Papa stayed at the window. Silence. We didn't know then that we would never see her again.

103

Bad news about the war raging in Europe happened every day. Mama and Papa had a way of swallowing it and getting back to our life in America. After Edward R. Murrow's broadcast from London, we ate dinner. Then, Mama, Papa, and I got ready to meet the Feldmans downtown to see a Shirley Temple movie. We stepped off our bus into a blustery rainstorm. Drops, big and heavy as oil, bounced off the sidewalk as we walked toward the theater, hunched under our umbrellas. We could be recognized only by the color of our raincoats. Safely under the marquis, with folded umbrellas leaving puddles on the floor, we met the Feldmans.

But Shirley Temple was not on the billboard that day. Instead, we saw a grotesque-looking man with a high forehead, sunken eyes, and a bolt through his neck. Mama looked around at the others and said, "Do you think this is a movie for little children?"

"I'm not little," I said. "Kids smaller than me are going in."

"*Ja.* Some kids are as little as me." Trudi was always on my side.

"I suppose its okay," Mitzi said. "The kids are right. It must be a children's movie after all." We bought tickets and went in to see *The Son of Frankenstein*.

From the beginning of the movie, I felt myself inside every scene. I was in Frankenstein's castle, feeling its bitter cold and fearful of the threatening force of its sinister, dark rooms. The sight of the misshapen face of the monster, Frankenstein, made the hair on my arms stand on end. I might as well have been in the graveyard with the evil hunchback Ygor, his broken neck pushing his head to one side, watching him rob corpses from their graves. I gasped for air. I felt what the child, Peter, must have felt when he was about to be thrown into a boiling cauldron of oil. The movie ended with me in a trance, my heart banging inside my chest. I walked through the doors to the sidewalk outside, where I was surrounded by jabbering kids laughing at how funny the monsters looked. *What's wrong with me? Why am I so scared? Why am I not like them?*

The following Monday, I was grinding coffee beans for Mama after school. A short man dressed in a dark blue suit, white shirt, and red tie entered our store to the sound of our creaking front door. He didn't look like a customer—no flannel Pendleton jacket or plaid shirt or khaki bomber jacket. He was a refugee from Berlin and our Zellerback paper-goods salesman.

Papa greeted him with a wide smile that plainly showed the gap between his two front teeth. He was pleased to meet this man, saying, *"Es freut mich sehr Sie kennen zu lernen."*

Papa offered Herr Meyer the desk chair in the back room, while he himself settled on a stack of canned goods. I leaned against Papa's shoulders, making my stomach stick out like an over-stuffed cushion. They exchanged stories about how they'd escaped from Hitler. Papa grinned, a little too wide and a little too long, telling me that he considered Herr Meyer a *better man*—someone who was either a professional man or someone who'd made a lot of money. In Herr Meyer's case, it was because he'd owned a successful leather goods factory in Berlin before Hitler came to power.

"I'm sure you heard that Hitler marched into Russia," Papa said.

"*Ja,* I did. But I don't think he can take such a big country. Nobody ever has," Herr Meyer said.

"I agree with you there." Papa would never have disagreed with anyone he considered *better,* even if he did. Then he bowed his head a little and added, "May I offer you a cup of coffee?"

Herr Meyer went through the customary routine of first saying, "No, it's too much trouble," then, "Aren't you nice to offer it," and finally, "All right, if you insist." While having their coffee, Herr Meyer took the order for paper towels, napkins, and toilet paper. When they finished, he smiled at me and said, "What a pretty girl."

I lowered my eyes and dug deeper into Papa's chest. Herr Meyer followed with, "What's your name?" and "How old are you?" and "Come sit on my lap." I kept leaning on Papa.

With the grin still on his face Papa said, "Go on, then."

I slid onto Herr Meyer's lap and was engulfed in a crisp, clean fragrance, perhaps like lemon, or pine needles. Herr Meyer pulled a Hershey Chocolate Bar out of his pocket. "This is for you," he said, putting his arm around my waist. I took it and looked at Papa.

"It's all right. You can have it," Papa said. My stiff back went limp and I sank back against Herr Meyer's chest as if it were Papa's, peeling the silver paper off my chocolate bar.

Herr Meyer couldn't have been a *better man* in Portland with only a job as a Zee salesman. But Mama and Papa treated him as if they were still in Europe. That's how it was with all the other Jewish refugees as well. Herr Goldberg had been an accountant and now worked as a cutter in a uniform factory. Herr Lipton sold insurance in Germany and now drove a taxi. Papa judged them all by what they had done in the old country. Papa considered himself *better* than all of them, since having been a doctor in Vienna got you a whole lot of respect, even if you didn't have any money.

Herr Meyer came into the store regularly to get his orders, always dressed as if he were going to a wedding or a funeral. He always had a candy bar in his pocket for me. Mama and Papa danced around him as if he were royalty, and I always danced around him for the chocolate bar.

The summer vacation that followed was like a year of Sundays put together, with nothing to do except work in the store. The only bright spot was being able to play with Dolores—that is, when her mother didn't make her go to church. On one such day, she jangled her way inside the store and asked if I could play.

"Mom," I said. "Can I go to Dolores's house to play?"

"Mom? Since when am I 'Mom'?" She put her hands flat on the counter and looked down at me.

"I don't know." I was as surprised as she was by what had escaped from my mouth. I knew she liked being "Mama" with all the rules that went with the title—the rules of having to love, respect, and obey her. "I don't know. It just came out like that. Nobody is called Mama here. Everybody is Mom. Dolores calls her Mama, 'Mom.'"

Mama didn't say anything for a while. Then, "All right then—Mom. You can call me Mom. Here in America everybody is Mom. *Aber* I'm still your Mama, no matter what you call me." I knew that changing her name didn't change the rules. "Now, you play with Dolores *aber* first you take these groceries to Mrs. DiGiulio's. She lives down by the railroad tracks. I'll explain to you where."

Delivering groceries was just fine with me. I hoped I'd get a nickel as a tip. Mrs. DiGiulio lived four blocks past the fire station and two blocks down along the railroad tracks. We delivered the groceries but didn't get a tip. Walking home I said, "Let's go watch the trains."

We sat down at the top of an embankment that led down to the tracks. A lumberyard on the other side had stacks of two-by-four, two-by-six, and two-by-eight planks on its platform, ready to be loaded onto the next train. We sat on a patch of saw-tooth weeds and grasses that made our legs itch. We bent our knees, wrapped our arms around them, and waited for a train, squinting against the glare of the summer sun.

"Let's get down to the tracks," I said after a while. "We can see better down there. Besides, I can't stand these itchy weeds." We stepped onto the middle of the track and walked along the wooden planks as if we were on a never-ending ladder. Before long we were on top of one of the steel rails, placing one foot in front of the other, like tightrope walkers at the circus.

"This is fun," Dolores said.

"Sure, it is," I said. "Let's see how far we can go before falling off."

We balanced our way down the track, heel to toe, eyes on our feet, arms extended like wings on a plane, rising and dipping from side to side. When we fell off, we'd climb right back onto the rail. The lumberyard was well behind us before we knew it. We stopped and looked around. The embankment we'd been sitting on that had been covered by low growing, itchy weeds, was now completely covered by blackberry bushes. Thorny vines crisscrossed one over the other to form a deep springy mass. Glossy blackberries, like onyx gems, beckoned us to feast on them.

"These berries are just like the ones Mom sells at the store," I said.

"I know." Dolores nodded. A few red spots appeared on her yellow shirt.

"Mom sells them for a quarter," I said. "If we put these berries into a box, they'd be worth a quarter, wouldn't they?"

"I guess so."

"Let's go get an empty box from Mom's trash and fill it up and see if Mrs. DiGiulio will give us a quarter for it."

Mom's face broke into a smile when Dolores and I told her our plan. "I don't think the customers would like it very much if zey knew their berries were coming *von* the railroad tracks. Besides, playing around the railroad tracks is not a good idea. What if a train comes along? Why don't you play on the lot across the street?"

Dolores and I sat down on the crab grass field across the street from the store and had a business conference. I said, "I don't see anything wrong with us getting an empty berry box from the garbage and filling it up with berries. Then we can find out if Mrs. DiGiulio would buy one."

Dolores said, "We'll have to tell her that they weren't from the store."

I said, "Sure—if she asks." We went into the alley behind the store and found an empty berry box. We were in business.

Dolores and I stood on the doorstep of Mrs. DiGiulio's house holding our box of berries. Dolores's yellow shirt was stained with red spots of various sizes, and her wiry hair stood on end. My blue shirt was out at the waist, and some of the hair from my blond pigtails had escaped, making them look like worn out hemp rope. We rang the doorbell.

"Would you like to buy a box of blackberries?" I asked, holding the box up.

Surprised, Mrs. DiGiulio clapped her hands under her chin, not knowing what to make of the sight. But when she saw the berries, she smiled. "They look beautiful. Perhaps I'll make a pie. How much are they?"

"Twenty-five cents," I said.

We'd made our first sale. We picked more berries, filled more boxes, rang more door bells, and collected a bunch of quarters—until there were no more berries to be picked at the tracks at ground level.

Dolores said, "If only we could get up there." She pointed to the shiny fruit we couldn't reach glistening high up on the embankment.

"I know. Why don't we get one of those wide wooden planks from the lumber yard and lay it down on the bushes and climb up there?" I said.

"Okay," she said and, after it was in place, "You go first."

"No. You go first," I said. Dolores shook her head as if to say no and sat down on the ground with her arms wrapped around her legs.

When she didn't budge, I started up the plank on my hands and knees and said, "Hand me the carton when I get up to them." Halfway up, the board tipped over and dumped me into the bushes. I screamed as the thorns tore at me like tiny sickles. They snagged and ripped my clothes and drew bloody lines on my arms and legs. Dolores squealed and reached up to steady me as I tried to free myself from the monster bush that wouldn't let go of me. I won the tug-o-war with the embankment, but paid a high price for my victory.

Mom shouted, "What happened? Just look at yourself! What've you done to your arms—and your clothes? Wait until Papa sees you."

When Dad—yes, Papa had become Dad that summer—heard the whole story, he said, "Why did you do that? Do you think I don't have enough money to support you? Do you think you have to go around like a beggar scratching for money? What will people think of me? How could you be so stupid?"

I felt like a whipped dog.

Aunt Dora and Uncle Max

Dad walked up and down the aisles in the back room taking stock of our inventory. I sat in the oak chair by the desk, rocking back and forth, swiveling round and round, as fast as I could. The chair objected with a loud, grating screech.

"Stop that noise!" Dad shouted from the back of the room. "Can't you see I'm counting?"

I tried to escape to the front of the store when I ran into Mom, standing in the doorway, shouting so Dad could hear her, "Put down on the order that we need another case of Campbell's Cream of Mushroom Soup."

"We don't need any more soup—we have half a case—that's enough," Dad said with his back to us.

"That's *not* enough," Mom said. "I don't want to run out."

"You won't run out."

"*Aber* if I do, our customers will go to another store to buy it. Then zey think we don't keep this store well stocked *und* don't come back."

I leaned against the doorjamb, my hands behind my back. *Why doesn't he just order an extra case? They'll sell it sooner or later.* I didn't say anything. I knew if I did, Dad would turn on me. And Mom would get mad at me for "mixing in." I hated for them to be at one another.

"Why do you always go against me? If I say black, you say white. What makes you think you're smarter than me?"

"I didn't say I'm smarter than you. I know the Americans use a lot of cream of mushroom soup in their cooking—not only for soup, but zey make gravy with it. Zey put it with green beans *und* zey make tuna casseroles with it. Zey buy lots of mushroom soup."

"You might know how to cook, but you don't know how to save money. You can't figure out that if we buy Campbell soups and we don't sell them, our money is sitting here doing nothing." Dad's voice got louder and louder with each word, as if he were raising the volume on a radio. "But anyone can see that you're too stupid to understand that."

They stopped arguing when the front door opened and our mailman entered. He was a tall, half-blond, half gray-haired man whose eyes looked as big as an owl's through his thick glasses. His bad eyes must have kept him from being drafted into the army. The only men who came into the store in our neighborhood were old, sick, or handicapped like our half-blind mailman. He set his heavy leather mailbag down and flipped one envelope after another onto the counter as if he were dealing a deck of cards. "So—how's the world been treating you?" he asked Mom when the last piece was down.

"Sank yoo. Verry goot." Mom spread her lips wide into a smile.

Why doesn't she learn to say thanks instead of sanks and good instead of goot?

Mom sorted through the mail, picked up a letter and yelled to Dad in the back room, "We got a letter from Max." She passed through the striped curtain with me right behind her. She opened it with a paring knife and read:

November 15, 1941

My dear ones,

We haven't received a letter from you in a long time and hope that everything is all right. We wish we could tell you that everything is fine with us. As you know, Dora has been working as a maid in the home of a rich lawyer, a certain Mr. Anderson. They treat her well but the work is very hard. She is not used to scrubbing floors and waiting on people. That must show on her face because they have already asked her if she can't make an effort to look more friendly when they entertain guests. I hope she won't lose her job there.

As for me, I don't know how much longer I will be able to work as a lumberjack here in Seattle. I have to stand in freezing cold water almost up to my waist and I am sick most of the time. Then pushing the logs into place so they can be tied up and floated down stream is such heavy work. I don't know if I will have the strength to keep my job. I don't know if the HIAS can find any other kind of work for me.

Please don't worry about us. We will try our best to keep our jobs. We send you our best wishes and hope to hear from you soon.

Max and Dora

Mom dropped the letter on the desk and said, "He's too sick to do that kind of work. The bullet he took in the war and the asthma he got in Siberia may not have killed him, but this work as a lumberjack will, for sure." Two lines appeared between Mom's brows, making the number eleven appear on her forehead.

"You're right. It will," Dad said. "We have to help them."

"How can we do that?" Mom said. "We can hardly take care of ourselves, let alone support two more people."

"I don't mean support them. We can't do that," Dad said. "Maybe if they were in Portland, they'd have a better chance to find some other kind of work. Maybe the HIAS here could help them more." Dad got up on his feet and started pacing back and forth—a sure sign that he was upset. "Let's write them and tell them to move to Portland."

"Why would you do that, Dad?" I said. "I thought you didn't even like Tante Dora, after all the fights you two had as kids. Besides, you said she was crazy. Why would you want a crazy person like her living here so close to us?"

Mom and Dad laughed, but I didn't know what was so funny. Then Dad said, "You're right. She is crazy. And she's mean. And she's a liar. She's all those things. But she's also my sister. She's family and family sticks together. We have to help one another no matter what."

"I'll write zem tomorrow *und* tell zem to try to move to Portland," Mom said, getting up on her feet. "After all, Max is my brother, too."

That night when Fred came home from school, I followed him into his bedroom and said, "Fredi, did you hear? Tante Dora and Onkel Max—I mean Aunt Dora and Uncle Max—might move to Portland."

"Fred. Not Fredi. When are you going to learn to say Fred?" He grabbed my shoulders and lowered his face down close to mine. "Fred! Fred! Can't you remember that? Fred!"

"All right—Fred then. You didn't hear one word I said. I said ... Tante Dora and Onkel Max ... I mean Aunt Dora and Uncle Max ... might move to Portland."

"Okay, so they're moving." Fred went to the closet to get into his "at home clothes."

"Why does Dad call her crazy? And why doesn't Mom like her? Why are they asking them to move down here?" I said. "We don't need to have a nasty, crazy old aunt here."

"She isn't going to hurt you. It's just that she doesn't like Mom because she thinks Dad married below his class. She thinks a doctor could have married somebody with money—not someone like Mom whose family didn't have a penny. She's just ..." Fred stopped to think for a minute, "... crazy. She imagines things and then starts to believe them herself."

"What things?"

"I only know a couple of things. I know she told a boyfriend—actually he was a friend of Dad's—that she had a large dowry. It wasn't true, of course, and when her boyfriend found out what a liar she is, he left her. And he didn't want to have anything to do with Dad anymore either."

"What's a dowry?"

"Money, Illy, money. Back in Vienna, everybody married for money—except Dad, who fell in love with Mom and didn't care what his family said. When you're older you'll see that in the end, everything boils down to money."

"So she made a mistake. I don't see why that makes her crazy."

"How about the time when she got mad at Dad and told him their parents in Poland had died? It was the only time I'd ever seen Dad cry."

"There's nothing crazy about crying when your parents die."

"But they weren't dead! She just said that knowing there wasn't anything that would hurt Dad more than losing his parents."

"That's crazy," I said.

It wasn't long before Aunt Dora and Uncle Max moved to Portland. Aunt Dora got a job as a maid for a doctor's family, but Uncle Max was too sick to do any kind of work. They moved into an apartment not far from us, just a short bus ride away. After they settled in, they invited us to dinner.

I was glad to be going somewhere on this Sunday—to have something to do other than helping Mom clean house or stack cans at the store. Often I'd see kids out in the street riding their bikes. I hungered for a bike. What fun it would be to speed downhill, slicing through the air, feeling it push my cheeks back on my face, closing my eyes into slits against the wind. I'd pretend that if I went fast enough, I could take off and fly like a bird. I envied other kids going places, doing things with their families. I'd see them get into their cars with straw baskets to picnic in the country. I imagined them to be filled with crusty fried chicken, crunchy carrot sticks, and chocolate-covered doughnuts. This Sunday was special. I had someplace to go, even if it was only to my crazy Aunt Dora's and sick old Uncle Max's apartment.

They lived on the top floor of an old wood-shingled building. Inside their entry, the air was musty and still. Aunt Dora wrapped her fat arms around me like a boa constrictor and kissed me on the cheek. Her mouth was open, and I could feel her wet teeth against my cheek. *Ugh!*

Inside their dark living room, I passed a round table covered by a crocheted cloth that reminded me of a huge spider web. Uncle Max sat in an overstuffed maroon chair—bald, long-eared, long-nosed, and wheezing from asthma. He was reading the *Vorwarts,* a New York paper listing people's names who'd survived the war. He never stopped looking for Oma. With a sugar cube between his teeth and a glass of hot tea in his hand, he said, "How's my favorite girl?"

Aunt Dora's double chin quivered like a bowl of Jello as she said, "Want to help me frost the cake?" I followed her over-sized body into the kitchen. She tended to four different pots and pans on her stove while I spread mocha frosting on an almond cake.

"It reminds me of when I was a little girl at home," she said, between stirrings. "Only our maid did all the work for us." She told me her parents were *better* people. They were rich. They lived on a huge ranch with hundreds of hectares. They had many heads of cattle and many horses. She stopped only for a moment to look at the roast in the oven before telling me her parents wore fine clothes and had tutors for their children. When they were older, Dad was sent to school in Trembovla where he boarded with a family, and Aunt Dora boarded at a convent school. After what Fredi had told me, I wondered how much of what she said was true.

When we were done, Aunt Dora called everyone to a small table in the middle of the kitchen. Uncle Max shuffled in with his barrel chest sounding like clogged bellows. He lifted a spoon full of mushroom-barley soup to his lips and then put it back into the bowl, overtaken by a coughing fit. He followed it by spitting phlegm into a paper towel and throwing it into a paper bag at his feet. I put my own spoon down and pushed my bowl away from me.

Aunt Dora served meatloaf, roasted potatoes, and red cabbage made from an old Viennese recipe. I was halfway through dinner when Uncle Max put his asthma inhaler to his mouth and filled his lungs with medication. I couldn't finish my meal. When he recovered he looked at me with almost colorless eyes and said, "Illy, eat … eat … why don't you eat?"

"I'm not very hungry, I guess," I said with a smile.

After dinner we said goodbye to Uncle Max, who was back in his stuffed chair, wheezing with each breath. At the front door Aunt Dora placed another slobbery kiss on my cheek and said, "I hope you'll come to dinner often."

I dried my cheek with the back of my hand. *Stocking canned goods at the store isn't so bad.*

Fredi's Love

Fredi enrolled at Reed College even though we needed the money he earned by working. But Mom and Dad were afraid he'd be drafted and sent to fight in either Europe or the Pacific. They knew being a pre-med freshman would keep him out of the military. I didn't understand why Dad tried so hard to keep Fredi out of the army when he was so proud of his own service in the First World War. He bragged about being an officer and being wounded and winning a silver medal for bravery. *Doesn't he think Fredi can do the same thing?*

Fredi had as much trouble making friends as I did. He joined the Octagonal Club, a Jewish social club for young people in Portland and was all excited about going to dances and meeting people. But each time he came home from one of their functions, he had a long, sad face. He said no one would speak to him. One time, the kids not only wouldn't give him a ride home, they even refused to give him a lift to the bus stop. He was so hurt that he almost gave up going again. But he didn't, and that's when he met Catherine Anne.

I was sitting on my bed in our room cross-stitching a napkin when Fredi came in all smiles, chanting and teasing me with that nonsense rhyme, "*Ilse, Bilse, niemand Willse.*" I hated that "Ilse, Bilse, no one wants her around" thing, but I was glad to see a face full of sunshine and roses instead of the usual dismal lines across his brow.

"Fredi, how come you're in such a good mood? Didn't you go to the Octagonal Club dance?" I put my stitching down.

"I thought I told you not to call me Fredi," he said, sitting down on the bed next to me.

"Okay. Fred, then. So, how come you're in such a good mood?"

"I met a girl," he said, trying to stifle a smile.

"What's her name? How'd you meet her?"

"Catherine Anne. Isn't that a nice name? Catherine Anne." Fred looked as if he were listening to himself. "I met her at the dance." He put his hand on my knee. "And guess what else ... she even goes to Reed."

"I thought you told me nobody would talk to you there."

"*She* did. She sat down next to me and asked why I looked so sad. So I told her how everyone ignored me. Then she said she wouldn't, and asked if I'd like to dance." Fred got up and crooked his arm around an imaginary girl and twirled around the room. "So we danced."

After that Fred and Catherine Anne were always together at school, and even saw each other on the weekends. I wanted to know what they did on dates but Fred wouldn't say. He only smiled. Mom and Dad didn't know a thing about Fred's girlfriend until one Sunday a few weeks later. Mom was in the living room mending socks. She would push a wooden knob against the hole, then weave a patch over it with a heavy thread. Once mended, it could be worn as long as any new sock. Fred came into the room and grabbed his jacket. "I'm going out."

Mom looked up and said, "Where are you running off to this time?"

"I'm meeting Catherine Anne. You don't know her." His hand was on the doorknob.

"So who's this Catherine Anne? Is she the one you spend so much time with?"

"Just a girl ... someone I see at Reed." Fred's head was turned over his shoulder.

"Oh." Mom's eyes were on her mending. "How old is she?"

"Eighteen. Just like me." Fred let his hand drop off the doorknob and turned around to face Mom.

"Oh." Mom looked up, but her face said nothing. "What about her parents?"

"What do you mean, 'what about her parents'?" Fred stuffed his hands into his pockets.

"I mean, what does her father do?"

"He's a dentist ... a credit dentist."

"What's that?"

"That's when you get your teeth fixed but don't pay for them until later." Fred shifted his weight from one foot to another.

"What kind of business is that?" Mom put her sock down on her lap and looked at Fred. "Either you pay or you don't pay, and if you don't pay, then there's something crooked going on there."

"It's not crooked, Mom," Fred said, lifting his hands palm up. "He's not a crook—he's a credit dentist. His picture's in the paper every day advertising what he does. Haven't you seen it? He fixes your teeth, and you don't have to pay until you have the money. It's like having him lend you the money, charging you some interest, and then you pay him back what you owe him, plus the interest, when you can afford it."

"Ah-ha! I knew it. He's like a moneylender. They're all crooks. Everybody in Vienna knew that moneylenders were crooks."

"He is not! He's a very rich man. Dr. Stemper is not a crook." Fred voice was loud.

"You don't have to yell at me," Mom said. "I just wouldn't get too close to those people." Mom picked up her mending and went back to weaving the hole.

"I'm leaving," Fred said, and disappeared out the door.

I wished Mom wouldn't say bad things about Catherine Anne or her family. I never liked it when Mom and Dad said Mr. Fabrocini was just a common worker. It made me worry that they thought Dolores wasn't good enough to play with me. I liked seeing Fred happy with his girlfriend and wanted them to get married and live happily ever after, just like in the movies.

But Mom and Dad didn't see it that way. They tried every which way to talk Fred out of seeing Catherine Anne. Dad didn't like Fred spending money on her, and taking time away from his studies. Mom was afraid he'd fall in love, and she thought he was too young for that. She wanted to keep Fred all to herself a while longer. He didn't care how they felt; he kept on seeing Catherine Anne.

One Sunday morning Fred walked into the kitchen in his pajamas, his hair tousled like a bird's nest. He blinked the sleep out of his eyes and said, "What's for breakfast, bacon and eggs?" The pungent aroma of bacon filled our apartment so that you could almost taste the salty, crunchy bits in your mouth.

"Can't you smell it?" Dad said … then, "So, when did you get home last night?"

"About twelve-thirty, I guess," Fred said.

"It was almost two," Mom said.

"See what I mean?" Fred said, throwing his hands up in the air and turning his back to us. "She stays up all hours to spy on me."

"What do you mean spying?" Mom said. "How can I sleep when I'm worried that something happened to you, out so late at night?"

"Oh, forget it!" Fred said. He grabbed a plate and fished some bacon out of the frying pan. "I guess I'll have to have gray hair before you'll stop treating me like a baby." He sat down next to Dad.

"So, how much money did you spend last night?" Dad asked.

"About ten dollars."

"Ten dollars! Ten dollars? Who do you think you are? Henry Ford? How can you go out and spend ten dollars on a girl just like that?" Dad lifted his hand in the air and snapped his fingers.

"That's what it costs, Dad. If a guy takes a girl out dancing to Tommy Dorsey's Band at Janzen Beach, that's what it costs. That's what my friends paid. That's what Davy Weinstein paid."

"How can you compare yourself to Davy Weinstein?" Dad was on his feet pacing to the far end of the kitchen. When he returned, he bent over Fred and said, "Are you the son of a rich lawyer like Sam Weinstein? No! You're ..." he pointed at Fred, "... the son of a struggling refugee—a greenhorn. That's what the American Jews call us, and if you think spending a lot of money will get them to accept you, you're wrong. They don't want to have anything to do with us. They wouldn't even invite us into their homes for a cup of coffee." Dad was at the far side of the kitchen again. "They'll help us with money all right—but that's all. And if you think otherwise, you're a fool."

Dad walked out of the kitchen without finishing his breakfast. I looked at Fred whose face had gone back to the old half-sad, half-mad one I was used to seeing. I didn't know if Fred was spending too much money or not. I only knew that I'd better get money of my own someday, so I could spend it any way I liked without having Dad yell at me.

"I didn't spend the money to get accepted by the others. I spent it to have a good time with Catherine Anne," Fred said, looking at Mom.

But he didn't get any understanding there either. Mom said, "What kind of girl could she be, to take your money like that when she knows you don't have it? Doesn't she know we spend every last cent we earn to keep you in school? If she really liked you, she'd be happy to go out for a cup of coffee with you, like I did with your Dad when we were young. She wouldn't let you take her to Janzen Beach."

"Mom, you just don't understand. It's different here in America." Fred said, and walked out of the kitchen.

Herr Meyer—A Better Man

The wars in Europe and the Pacific actually helped Dad get a job. We had a shortage of doctors at home since most of them were in the armed services. That's why Coffey Hospital gave him a job working the graveyard shift—overlooking the fact that he didn't have a medical license in the state of Oregon. He could treat patients and write orders without supervision, as long as a staff doctor co-signed everything he did. That was okay with him—Dad could be a doctor again. He didn't even mind the long hours he worked—all night at the hospital and a good part of the day at the store doing paperwork.

Dad slept a few hours in the afternoon. I made the mistake of coming to the apartment after school one day, instead of going to the store. I helped myself to some peanut butter cookies and took a bottle of milk out of the refrigerator. It slipped out of my hand and hit the floor like a bomb. The explosion made me freeze in place as a free-form puddle of white, dotted with shiny glass shards, formed around my ankles.

Dad's voice boomed out of the bedroom. "What was that?"

"Nothing, Dad."

Dad yelled, "That wasn't 'nothing.' Why are you making such a racket when you know I'm sleeping?" His voice sounded like it came through a loudspeaker. "All you think about is yourself. You never think about anybody else. Can't you see how hard your Mom and I work? All you have to do is be quiet, and you can't even do that right."

I bit my lower lip. I didn't want him to see my eyes flooding. Dad passed through the kitchen door to find me glued to the floor.

"Just look what you've done! How stupid can you be? Can't you even hold onto a bottle? Do we still have to do that for you, too?" Dad picked up a broom, and started to sweep the glass shards away from my feet, shouting, "When the hell are you going to grow up?"

I was stung by his calling me "stupid," the worst of all crimes, and began to choke up. I swallowed and said, "I'm sorry, Dad. Can I go to the store now?"

"*Ja*, go, just go!" Dad's arm swung forward as if it were the broom sweeping me out the door. My being in the apartment with him was like putting a canary

118

and cat into the same cage. After that, I spent most of my after-school time at the store.

Dad continued to work that schedule until Henry J. Kaiser asked him to take care of the shipyard workers who were building warships for the navy along the Columbia River. He jumped at the chance, and became one of the original doctors for the Kaiser Permanente Health Plan. He still didn't have a license to practice medicine in either Oregon or Washington.

Dad's new job meant Mom would be running the store by herself. Even with the help of Mr. Wirth and Mrs. Amato, she still worked a twelve-to-fourteen hour day. Sales had doubled since Mom and Dad had bought the store, and even though she was always tired, she often had a half-smile on her face. Everyone liked Mom and respected her—something she couldn't get from Dad, who needed to have all the praise for himself.

With Mom making money at the store and Dad having a steady job, they could afford to buy a used, burgundy-colored 1942 Pontiac. With white-wall tires like giant spinning peppermints, it shone like ripe plums under the summer sun. Its leather upholstered seats were nicer than any piece of furniture in our apartment. We felt like the Americans who wanted to have nothing to do with us.

Fred was the first one to learn how to drive—Dad didn't have the time. Fred drove Dad to work during the week and gave him driving lessons on the weekends. The rest of the time, he was supposed to help Mom by picking up stock goods from the warehouse downtown to save any delivery charges. He didn't mind because he could also slip away and see Catherine Anne. This worked out well for everybody, until the day he didn't return with the two cases of Del Monte fruit cocktail Mom needed.

"I don't know what's keeping that boy," she said, strands of hair clinging to her moist neck. Mom walked through the screen that took the place of the front door in the summer heat, and stepped onto the front landing. Looking first left, then right, she said, "He should have been here an hour ago."

I'd taken an orange Popsicle out of the freezer and was sucking the juice out of it. "He'll be here—he said he would," I said with a slurp.

Mom had sent Mr. Wirth and Mrs. Amato home that afternoon, counting on Fred to be there to help her. She was somewhere between being mad and being worried, when Fred showed up at the store two hours late. His plaid shirt clung to his chest as he carried the boxes into the back room. "What happened to you?" she said, "I expected you two hours ago."

"Oh, I just stopped off at Catherine Anne's for a few minutes. It was on the way," he said.

"Catherine Anne?" Mom shouted, hands on her hips. "Why are you doing this? Why do you run after her all the time? Aren't the weekends enough for you? I want you here in the store helping me."

"You're not going to keep me away from her," Fred said, his face flushed. "I love her."

Mom turned around and looked at Fred, as if she were nearsighted. "Love her?" she said. I stopped licking my Popsicle. *Love? How exciting!*

"Yes—love her," Fred said, turning around and walking past Mom straight out the front door.

Mom glared at his back, saying, "That girl is going to ruin his life." She turned to me. "Forget about him—let's get to work." She told me to package elbow macaroni into half pound bags. She went off to grind hamburger behind the meat case. Hidden behind the bread island with the macaroni sack in front of me, I ran my fingers through the little yellow tubes and thought about Fred and Catherine Anne. I pushed the hanging scale in front of me and watched it swing. I filled the silver scoop with a few macaroni pieces and let them plunk onto the scale's tray in a slow steady stream—ping ... ping ... ping. *I wish she'd leave Fred alone about Catherine Anne.*

A blue-nosed fly buzzed past my head, bringing me to my senses. One of our sticky, yellow flypaper spirals, hanging from the ceiling, beckoned it like a seductive siren. A momentary silence—I watched the fly walk on our front window—then buzzing again. I placed four pieces of macaroni on the scale's tray and arranged them into a square. I added four more, placed at the joints of the others, and studied my creation ... *perhaps a maze.* Four more pieces ... *a rose!*

The screech of our screen door brought me out of my reverie. Herr Meyer entered—all dressed up. Every hair on his head lay in its place. Only a slight dampness glistened on his forehead, despite the clammy heat outside. No wonder Dad considered him a *better man.*

"*Wie geht es Ihnen, Frau Fell?*" he said, walking up to the counter and extending his hand.

"*Sehr gut, Danke.*" Mom said. "I have your order ready. It's on my desk." She extended her arm, inviting him into the back room. Her face was still stiff, as if she hadn't stopped thinking about Fred and Catherine Anne. I shoved the silver scoop into the sack of macaroni and followed them.

"*Ilse, Bilse, niemand willse. Wie geht's, Illy?*" he said, smiling and reaching over to poke me in the ribs.

His tickle made me giggle before I answered, "*Gut, Danke.*"

Mom stood at the desk pushing papers around, trying to find the order form for Zellerback items. The screen door squeaked and banged again, followed by footsteps to the checkout counter. Mom pointed to the slatted chair, "Please sit down. I have a customer now, but I'll be right back." The flypaper spiral swung as she slipped through the striped curtain.

Herr Meyer sat down, his knees parting into a navy blue V. He smiled at me and patted his right knee twice, inviting me to sit on his lap. I smiled back and approached with my arms close to my body, so that he couldn't tickle me another time.

"*Nein, nein*, I won't do that again," he said, laughing. I spun around and settled on his right knee. The white collar of his shirt was stiff and tight and dug into his neck. His clean, pungent scent wrapped itself around me. I waited for my candy bar.

"So, Illy, are you enjoying your summer?" he said, putting one hand around my waist, another on my knee.

"*Ja,*" I said, leaning back against his chest.

"*Ach*, I almost forgot," he said. He put his left hand into his pocket and pulled out a Hershey Chocolate Bar. "Would you like to have it?"

"I would!" I said.

The screen door screeched and banged again as another customer entered. Mom's footsteps were clumping across the wooden floorboards all over the store. She was busy out front, and I knew she'd be happy about that.

I peeled the silver foil off my chocolate bar with great care so as not to tear it. I saved it for the war effort, and already had a ball as big as an orange. When it was as big as a cantaloupe, I would sell it. It was a way for me to get some money of my own, beside the tips I got for delivering groceries. I ironed the sheet of silver foil with my hand on the top of Dad's desk, so that it looked like a silver-plated tray, and took a bite of chocolate, coating my tongue with its sweet creaminess. I didn't hear the *bzzzzz* of our blue-nosed fly or feel Herr Meyer's hand on my leg.

"So, Illy, how are you spending your time this summer? I mean, when you're not in the store?" Herr Meyer turned a smiling face toward me, crinkles around his eyes. His hand stroked my leg, up and down, as if he were petting an adorable puppy.

"Sometimes I play with Dolores," I said, taking another bite of chocolate. Herr Meyer's hand kept stroking, a bit higher up my leg each time, and I became aware of it. I didn't like it.

"Who is Dolores? Tell me about Dolores," Herr Meyer said.

"She's my friend," I said and stopped chewing my chocolate bar. His thumb had lifted the elastic of my panties to allow his hand to roam further.

I was in shock, feeling as I'd never felt before. The hair on my arms rustled. A shiver passed through my body. I no longer tasted the glob of chocolate in my mouth. I felt Herr Meyer's hand on my stomach, stroking, moving toward—I didn't know where—toward a place I didn't know anything about. I began to pant like a dog. The *bzzzzz* of the fly passed my ear, then a zap, and silence. I was as terrified as I'd ever been. I didn't understand what was happening to me, or what I was feeling. I gulped down the chocolate in my mouth, jumped off Herr Meyer's lap, and ran through the striped curtain, shouting, "I have to help Mom."

Mom was wrapping two pork chops for Mrs. Versace when I ran to her side, winded. She didn't notice. I wanted to tell her about Herr Meyer. *She'd never believe a better man would do a thing like that.* Still breathing deeply, my shoulders rising like wings, I said, "Mom, can I help you? What can I do?" *She'd think I was lying.*

"Nothing much, Illy. We're almost done here. Why don't you go into the back and keep Herr Meyer company?"

"No!" I shouted. "I can box this order, Mom." I grabbed a large paper bag and slapped it open. "Let me put this together for Mrs. Versace." Before Mom could say another word, I had the canned goods at the bottom of the bag and was reaching to pack the Wonder Bread next.

"I can do that, Illy," Mom said. "Go on back with Herr Meyer. We shouldn't keep him waiting."

"No! That's okay," I said. "I can do this. I'm almost done." I put a bag of potato chips on top of the bread while Mom collected the payment, rang it up on the cash register, and said goodbye to Mrs. Versace.

"Now let's go back," she said.

"No!" I said. "I'm going to see if Dolores can play." I ran past the meat case and out the front door, not allowing Mom to keep me from seeing Dolores. She looked puzzled, but just for an instant. She had to tend to Herr Meyer—*the better man.*

No More Best Friend

In September, as if a start bell had rung, the storms over the Pacific blew in over Portland, and dumped the first of nine months' worth of water on us. I welcomed them, because it meant the boring days of summer were over, and I could go back school. I'd learned to speak English quickly, and passed through the first three grades to catch up to my class. When I raced through my assignments at the start of the fourth grade and spent most of the class time looking out the window, they skipped me out of 4A into the 4B class. Once again the kids considered me an outsider.

A couple of weeks into the semester, I sat down for lunch, plopping my brown paper sack down on the table in front of me. A girl with a pageboy haircut framing a face round as a plate sat down next to me. She watched me take out a sandwich and said, "Hi, my name's Maria. What did you bring for lunch?"

"Salami," I said.

"Salami?" She wrinkled her nose. "I don't like salami. I've got peanut butter and jelly. Want some?"

I wrinkled my nose. "No."

She laughed, showing two deep dimples—like craters in each of her cheeks. I thought she was beautiful. After a few bites, she said, "You're Austrian, aren't you?"

"Yes. How do you know?"

"Everybody knows. The teacher told us. I'm Austrian, too."

"Really?"

"Yup, both my parents are Austrian. My last name's Jaeger."

"Jaeger?" I said. "It means "hunter" in German."

"I know," she said. "My parents told me."

"My last name's Fell. It means "fur" in German."

"Fur?" she said, dropping her chin to her chest and looking up at me. "Fur? What kind of fur are you? Cat's fur? Dog's fur?"

"Any kind of fur." We both laughed out loud.

"Come on," she said. "Let's play dodge ball."

The shock of anyone at school asking me to play rendered me immobile.

123

"Come on," she repeated, grabbing my hand and pulling me to my feet.

After that, we were together all the time at school. We'd choose each other for teams and school projects. We'd gossip about other girls and whisper about boys. I loved Maria—we were best friends. The weeks that followed were the happiest I'd had since coming to America.

Then one day, she said, "My Mom and Dad say that Austria is a beautiful and wonderful country."

"Yes, it is," I said, feeling the muscles in my jaw tighten. Austria might have been a wonderful country for her family, but not for my Jewish family. I didn't want her to ask me any questions about what it was like, or why we left. I said no more. I didn't want to risk losing her friendship. I said, "We'd better get back to class." Nothing more was said and we went on being best friends—until seventh grade. That's when we started to have Religious Study every Friday and everyone went to their church for instruction. I didn't have anywhere to go—there was no synagogue in my Italian neighborhood.

Dad said, "Why would there be a synagogue in our neighborhood? There are no Jews living here." He said there were only a couple of thousand Jews in all of Portland—out of four hundred thousand gentiles.

The kids who had nowhere to go were sent to the gym for that period. There were four of us there—three boys and me. One was a tall, sandy-haired boy from Texas named Chuck, another was a boy so clumsy he had yet to catch a softball, and the third was so fat, he was the last one to be chosen for any team. The gym teacher, a hefty young woman with a whistle around her neck, told us we could use the sports equipment and left the room. We looked at one another without speaking. Finally Chuck said, "So, how's it y'all ain't goin' to church some-where?"

"I dunno," the fat boy said, looking down at his shoes. "Guess my folks don't belong nowhere."

"We don't believe in no religion," the other boy said. "My mom and dad say all the church wants is your money." He walked over to the equipment bin, picked up a dodge ball, and bounced it along as he walked back toward us. We stood around not saying anything, listening to the bounce of the ball and its echo against the walls of the gym. Chuck looked at me and said, "How's it yer here?"

I said, "I don't have anywhere to go either." *He doesn't have to know I'm Jewish.* "Come on," I said. "Let's play dodge ball, two on each side."

Gym was one of my favorite classes in school. I was good at sports, better than most of the girls, and as good as many of the boys. An extra gym period would have been fun, but not with these three boys—kids on the outside of things like me. I wished I wasn't Jewish so I could go to church.

One Friday Maria and I stood in the hallway by our lockers—she was getting ready for Religious Study. She banged her door shut, put her combination lock through the handle, spun the dial around, and said, "You never go to church, do you?"

"No," I said, with a start.

"Why not?"

"Just because." I looked away.

"But why not? Doesn't your family belong to a church?"

"No." I started to walk away.

"Wait," she said, pulling me. "Why not? Why don't you go to church?"

"Because … because. I've got to go now." I turned away from her, but she grabbed my hand and pulled me back.

"I don't understand. Everybody else goes to church. Why don't you?" She lowered her brows down over her squinting eyes.

"Because I'm Jewish," I said, standing up straight. The second those words slipped out of my mouth, I knew I'd made a mistake. I remembered Mom and Dad saying I should never tell anybody anything about us. And when I looked at Maria, I understood why. Her eyebrows shot up on her forehead, her eyes like blue marbles. The silence that passed between us was like an axe splitting us apart.

"Oh, I didn't know …," she said, her voice fading in tone. She looked down the hall, back at me, and attacked. "You killed Christ."

I knew then that our friendship was over. I blurted out, "I did not! I didn't kill anybody." I felt my face flush.

"The Jews killed Christ," she insisted.

"They did not. The Romans killed Christ." Dad had told me so.

"My priest told me the Jews killed Christ." Maria's voice was louder; her body bent forward.

"Well, they didn't," I said, my fists clenched at my sides.

"Are you calling my priest a liar?" Her cheeks were flushed as she bobbed her balloon-shaped head up and down.

"I've got to go," I said, walking away from Maria for what I knew would be the last time. Dad warned me to never discuss religion or politics with anybody. If they disagreed with you, you've lost a friend, or your job, or like Opa—your life. The rest of the day at school, I fought with myself to keep from crying in front of the rest my class.

125

When the last bell rang to announce the end of the school day, a noisy roar filled our classroom. Books slammed shut, papers were crinkled and tossed away. A squad of stomping feet raced through the door, leaving me behind at my desk in silence. I took a deep breath and swung my feet into the aisle. I stood up as if I was lifting the weight of a buffalo. I was in no hurry to get home.

Inside the store, I found Mom standing in front of our striped curtain, feet spread apart, fists planted on her hips, fingers opening and closing in a nervous rhythm. Mrs. Di Giulio was in the middle of the store holding a fishnet bag filled with groceries, saying, "I told her straight out—if you don't get your grades up, you won't get into college. It's as plain as that." Her face moved from side to side.

I walked past Mrs. DiGiulio toward the back room. "'lo, Mrs. DiGiulio ... 'lo, Mom." I slipped past them without waiting for an answer, grabbed a doughnut out of a package, and went back out front.

"*Ja*, sure. You have to tell these kids straight out," Mom said, her fingers pumping away.

"It's not that she can't make good grades. She spends too much time with her boyfriend," Mrs. Di Giulio said.

"*Ja*, that can be a problem."

"It's not that I don't like her boyfriend. He's a very nice boy. It's just that she needs to study."

"Of course, you're right," Mom said, trying to make herself sound interested.

"I talk to her all the time. She just doesn't listen."

"She should listen. It's for her own good."

"Well, I better get home," Mrs. DiGiulio said.

After she left, Mom said, "What do I care about her daughter, and her bad grades, and what she does with her boyfriend? I have so much work to do here. And she keeps me standing there, with a smile on my face, as if I cared about her problems." She walked over to a burlap sack full of kidney beans and sliced it open. A few of them fell onto the floor to the sound of a series of pings. "*Gott sei Dank*, I don't have problems with *my* daughter."

Mom is so overworked—how can I bother her with what happened at school? "No, you don't have to worry about your daughter. Can I go home now?"

I slid the key to our apartment into the lock and found Fred sitting in a stuffed chair, a textbook open in his lap, a pen in his right hand underlining a phrase. "Hi," I said, on my way to the bedroom.

"Aren't you even going to talk to me?" Fred said to my back.

"No ... not today." I kept on walking.

"Why not?" Fred said.

126

"Because …," I turned the corner into our bedroom, kicked off my shoes, and sat down cross-legged on my bumpy chenille bedspread.

Fred appeared at the entry to my room and leaned against the doorframe. "What's wrong?"

"Nothing," I said with my head hanging down, trying to hide my shiny eyes and a chin that wouldn't stop trembling.

Fred sat down next to me and said, "Come on, it's not 'nothing.' Tell me."

A drop rolled down my cheek and fell onto the bedspread. "Some kid at school said we killed Christ." I rubbed the wet spot on the bedspread in front of me.

"Oh, that," Fred said, taking hold of my hand. "That's not the last time you'll hear that. You might as well get used to it right now and learn not to let it bother you. Just forget about that kid—stay away from her."

"But that kid was my best friend!" Another drop spilled onto the bedspread.

"That kid wasn't your best friend," Fred said. "Your best friend will never be somebody at school. Your best friends are right here—here in this apartment. Only your family can ever be your best friends." Fred put his arm around my shoulders and held me close. He lifted my chin up and looked me in the eyes. "Come on. Forget about that kid. Let's get you something to drink."

I'm so lucky to have a brother like Fred.

Dad's Suspicions

I made chicken-in-a-pot on the wood-burning black stove for dinner that night. At age twelve, I knew how to make all Moms' recipes on my own. It was almost dark when Mom, Fred and I walked back to the apartment. Dad was still at the hospital with a sick patient. We turned down our street but Fred stopped at the corner and said, "You go on ahead—I'm going to the bus stop. Catherine Anne and I are going to study tonight."

"Again?" Mom said. "You should study at home and stop running around."

We'd stopped under a yellowish street light that shone down on us like a spotlight on a stage. Long black shadows lay on the sidewalk next to our feet like dead ghosts. In the dim light, two purple loops under Mom's eyes showed the strain of her day's work.

"Mom, I don't run around. I study with Catherine Anne." Fred turned his back on Mom and stepped away from her, his right hand pushing his hair back out of his face. He swung around to face her again and said, "Wait 'till you meet her. You'll see what an intelligent girl she is. Sometimes, I think she's smarter than me."

Fred brought Catherine Anne to our apartment for lunch one Sunday. Mom cleaned the apartment, cooked the meal, and got into her best dress—the black one with roses as big as cabbages. *It looks like drapery material.* Her hair was slicked down on her head and anchored at her neck. *I wonder of she's ever going to change her hairdo?*

Not having a best dress, I picked my favorite school outfit—a pair of forest green corduroy pants and a pink blouse. Dad, as usual, looked like he was going to the hospital. He kept pulling his watch out to check the time, and Mom kept cleaning, even the things she'd already cleaned. Over the radio we heard Arturo Toscanini conducting the NBC Orchestra from New York. I was at the window peeking through the Venetian blinds when I saw them. "They're coming! They're here!"

Catherine Anne was much shorter than Fred and had more than generous hips. She entered wearing the uniform of a well-to-do bobby-soxer—saddle shoes, wool skirt, and a cashmere sweater. Settled inside our living room, she reached inside her purse and pulled out a small box wrapped in shiny yellow paper. "This is for you," she said.

"Thank you," I said. My present was a set of silver jacks. *How nice ... now I have another game I can play by myself.*

We sat around the table eating fried chicken and French fries. Mom wanted us to look as American as possible. Dad asked a lot of questions about Catherine Anne's family, about her Dad and her brothers. She answered each one, looking either to the left or the right of Dad's face, but never at him. She asked Mom and Dad nothing. In between Dad's questions the booming, forceful melody of Beethoven's Fifth Symphony filled the room. The minute we finished eating, Fred and Catherine Anne excused themselves and left—like they wanted to escape from any further grilling.

Mom was ironing one of Dad's shirts when Fred came home that night. She wouldn't have spent the money for a Chinese laundry to do that for her. Dad sat in his usual place next to the radio. I sat on the floor, practicing bouncing the small red ball from my present, picking up a jack, and catching the ball before it bounced again.

"So, how'd you like her?" Fred said.

No one said anything for a while. "She's all right," Mom said, without looking up.

"Well, do you think she's pretty?" Fred asked, sitting down in a stuffed chair.

"*Ja.*" Mom lifted one shoulder and tilted her head toward it. "I wouldn't exactly say she's beautiful. But *ja*, I guess she's pretty." Mom raised her elbow over the iron and pushed down hard.

"But ... do you like her?" Fred's eyebrows rose.

"How can I say if I like her or not? She never looks you straight in the eyes so that you can tell what she's thinking. How can you know what a person's like if she doesn't ever look at you?" Mom picked the shirt up and arranged a sleeve along the length of the ironing board.

"Well, I like her," I said from my cross-legged position on the floor. "And I think she's really pretty, Fred." I bounced the rubber ball, grabbed two jacks, and got my fist under it in time to catch it. "I did it! I did it!" Fred's blank face broke out into a grin. I was happy Fred had Catherine Anne as his girlfriend. I wished I had a friend, but I was too busy making sure nobody would ever hurt me again like Maria had done. I kept to myself at school, waiting for summer vacation, when I could go back to playing with Dolores.

On a hot day in July, Dolores ran into the store, her chest rising up and down with each long, deep breath. In the window, a newly delivered crate of strawberries filled the room with its sweet, acrid aroma. She pulled me into a corner behind the red coffee grinder and whispered, "Ask your Mom if you can come for a ride in our car."

"How come?" I said. "Isn't your Dad at work?"

"My brother Dale's home. He's not in the Army anymore. He'll take us for a drive." Dolores' breathing slowed. "Go ask your Mom."

"Where is your brother taking us? When will we be back?"

"He's driving us around the neighborhood. He wants to see if any of his old friends are still around."

Mom finished waiting on the black mound that was Mrs. Carbone. She then went to the vegetable stand and began cleaning the display lettuce. I put my hand on her arm, my eyes up to her face, and asked, "Can I go for a ride with Dolores?"

She pulled a slimy, mildewed outer leaf off the green ball in her hand and took a deep breath. She looked down at me with a colorless face, lipstick worn off hours ago, eyes half open. "*Ja ... aber komm schnell zuruck.*"

I turned to Dolores. "I can go. I just can't be gone long."

Dolores and I ran around the corner and climbed into the back seat of the Model T Ford parked outside her house. A tall, skinny kid with a caved-in chest hopped down the front steps two at a time and slid into the driver's seat. A crew cut made the top of his head look like a black brush. Dale said, "Hi, Elsie." I watched his Adam's apple ride up and down his neck.

Dale turned the key to start the car. We heard a cough, a sputter, and then silence. "What the hell." A grinding noise followed, then quiet again. "Goddammit! Didn't anybody drive this thing while I was gone?"

When the motor finally caught, we drove past the railroad tracks, past Mrs. DiGiulio's house, across the tracks to where his friend lived. No one was home. We drove past my apartment, past Dolores' church, and past Dale's high school. We rolled down the windows and let the wind push our hair back and felt it flapping free behind our heads. *What fun!* I hadn't ridden in a car since the time we crossed the border into Latvia. But this time, I was having too much fun to get carsick.

At dinner that night, Dad said, "So, I heard you got a ride in the Fabrocini's car today."

"*Ja.*"

"Where did Mr. Fabrocini take you?"

"No place. It was Dale who took us."

"Dale? Who's Dale?"

"Dolores's brother."

"Isn't he supposed to be in the army?"

"He's out of the army. He's home for good."

"Nobody's out of the army now. They need every able-bodied man they can find for the war." Dad pursed his lips, a circle of wrinkles appeared around his eyes. "… unless he was kicked out … unless he did something wrong … unless they gave him a dishonorable discharge."

"Gee whiz Dad, Dale's really nice. He wouldn't do anything wrong."

"Don't argue with me. That's the only reason anybody could get out of the army … unless they were wounded, of course." Dad looked straight at me. "He isn't wounded, is he?"

"No-o-o." I wasn't sure about that. "He's really nice, Dad." I felt sure about that.

"How nice could he be if they kicked him out of the service? You better stay away from him. I don't want you to go over to the Fabrocinis anymore."

I felt I'd been hit again—I'd lost Maria and now Dad wanted me to give up Dolores. There was no one, except perhaps Trudi—who lived all the way across town—who was four years younger—who I saw only on rare occasions—that I could call a friend. I fell back into my chair, defeated.

"Bobi, that's not fair," Mom said. "Dolores is a nice girl. There's no reason why Illy shouldn't play with her. She shouldn't be punished for something her brother did—or didn't do."

Dad's eyes were still on me. "He could be a bad influence on the girls. I don't want Illy to go to the Fabrocini's house again. If she wants to play with Dolores, she has to do it here."

But we couldn't have played in the store. What Dad had done was force us to play outside, all over our whole neighborhood, without any supervision whatsoever.

PART III

Fear and Withdrawal

Mom and Dad thought I should learn to swim. Mitzi told Mom the lessons at the Y were free and that Trudi already knew how. Mom signed me up and sent me off with a one piece red swimsuit and white rubber bathing cap. I changed in the locker room, pulling more than one hair out by the roots as I pulled the cap over my head and stuffed my braids into it. On the way to the pool, I passed a full length mirror and saw myself in my red swimsuit, looking like a giant tomato. Ashamed of how I looked, once again, I hoped to get into the water before anyone could see me. Inside the pool room, I almost gagged with the amount of chlorine gas in the air. When the rhythm of my breathing settled into a survivable pace, I looked around the room. At the bottom of the large rectangular pool, long black lines, meant to mark the swimmer's lanes, seemed to move like garter snakes. Echoes boomed off the walls, "Kick, kick, breath ... kick, kick, breathe." I stood by the door, wishing I could go home.

At the far end of the pool a college-aged kid, his blond hair tinged with green, yelled at me, "Elsie ... over here. Come on over." I splashed my way across the wet deck toward my instructor. "Hi. My name's Erik. And this is Mike and Sandra." He pointed to a dark-haired boy in the water whose black trunks looked like an irregular ink blotch. Next to him, a red-haired girl without a drop of fat on her body and dressed in a yellow bathing suit, stood straight as a rod. "Come on. Get in the water," Erik said.

I slid into the pool and felt as if I'd jumped into the Arctic Ocean. The cold made me gasp for air; my body broke out in goose bumps. I lifted my arms up to my shoulders, ready to push the water down if it came anywhere near my face.

Erik lined us up facing the side of the pool, told us to put our hands on the edge, and put our faces in the water. I squeezed my eyes shut, wrinkled my nose, and dunked my face into the dreaded liquid. It went under my cap, into my ears, and up my nose. I couldn't see ... I couldn't hear ... and my hair was soaking wet. I pulled my head up out of the water and gasped for air.

Much as I hated every minute in the pool room I was determined to learn how to swim. "*If Trudi can do it, so can I.*" I took the first few lessons doing what I was told to do, but with arms and legs stiff as sticks.

135

On the day of our fifth lesson, Erik walked us down to the deep end of the pool, told us to jump in, and swim to the side. He guaranteed the water would push us up to the surface and, since we already knew how to do the crawl, we wouldn't have any problems getting to the side. Mike jumped in feet first and left a patch of bubbles behind. When he came up, he gasped for air and dog paddled to the side, forgetting to do the crawl, which we'd spent four lessons learning.

"Good, Mike. Good, only next time, remember to do the crawl to the side. You know, big arms … pull … pull." Erik paced back and forth, his arms swimming in the air, his voice bouncing off the walls.

Sandra jumped in and came right back up, her hands at her sides, her red hair breaking the water first like the eraser end of a pencil. She broke into a wide grin and swam the crawl to the side exactly like Erik had taught us.

"That's the way. Great!" Erik walked past us, clapping his hands.

My turn was next. "*If they can do it, I can do it.*" I stood at the side of the pool with my toes bent over the edge and looked into the water. I might as well have been looking into the jaws of a shark. I couldn't jump. The others stared me, waiting.

"Go on. Jump. It's fun!" Sandra yelled. She sat on the edge of the pool with her feet splashing the top of the water.

Erik and Mike stood next to one another on the deck, watching. "Go on. Jump," Erik said.

I couldn't move. Out of the corner of my eye I saw a black shadow streak across the wall behind me. It was Mike—who pushed me into the pool. I sank to the bottom like a boat anchor, past greenish bubbles like those inside a large bottle of soda. I began to flap my arms up and down, trying to come to the surface. But every move I made pulled me back down. My lungs seemed to be in a vise. *I'm going to drown.* Panicked, my arms flayed faster and faster until, exhausted, I went limp.

I felt an arm wind itself around my chest and pull me up to the surface. It was Erik who brought me to the side of the pool and dumped me over the edge, as if I were a sack of potatoes. I sputtered and coughed and sucked in air with deep, raspy croaks that might have come from a frog.

"Why did you do that?" Erik said. "By doing this," he flapped his arms like I'd done, "you were actually keeping yourself down. If you would have let your arms hang at your side, like Sandra had done, you'd have come up to the surface." I was still panting when I noticed that Mike and Sandra were staring at me, poker-faced. *Why can't I be like them?*

I never went back to swimming lessons.

Our radio had been on all evening, but no one paid much attention until we heard the newscaster say, "It has been confirmed that Smolensk is now in Russian hands."

"Ha!" Dad pounded his fist on the armrest of his chair, "Hitler didn't know what he was doing when he attacked the Russians. He made a big mistake by fighting on two fronts." Hitler's blunder put Dad into a good mood. He turned the radio off and said, "Jenny, let's tell her now."

"Tell me what?" I kept my eyes on my jigsaw puzzle.

"We think it would be good for you to go to Sunday school," Mom said. "So you'll be going to Temple Beth Israel next Sunday at ten o'clock."

My muscles tensed and I stopped moving. Before I could say anything, Dad said that Fred would drive me there and back. Now that we had the Pontiac, the distance to the temple, all the way across town, over the Hawthorne Bridge, and past the downtown area, wasn't a problem.

"I don't mind driving," Fred said.

Sure—so you could have the car to go see Catherine Anne.

To me, it was another place away from the safety of home. I wouldn't know anyone. I'd be a stranger again. Everyone would stare at me. No one would talk to me. I didn't want to go.

"Why do I have to?" I said.

"Because you should know what it is to be Jewish," Mom said. She moved over to her Singer and picked up the blue corduroy fabric for my new pants.

"I already know what it is to be Jewish. People call you names, or think you're weird, or think you killed Christ," I said. "I don't want to be Jewish. I want to be like all the other kids at school."

"But you're not like them. You're born Jewish, whether you like it or not. So you better learn what Jews believe in and what makes us different from the others." Mom put the fabric under the needle and lowered the foot over the seam. The loud whirr of the sewing machine seemed to emphasize her point.

"I know that already," I shouted over the noise. "We believe God is God and the others believe Jesus is God." I stood beside Mom and watched the needle skip along the seam.

"It's not as simple as all that," Mom said, taking her eyes off her sewing. "Besides, you should get to know some Jewish kids, not just all the *goyim* at school and around here. You should know what Jewish people are like."

"I already know what Jewish people are like. They're like the Feldmans and the Scheins and the Cohens. They're just like anybody else except they look and talk funny."

"That's because they're not American. It has nothing to do with being Jewish. Now don't argue with me." Mom stopped the needle from whirring and sat back in her chair. She looked me straight in the eye and said, "You just have to go and that's final. Now let me finish these pants."

Dad took his attention away from the radio by his side and said, "Don't look so sad, Suzinka. We're not sending you to jail."

"I know," I said. "I just don't know why I have to go to temple, when *you* never go." I sat down next to him and he pulled me close.

"I do go. I go to synagogue—on Rosh Hashanah."

"Why do you even go then, just on that one day, when you don't believe one word they say?"

"I go to say Kaddish for my parents. It's a prayer for the dead."

"But Dad, you say God doesn't listen. So why do you say Kaddish when God doesn't listen?"

"Because my parents would want me to. I do it to honor them. That may not make any sense to you, but it does to me. Someday you may understand."

There was nothing more to say or do that day, except watch the everlasting rain leave polka-dot drops on our windowpanes. The following Sunday, Fred took me to Temple Beth Israel, a large building with two massive front doors. I noticed immediately that all the girls were dressed in embroidered silk blouses or cashmere sweaters or velvet dresses. I was in a corduroy skirt, cotton blouse, and wool cardigan. *I always look different than anybody else.*

Fred picked me up and after looking at my glum face said, "Come on—cheer up. We're going to Aunt Dora and Uncle Max's house for lunch."

Aunt Dora opened the front door with an embroidered apron tied around her paunchy stomach. The smell of onions, garlic, peppers, and tomatoes floated out of the kitchen. I braced myself for a wet kiss, but Aunt Dora was in no mood for that. She pointed towards the living room with a face as wrinkled as a prune, and said, *"You* talk to him. He's impossible!"

"What do you mean?" Fred said.

Uncle Max said, "*Ach*, she's talking crazy again, digging up old problems that don't matter anymore." He thrust his hand in her direction, sending ashes from his cigarette onto the carpet.

Aunt Dora stood in the middle of the room with her hands on her hips and said, "He won't admit the truth, that's all. He always thinks he's right."

Fred and I looked at one, then the other, and Fred said, "What's going on here? What's all this about?"

"He just won't admit that our clothing business in Vienna failed because it was the depression. Nobody had any money to buy new clothes. That's why our tailor shop went bankrupt," Aunt Dora said.

Uncle Max took a handkerchief out of his pocket and wiped the shine off his bald-as-a-billiard-ball head. "She didn't bother to tell you that she took all the cash we had and ordered a dozen suits made to her own body measurements. Now tell me, how many women do you know who have bodies like that?" His yellow-fingered hand flew in Aunt Dora's direction again. "How crazy is that, I ask you? We didn't sell one suit."

Aunt Dora's body was in fact shaped like a squash—narrow shoulders, no breasts, and a big, round belly. Embarrassed by our stares, she stormed out of the living room.

After lunch, as Fred and I stood by the front door, ready to leave, she said, "He always thinks he knows everything better than anybody else."

From the living room, Uncle Max shouted, "I know better than you! But what's the use of talking. Nobody can live with a woman like that."

Aunt Dora held the front door open for us. As we passed the threshold we heard her shout, "Kiss my ass!"

"*Chob Dir in d'rayard!*" Uncle Max answered.

As soon as Fred and I were in our Pontiac driving home, I asked, "Fred, what does '*chob Dir in d'rayard*' mean?'"

Fred burst out laughing, as if I was as funny as Abbott and Costello.

"What's so funny?" I said.

"Nothing," Fred answered, trying to swallow the hilarity. "It's Yiddish," he said, "it's like saying, 'go to hell.' Those two are crazy. Can you imagine ordering all those suits to fit *her* body? See what we mean when we say she's crazy?"

I hope no one ever finds out how crazy some people in my family are.

Mom must have known how embarrassed I was going to Sunday school in my cheap, everyday clothes. She came home one day with a beautiful, new, navy blue silk dress trimmed in white. I wore it the following Sunday, but it did nothing to make me feel that I belonged.

I tried to learn about the Jewish holidays. They spoke about the miracle of Chanukah when the lamp burned for eight days when it only had enough oil in it for one day. *They must have made a mistake in seeing the amount of oil in the lamp.* They told us to ask God to forgive our sins on Yom Kippur. *I haven't committed any sins.* And at Passover, the Red Sea parted to allow Jews to escape Pharaoh's bondage. *How could that be?*

Still, I went to Sunday school—until the day that Fred forgot to pick me up. I sat on the steps in front of the two massive front doors to the temple, watching one kid after another being picked up by their parents, until there were only three of us left. A few minutes later, a shiny black car stopped in front of us and swallowed up my two companions. Still, our Pontiac was nowhere in sight. I was alone. *Where is he?* I felt like a block of cement rested on my chest. *What shall I do?* My stomach began to churn. *What if he doesn't ever come?* I felt sick.

I tried opening one of those heavy temple doors, but it was locked. I went back to my place on the top step and wrapped my arms around my knees. The sky darkened and it began to drizzle. *Fred isn't coming for me.* A swirling wind picked up several crinkled brown leaves on the street and sent them into a restless dance. A clap of thunder brought a downpour, and my head fell down onto my knees. *Who will take care of me?* I was in a state of panic and remained in a near fetal position for about an hour before our plum-colored Pontiac pulled up at the curb. At home, sobbing and hysterical, I screamed that I would never go back to Sunday school.

Sex Education

At age twelve, I was one of the tallest kids in my class due to a pair of long, skinny legs that came together at the knees in a perfect X. Fred was the first one to notice this abnormality, which everyone hoped would be corrected by my wearing arch supports. Sadly, the inserts made my feet slip off to the side, making my shoes look like flippers, and did nothing for straightening my knock knees. Next, Fred noticed two soft pancake-shaped forms pushing the front of my sweaters out.

"Mom, have you talked to Illy yet?"

"About what?" Mom was at our dining table hand-ironing a length of fabric. She pulled a piece of marked tissue paper out of a Simplicity pattern envelope.

"*You* know," he said, nodding his head in my direction.

"No, not yet," she said, "but I will. I will." Mom opened the sheer pattern, laid it down, and ironed out the creases with her hands.

"Talk to me about what?" I asked.

"Nothing," she said. "Illy, hand me that piece over there." She pointed to a pattern piece that had slipped off the table onto the chair next to me "Over there—that one—the belt piece."

"It's high time you told her," Fred said, "if you don't want to do it, I will."

"*Nein. Nein*, it's not your place," she said. "I'll do it ... but not *now*." She reached over the table to get a hold of the pattern in my hand.

I raised my voice. "Tell me *what*?" Mom grabbed the pattern in my hand and in doing so, ripped it in two.

"Now look what you've done," she said, holding half the belt pattern in her hand.

"I ... I'm sorry, Mom," I said, biting my lower lip.

"Go get the scotch tape," Mom said, inhaling deeply, sitting down in her chair, and letting the air out slowly through her lips. "Maybe I can fix it."

I came back with the scotch tape and said, "Can you?" With my mind on my skirt, I forgot all about what it was that Mom was supposed to tell me.

The next day I was in the Fabrocini's kitchen with Dolores, her sister Angela, and her mom. Angela was as beautiful as Dolores was homely. She had skin the color of egg shells, and a perfectly oval face framed with chestnut color hair down to her shoulders. The minute she turned sixteen, she got an after-school job as a waitress, where she had to wear a red-and-white uniform that made her look like a peppermint stick.

"Elsie, here … have a sweet." Mrs. Fabrocini held a plate of bear claws under my chin.

"Thanks," I said, savoring the one American pastry I liked—besides chocolate covered doughnuts.

"Come on," Dolores said. "Let's go to my room." She tugged on my sleeve. "Want to play checkers?"

Sitting on her chenille bedspread, I said, "How come Angela's home? Isn't she supposed to be at work?"

"She's not going back to work." Dolores pulled the checkers out of a knotty-pine chest.

"How come?"

"She's going to have a baby."

"What?" My chin dropped.

"She's going to have a baby." Dolores repeated herself in a matter-of-fact tone, as if she'd told me her sister bought a new dress.

"How can she? She's not even married," I said, wide-eyed.

Dolores laughed and said, "You don't have to be married to have a baby. She's been fooling around with Hugh."

I'd seen Angela and Hugh leaning up against the Fabrocini's Model T Ford, with Hugh's arm around Angela's shoulders. "Really? What do you mean *fooling around?*"

"*You* know." Dolores gave me a look as if to awaken an understanding I didn't have. I had no idea what she meant, but didn't want her to know just how ignorant I was. Quickly, I said, "Come on, let's play."

I told Mom about Angela's baby, and she was shocked, listing all the reasons that is was a catastrophe—for Angela, who would become unmarriageable, for the Fabrocinis, who would have to live with the shame as well as the burden of supporting the child, and the baby, who would be branded the worst of all things … a bastard. I tried to digest the impact of each of these horrors, while still trying to understand how one could get pregnant without being married.

That night at the apartment, I stepped in front of Mom and demanded, "Now, tell me!"

"All right. All right. *Aber wart' eine Minute.*" Mom said. "Let me at least get my shoes off." Mom came out of the bedroom and sat down on our lumpy couch. She put her elbow on the armrest and held a handkerchief in her hand.

"Well?" I said from my seat on the sofa chair facing her.

"Now," she took a deep breath, "when a man and a woman get married, they get into the same bed and they put their bodies together ..." Her eyes were on her handkerchief, her fingers twisting it, rolling it, and squeezing it until it looked like a wrinkled prune. *Why is she so nervous?* Mom's chest heaved as she took a deep breath. "Well, they put their bodies together ... like ... like ... like your jigsaw puzzle!"

"Jigsaw puzzle?" I opened my eyes wide. "What do you mean?"

"Just imagine putting two pieces of your puzzle together." She picked up the twisted, crumpled handkerchief in her lap and stood up. "Now, I have to fix some dinner."

"Wait," I yelled. "Is that *fooling around?*"

"*Ja!* Same thing—fooling around ends up the jigsaw puzzle."

Confused, I sat back in my chair and pictured Angela and Hugh putting a jigsaw puzzle together.

The Camel Hair Coat

Dad opened the screen door to the sound of a grinding screech and said, "Where's Mom?" The sticky flypaper hanging from the ceiling swung in the draft.

"She's gone downtown shopping," I said from behind the checkout counter. Mrs. Amato was next to me, waiting on a customer. Everyone liked near-sighted Mrs. Amato, whose plastic-framed glasses sat on her nose like the wings of a bird. Ever since her husband left for France to fight the Nazis, she was available anytime Mom needed her to work in the store.

Mrs. Amato had me running all over, fetching Wonder Bread, Folgers Coffee, or Del Monte Peaches for our customers. She even let me push the alabaster buttons on our brass cash register. It made me feel grown-up, not like a twelve-year-old.

"Downtown again?" Dad asked, his tie loose around his neck like a necklace, after having finished his shift at the hospital. "I don't understand her. How can she go downtown when she has a store to run? Doesn't she know it costs money to hire help?" He glanced at Mrs. Amato as he passed her on his way to the back room.

Our little mom-and-pop grocery store, which looked like a Norman Rockwell illustration on the cover of the *Saturday Evening Post,* made money for our family. It was mostly Mom's doing, and I could tell she was proud of herself. Mom had changed. She was no longer the poor refugee woman from Vienna, who worked fourteen hours a day, couldn't speak English, and wore funny-looking clothes. She told me one time that she thought her job was just as hard and important as the work women like "Rosie the Riveter" did, making airplanes and tanks. I even noticed that she'd learned to say "but" instead of "*aber*," and "from" instead of "*von*"—even when she was nervous. There were no more puffy crests under her eyes, and the dash that had been her mouth was now a wide, shiny red line.

Mom came back from her shopping trip wearing a beige raincoat and brown fedora, its feather standing straight up like an antenna. In her right hand, she held a large shopping bag.

"Let me just put this bag in the back, Mrs. Amato. I'll be ready to take over in a minute." She slipped through the striped curtain with me on her heels.

Dad sat at our oak rolltop desk with his eyes on a bill. I skipped behind Mom as she walked to the back of the room through the tunnel formed by stacks of cardboard boxes. When we reached the table and chairs pushed against the back wall, she plunked her shopping bag down and pulled the hatpin out of her fedora.

"Let me see," I said, reaching inside her shopping bag.

"Wait a minute," she said, with a smile that pushed a dimple into her cheek. Then she pulled a long camel hair coat out of her shopping bag and lifted it to her shoulders. It was fitted at the waist with two rows of tortoiseshell buttons down its front.

"Isn't it beautiful?" she said, her eyes shiny.

"It *is*," I said. "Put it on."

Dad left his desk chair and came to stand in front of Mom while she buttoned her coat. His eyes swept her up and down, from neckline to hem and back again, until he met Mom's hazel eyes.

"Another coat?" he said. "You just bought a raincoat a couple of weeks ago. What do you need another one for?"

"I don't really *need* it," Mom said, "but it was on sale. And Adele—you know Adele, Martha's friend. Well, Adele works at the store and gets a ten percent discount. And Adele gave me her discount. So I got a double discount, one from the sale, and another from Adele. So I bought it!" She cocked her head to the side and twirled around, so that Dad could see the back as well as the front. "Do you like it?" she asked, flashing her dimple again.

"It doesn't matter whether I like it or not. You're taking it back." Dad's nostrils flared. "I can't imagine what you were thinking of to buy two coats. Who do you think you are? Mrs. Rockefeller?" Dad shook his head and, with a sweeping hand motion, he dismissed her, saying, "Just take it back," and returned to his desk.

Mom didn't move from where she stood. With two fists at her side, she shouted, "I'm not taking the coat back." She let the coat slide off her shoulders and put it back into the shopping bag. "I wouldn't know what to say to Adele after she was so nice as to give me her discount. I'd be embarrassed. Besides, I like the coat. I'm going to keep it."

Dad came back to face Mom again. "It doesn't matter if you like it or not. That coat is going back to the store." My stomach was doing summersaults. If

145

Dad hadn't been standing in my way, I'd have run up front to help Mrs. Amato. Every word they said to one another seemed like a slap.

"Well, I'm keeping the coat, no matter what. I work hard enough around here that, if I want to spend a little money on myself, I have the right to do it." Mom's chin quivered.

"*You* have the right? Since when do *you* have the right?" Dad's face was close to Mom's. His thumb bounced off his chest a few times. "*I'll* tell you what rights you have here. *You* don't have any right to make decisions unless *I* say so."

Mom's chin looked like cottage cheese and her voice sounded like her throat was flooded. "All right … all right … if that's all I'm worth, let's see how you do without me." She grabbed her purse, walked past Dad, through the store, and straight out the front door.

I swallowed hard and didn't know if I should follow her. If I did that, Dad would have gotten mad at me. Not knowing what to do, I did nothing. I thought Mom shouldn't have made Dad mad by buying the coat. But I knew she had every right to it, after having supported our entire family for almost a year while Dad was out of work. I should have gone out the door with her. Now it was too late. My head spun. I couldn't choose Mom over Dad, or vice versa. I needed for them to be on the same side.

Dad walked past me saying, "Don't worry. Let her cool off. She'll be back." He paid Mrs. Amato for working in the store and took her place behind the checkout counter. He began pacing back and forth. Sometimes he stopped at the front window and looked out under the letters that said *Fell's Grocery*. He lit one cigarette after another.

Mrs. DiGiulio came in and Dad waited on her. Afterwards he stepped outside and paced in front of the store, a wavy gray ribbon of smoke trailing behind him. Every so often, he pulled his gold watch out and looked at the time. Finally he stomped his cigarette out with his foot, stepped back into the store to the sound of the screeching screen door, and said, "Suzi, you stay here. I'm going out to look for her." The muscles around his eyes were taut—as if he couldn't focus.

I fell back into the desk chair and grasped its arms until my knuckles turned white. I was afraid to be alone, and didn't know what I'd do if a customer came into the store. The front door screeched again and I ran to see if it was Mom or Dad. It was only Mrs. Riveti with her grocery list. I said Mom and Dad had stepped out for a minute, and could I help her. Her eyes got big and round. She thought a bit and said, "Well, I don't know—I guess so."

I knew where all the grocery items were stored—I had stocked most of them myself. I'd watched Mom grind hamburger, cut pork chops, and cube stew meat.

I'd seen how she wrapped meats in white butcher paper, as if she were putting them in an envelope. I knew how to work the cash register, and make the right change. I waited on Mrs. Riveti and was proud that I'd done it right all by myself. I wanted to tell Mom and Dad—but I was alone.

At six o'clock, Dad came back to the store, his face pale. He hadn't found Mom. I wanted to tell him about waiting on Mrs. Riveti, but he walked by me so fast that I couldn't. "Let's close up and go home," he said.

At our apartment Dad hung his coat on the back of a chair, opened the Venetian blinds, and looked out onto the sidewalk. His hands were clasped behind his back and I noticed they were trembling. *Is Dad afraid?* It was the first time I'd ever seen Dad looking like he wasn't in control, and it scared me.

Fred came home from college a little while later, dropped his books on the dining table with a crash, and said, "Where's Mom?"

"She's gone crazy," Dad said. "She just had a fit and walked out the door."

"What do you mean, 'she had a fit'? Why would she have a fit?" Fred swiped a wave of his dark hair off his forehead.

Dad looked over his shoulder and said, "You know how she is. She doesn't like anyone telling her she's wrong. She would never admit making a mistake. She just went crazy and walked out."

What did Mom do that was wrong? Why doesn't he tell Fred that he wouldn't let her keep her camel hair coat? Is he afraid Fred will see him in a bad light?

Fred didn't say anything. He knew that when Dad got mad, saying anything at all suggesting you didn't agree with him would throw him into a fury. Then Dad would turn on you and say things that could hurt for a long time. Mom had taught us to keep our mouths shut—think whatever you like—but keep your mouth shut. Fred did.

When it got dark outside, Fred asked, "Is anybody hungry?"

Dad shook his head no, but I said yes. Fred and I had a salami sandwich and then put the radio on. We heard the big belly laugh of *The Great Gildersleeve* fill the room and Dad shouted, "Turn that damn thing off." He slouched down in his place on the couch with his hands in his pockets. The light next to him was turned off. He just sat there in the dark, staring out at nothing at all.

What's he thinking? Is he afraid Mom left for good? Is he sorry about how he treated her?

For the rest of the night, Fred and I played a game of gin rummy until I went to bed. The next morning, I woke to hear silverware scraping on plates and some muffled conversation coming from the kitchen. I found Mom at the breakfast table, lifting a spoonful of cornflakes to her mouth. She wore a faded yellow blouse and brown skirt frayed at the pockets—her "store clothes"—ready to go to work as if nothing had happened.

"Mom, where've you been?" I said, running to her side. She wrapped her arm around my waist and kissed my forehead. I could see the dimple in her cheek.

"Never mind that," Dad said. He was leaning against the kitchen doorjamb with his face inside the morning newspaper. "Sit down and eat your breakfast."

Dad is back to his old self—in charge, giving orders, and always, always right.

We ate in silence. Later that day, after Fred came home from school, he told me that Mom had gone to the movies the night before and wasn't home until midnight. Neither of us ever knew what Mom had said to Dad, or what Dad had said to Mom, when she came home. I only knew that the camel hair coat remained in her closet.

Becoming Alice

Mom's sewing needle galloped over the brown taffeta material as she sat at the Singer making the dress I would wear to my grammar school graduation party. I didn't like it. It was brown instead of red or navy blue, like the other girls would be wearing. But Mom said the brown taffeta material was on sale at the department store and the other colors weren't. So that was that.

Our party was held in the gym at Abernethy school, where the strains of Glenn Miller's song, *Little Brown Jug,* filled the room. I spotted the girls, bunched together in one corner, as if they'd been herded there by an Australian sheep dog. *I'm dressed different from any one of them.* The boys were in a cluster on the opposite side. I sat down in one of the folding chairs lined up against the walls.

Our teacher gave each girl a single white gardenia corsage, looking like it had been carved out of Ivory soap. Its aroma was clean and fresh at first, but it wasn't long before the scent became so strong and overbearing, that I wanted to take it off. While I searched for the pearl-tipped floral pin behind the flower, I hardly noticed Norman walking across the gym floor toward me. Norman had been in my class all along, but this day he seemed taller, strong, and handsome. I began to breathe deeply. *He'll ask me to dance.* I held my breath, winding my fingers over the edge of my chair, and leaned forward.

Norman angled to the right of me and stopped in front of Ginny, a beanpole of a girl whose neck was as long as a swan's. I let go of the edge of my chair and sank back into my seat. The girl sitting to my left whispered, "They know each other from church. They're Mormon." I wished I were Mormon and not the only Jewish girl in my school.

After graduation, I never saw any of my Abernethy School classmates again. Mom and Dad sold the little grocery store in our Italian neighborhood and bought a bigger one on Southeast Twenty-Sixth Street. Mom thought she could make more money there. I was sorry to leave. That store, that empty lot, those railroad tracks, had been my home ever since we came to Portland. And I felt sad to never be able to see Dolores again.

We moved into a small, long and narrow, two-bedroom house almost directly across the street from the new store. Hardy junipers, which needed no pruning, leaned against the horizontal wood slats that made our house look like a giant writing tablet. Along one side, a driveway led to a separate garage behind the house.

The customers who shopped at our new store didn't have Italian names like Fabrocini, DiGiulio, or Amato. Instead, we had Johnsons, Krugers, and Sorensens. Certainly, no one named Goldberg, Kaplan, or Siegel ever came into the store. The few people in Portland with names like that were sprinkled over the entire city.

Mom and Dad didn't actually sell our old store. The new owners were Aunt Dora and Uncle Max, and they didn't have any money. Uncle Max was too sick to get any kind of job, and Aunt Dora could barely make a living working as a maid. So Mom and Dad let them run the old grocery, with the agreement they'd pay for it whenever they could. Dad said that families had to take care of one another. "No matter how crazy they are, they're yours. They're family. And families have to stick together and help each other. Having a crazy family is like having a clubfoot. You can't change them—so you might as well accept them as they are. Just don't tell anybody how crazy they are."

Aunt Dora and Uncle Max hadn't seen our new house, so we invited them to come to dinner one rainy Sunday at six o'clock. All four of us waited for them in our living room. I sat on the floor next to Fred's feet, with a game of solitaire spread out in front of me. Dad listened to the radio tuned to a news report on KOIN, telling us the Allies were gaining on the Germans in the Battle of the Bulge. In the kitchen, Mom's pink slippers swished across the floor as she skated from place to place preparing dinner.

"What time is it?" she asked, coming into the living room. "Shouldn't they be here by now?"

"They should. It's six-thirty already." Dad had his gold watch in the palm of his hand.

"I'm hungry," I said. "The chicken will be all dried out if they don't get here soon."

"They'll be here," Fred said. "They're just a little late, that's all." His mouth was the only thing that moved on his face. Silence again.

"*Ach*, something must have happened to them," Mom said. The wind was wailing outside—sheets of water bombarded our window pane. "They're never late. What time is it?"

"After seven," Dad said. "What are you looking outside for? That's stupid. It's pitch black out there, with rain coming down in buckets. You can't see a thing."

I knew Dad was worried—as soon as he lashed out at Mom and called her stupid. She said, "What are you yelling at me for? Is it my fault that they're not here?"

"Something must have happened to them," Fred said, frowning. "Maybe they had an accident."

"I wouldn't be surprised. Dora's such a terrible driver." Dad was up on his feet, pacing.

"What time is it?" Mom said. "Maybe we should call the police."

"Will you stop asking what time it is?" Dad yelled at Mom. He pulled his watch out of its pocket and said, "Seven-thirty." No one spoke anymore.

More time passed before the doorbell rang. We all jumped up. Dad got to the door first. There was Aunt Dora, closing her red umbrella, while Uncle Max stood behind her, shaking the water drops off his hat.

"Where've you been?" Dad shouted. "What happened to you?"

"She got lost," Uncle Max said, taking his raincoat off and walking past Dad.

"But we told you how to get to our house," Mom said.

"*I* know the way to your house," Uncle Max said, easing himself into a chair.

"If you know the way, how come you're so late?" I said.

"I made a wrong turn," Aunt Dora said. "And the *meshugener* wouldn't stop me and tell me the right way to go."

"She should know the way by herself," Uncle Max said.

Mom and Dad said that was crazy but Uncle Max only shrugged his shoulders. We all sat down at dinner—as if nothing had happened, as if acting crazy like that was normal. Afterwards we moved into the living room. Fred slumped into a place at the end of our couch, his elbow on the armrest. I pushed his elbow off and straddled the armrest as if I were on horseback. "What's a *meshugener*?" I whispered.

Fred's lips grew wide with a smile. "It's a crazy person," he whispered back.

I looked around the room and thought all of them, not only Uncle Max, were crazy. I thought about Aunt Dora considering herself a *better* person, when her parents were nothing but farmers. I thought about her promising a suitor a dowry, when she didn't have one. I thought about her accusing Uncle Max of having affairs when he was so sick, he could hardly breathe.

I looked at Mom in her pink slippers, brown-striped skirt, and floral blouse. *She looks like a kaleidoscope.* I thought she was crazy to let Dad call her stupid at every turn without answering him back.

Dad had lit a cigarette and stood in the middle of the room, rocking back and forth on his heels. He said General MacAuliffe didn't handle the Battle of the Bulge right. If he'd been the general, he would have given different orders, ones that would have kept the Germans from advancing so far against the Allies.

Uncle Max said he didn't think McAuliffe did such a bad job—he pushed the Germans way back, farther than the line they held in the first place. That was a mistake. Uncle Max should never have disagreed with Dad.

"What do *you* know?" Dad said. "Since when are you such a brilliant strategist?" He took a drag off his cigarette. "If you were such a great soldier, how come you took the first bullet they fired in the First World War? How come you were the last one to come home from Russia? What makes you think you know more about fighting a war than me? Were *you* ever an officer? Were *you* ever decorated with a medal? What makes you think you're so smart?" Dad's face was red. Saliva bubbled in the corners of his mouth.

"Norbert, I didn't say I was smarter than you." Uncle Max hung his head. "I thought ..."

"Better you shouldn't think," Dad said. "You don't do that so well."

Uncle Max said no more. The whole time Dad attacked Uncle Max, no one said anything. They wouldn't dare, knowing Dad would turn on them instead. Uncle Max stood up and said, "Dora, let's go home."

When Dad got mad, he had a look in his eyes like a mad dog in a fight. He even looked like he was about to hit you. Although he never struck any one of us, we were never sure that he wouldn't do it. He was like that the day we became citizens. We'd been in this country five years and were eligible to get our citizenship papers. Fred had gotten his a year before, when he'd reached his five year milestone. I, being a minor, would get my citizenship automatically with my parents.

The three of us had to appear before a judge in a Portland courtroom and answer questions about U.S. government and history. Mom and Dad needed to study those subjects before their day in court. Actually, Dad studied the material first and then taught it to Mom. I don't know why they didn't do it at the same time. Perhaps Dad thought Mom couldn't understand the books written in English—which was true—or he needed to look like he was smarter than she—which was also true.

It was Mitzi who told us I could choose any name I wanted for my citizenship papers. She was going to put Miriam down for her first name, instead of Mitzi. She didn't know then that all the refugees would still call her Mitzi just the same. When I found that out, I was excited.

"You mean I don't have to be Elsie anymore?" I said.

"You can change your name to any one you want. You only need to have a lawyer draw up the papers." She giggled. "It's cheap—only fifty dollars."

Mom and Dad knew how much I detested the name Elsie. It stood for the frightened and anxious foreign child that didn't fit in anywhere. They let me choose my new name, encouraging me to pick one that was similar phonetically to my real name, Ilse. After choosing and discarding the name of every famous movie star of the time, I settled for Alice.

On a normal gray and rainy day in Portland, Mom, Dad, and I appeared in court. We wore our best clothes. Dad said, "Who'd want to make American citizens out of a bunch of *schleppers*?" We entered the courtroom, as instructed, at our appointed time. The room was filled with people there for reasons unknown to us. Facing us from behind a desk on a raised platform, a judge in a black robe looked at us, wearing his authority on his sleeve. Dad's body stiffened. Mom took a handkerchief out of her purse, blew her nose, and proceeded to knead it in her lap. A musty odor permeated the room, as if no fresh air had entered since the courthouse had been built.

The judge called Dad's name and he stepped forward. He was asked several questions, which he answered correctly and returned to his seat, no longer stiff as a rod. Mom was called up next. She, too, answered all the questions perfectly and brought a half-smile to the judge's lips. She turned toward her seat when he added, "Very good, Mrs. Fell. One last thing … do you belong to any subversive organizations?"

What little color Mom had in her face, disappeared. She had no idea what the judge meant. She reverted to the age-old rule of pleasing people by agreeing with them. She hunched her back, clasped her hands at her waist, tilted her head forward, and looked up with a smile. "Oh, yes sir. I belong. Of course I do. Yes."

Dad bolted out of his seat and ran to her side. He put his arm around her shoulder and grabbed her hand, holding her close. "Oh, no! Please, sir, she doesn't know what she's saying." The others in the courtroom laughed as loud as any audience watching Jack Benny, the cheapskate comedian, playing his violin at the movies. The judge himself had a broad smile across his face.

"I can see that plain enough," he said, trying to stifle his laughter. "Citizenship granted."

But afterwards, when we walked back to the car, Dad didn't think it was funny at all. "How could you be so stupid? How could you do that? Why didn't you say you didn't understand him, instead of risking our citizenship? You just do one stupid thing after another. I never know what's coming out of your mouth next."

Dad was relentless. He berated Mom all the way home. I could never understand how he could put his arm around her shoulder, protect her, support her, care for her, one minute—then attack her so hurtfully, the next. I tried to tune out his barrage—I was busy enjoying the fact that from then on, my name would be Alice.

The Importance of Money

In January, I enrolled at Washington High, a somber, rectangular, two-story building that sat on its lot like a brick. I'd take a bus most of the way to school and then walk another five blocks under my beige umbrella, looking like a moving mushroom. I'd deposit my dripping rainwear into a clanking metallic locker, and exchange "Hi's" with someone, but only if that person spoke first.

Other than doing my school work, I was busy staring with envy at almost everyone. I gawked at Sandra Owing, who was as beautiful as Elizabeth Taylor. I ogled Gloria Jenkins, who wore a different color cashmere sweater every day. I was jealous of Lucille Ballard, who played the oboe, and I even wished I could type as fast as Betty Kendall. I got good grades, but that wasn't worth anything—smart kids were considered jerks.

I wanted to look like the kids at school but didn't have the money to do so. I cut my chestnut-colored hair into a bob. I wore Shetland wool sweaters that were styled like cashmeres. I sewed my skirts to look like the store-bought ones. Shoes were no problem. I couldn't afford to buy cream-and-tan saddle shoes, so I bought inexpensive brown loafers with copper pennies, which many of the kids wore. The simplest change I could make was to start wearing lipstick.

"Dad?" I said. His ear was close to the radio.

"Shush!" he shouted, waving his arm at me to shut up.

We heard, "This is Edward R. Murrow, reporting from London." Mom came out of the bedroom in a paisley-print housedress. Mr. Murrow said Soviet troops had liberated the Polish town of Auschwitz and found a Nazi death camp. They found piles of corpses, and gas chambers used for human extermination. They saw emaciated men in black-and-white striped uniforms, staggering around like living skeletons. Most of them were Jewish. The liberating soldiers were so distressed by what they'd seen, they vomited at the sight. After he signed off, the room was silent.

Mom and Dad didn't move. They looked at one another knowingly. Then Dad said, "That could have been us."

"I know." Mom dropped into a stuffed chair. "Do you think Oma was there?"

Dad took a long drag off his cigarette. Whiffs of smoke escaped from his lips as he said, "If she, at her age, was sent to Auschwitz in one of those cattle cars, she would never have survived the trip."

Mom got to her feet and looked down at Dad with glazed eyes. "We have to find out. I have to know what happened to her. I'll try writing to my cousin again—maybe Regina knows something."

Dad sent a last plume of white smoke into the room before punching his cigarette out in his ashtray. "You can try, but God only knows if Regina is there anymore." Silence followed. I didn't dare say a word.

I could hardly remember Oma—it had been over six years since I'd seen her. When we were at her apartment in Vienna, she'd be in the kitchen most of the time cooking for all of us. She spent hours peeling potatoes by hand for four grownup sons, a daughter, and all her grandchildren. Opa was the one who played with me, and I remembered exactly how he looked. When I thought of him, I felt warm all over. But I couldn't even picture Oma. I saw the anguish Mom and Dad felt after hearing that broadcast, and I knew that I should have felt the same pain. But I didn't.

After a long silence, Mom took a breath, as if waking from a deep sleep. "There's still a little daylight left. I think I'll cut the grass."

I followed her outside, sat down on the top step of our porch landing, and wrapped my arms around my knees. I watched Mom push the lawn mower across the coarse crab grass that was our front lawn. An apron was tied in a bow around her waist, its long ends bounced up and down her backside like the tail of a dog.

I couldn't control myself any longer. "Mom, can I have some money to buy lipstick?"

"What?" Mom stopped pushing the lawn mower and looked at me as if she hadn't heard me. I could tell that she hadn't stopped thinking about Oma.

"I need some money for lipstick."

"Lipstick?" The two lines, the eleven, reappeared between her brows. "How can you think about lipstick when your own grandmother might have been killed—and in the worst inhumane way?" She looked at me with a loathing I'd never seen before and then turned her back to me as she pushed the lawn mower down the driveway toward the garage. "Don't you have any feelings at all?"

I felt my eyes water and swallowed hard. I did have feelings, but they weren't for Oma, or the millions of people being killed. I only felt my own shame for being so different from everyone at school. I said no more and hoped Mom wouldn't say anything to Dad about it. As hurtful as the look of loathing was from Mom, it would have been twice as hard to bear from Dad. I wouldn't have wanted to tamper with the special feelings I knew he had for me.

On the following Monday, I crossed the street at school to buy a bottle of Coke for lunch at the school hangout. I fingered the money in my pocket and got an idea. If I didn't buy my drink and drank from the school's water fountain instead, I could save enough in a few days to buy my own lipstick, without Mom and Dad knowing anything about it. I could put it on in the school bathroom in the morning, and take it off before I went home.

Two weeks later, I biked to Fred Meyer's store and bought the same fuchsia color lipstick that Sandra Owing wore. I felt no guilt about keeping that cold metallic tube, shaped like a Tootsie Roll, in my locker and rushing into the girls' bathroom the minute I arrived at school. The first day that I spread the creamy color over my lips, it almost tasted like chocolate to me.

The semester went by with the same routine. I went to class, did my school work, and got good grades without participating in any extra-curricular activity. The week school let out for summer vacation, I read a bulletin outside the school office. Oregon's Department of Agriculture was looking for students to harvest our summer crops. Even though the Soviets had taken Vienna in April and the German High Command had surrendered unconditionally in May, our men still weren't home, and we had a labor shortage.

I wanted to have money of my own, money that I could spend any way I liked without getting Mom and Dad's permission. I found Dad sitting at the dining room table, taking notes out of a college chemistry book. He'd finally been allowed to take the tests required in the state of Washington to be licensed as a physician. At age forty-seven, he was studying basic sciences at the college fresh-man level all over again, just for the privilege of being able to practice medicine again as a licensed physician.

"Dad?" I said in a low voice, coming into the room and sitting down next to him.

"Suzinka!" Dad's face lit up as he looked at me. He closed his book and put it back into the knotty pine bookcase on the wall behind him. Our dining room had been used for two things, as a place for us to eat and as Fred's bedroom. His roll-away bed, covered by a mustard-colored floral chintz throw, was pushed into a corner. Now it had a third purpose—it was Dad's study.

"Dad, I want to go work in the fields this summer. I want to pick strawberries and raspberries and beans and … and whatever else needs picking. I want …"

Dad interrupted, "Why in the world would you want to do a thing like that? What kind of work is that for a thirteen-year-old girl?"

I saw Mom out of the corner of my eye leaning against the doorjamb of the door. "It's good work, Dad. With our men still not home, they need our help picking the crops out on the farms. They wouldn't have put the notice up on the bulletin board if they didn't think we could do it. The bulletin said...."

"Now wait a minute. I don't want you working like a common farm hand. No, no! You're not going to pick berries."

"But Dad, they really need workers. And I could make some money as well."

I glanced up at Mom, whose eyes were on the floor. *No help there.*

"Suzinka, I don't care about the money. I still make enough to support you."

"I know, Dad. But I want to do it. I have nothing to do all summer. I don't have Dolores in this neighborhood, and no one else either. I don't see one reason against it."

Dad leaned back in his chair, put his hand across his lips, and stared at me without saying a word, as he always did when he was thinking. I felt my heart pound. He glanced at Mom, who looked like she was in pain, trying to keep from saying anything. "Well, we can try it. But if I don't like what I see, you'll have to quit."

When the alarm clock rang at three o'clock in the morning on my first day of work, Mom and Dad came running out of their bedroom. They hadn't counted on my leaving the house in the dead of night. Dad said, "You're not going anywhere."

"But I promised," I pleaded, bent forward with my hands clasped between my knees. To Mom and Dad, breaking one's word was as big a crime as lying or stealing. They looked at one another for an answer.

"Well, just for today, then," Dad said.

I left my house in old, tattered clothes and rode to the fields in the back of an open-air truck with wooden side-slats. Long, straight rows of strawberry bushes, no higher than the tops of my bobby-sox, spread out before us like an enlarged piece of corduroy. We crouched down low to the ground for hours, and picked the succulent red fruit, big as ping-pong balls. By two o'clock in the afternoon, my legs, which had been folded under me like the frame of an umbrella, began to ache. I ignored them, thinking only about the money I was earning.

On the bus back to my house, spasms sharp as spears shot through my groin. My legs were in knots. I walked down the street toward my house like a spastic person. *I can't let Dad see me like this.* I clamped my teeth together as if I had lockjaw, and stretched my calf muscles out so that I could take a step, then another. I found Dad studying chemistry with Doctor Schneider, a handsome man wearing a turtleneck sweater. He was also a refugee trying to get his medical license. *I wish Dad was as good-looking as him.*

"*Mein Gott!* Look at yourself! You're filthy!" Dad said.

I was grateful that he'd only noticed my dirty clothes and not my crippled gait. "I'll get cleaned up," I said, trying to hide a waddle on the way to my room.

"Norbert," Dr. Schneider said with a smile. "Isn't it wonderful how patriotic the kids are today—helping our farmers during our labor shortage? You must be so proud of her."

Dad's head bobbed. He hesitated, as if to find the right words, "I am, Ernie, I am."

While Dad's eyes were on Ernie, I said, "Please excuse me. I'm going to take a bath."

What luck! How could Dad forbid me to go back to the fields after Doctor Schneider's complimenting me like that? He wouldn't want to look bad in the eyes of his colleague.

I poured some lemon-scented bubble bath into the tub and filled it with water as hot as I could bear. I lowered myself into it, feeling my muscles relax. A thick layer of iridescent suds lay on top of the bath water and flashed a momentary color this way and that before disappearing. I stuck a finger in one bubble after another as if I were a toddler, and thought about the money I was earning. I leaned my head against the back of the tub and imagined buying a different color lipstick, perhaps with a copper hue—or a string of graduated fake pearls—or argyle bobby-sox—or....

My Plum Tree

I'd been back at school for about three weeks in the fall when I woke up one morning with my throat feeling like sandpaper. It was like every sore throat I had yearly, one which eventually turned into tonsillitis with fever and chills, and required a two week stint in bed. Mom and Dad had been so frightened by my bout with rheumatic fever at age two that they went into a minor panic each time I had tonsillitis. This time, as usual, I recovered and returned to school. Two days later, I had trouble zipping my skirt. I wondered if I were becoming fat like Aunt Dora—and shuddered at the thought. I shrugged, sucked in my stomach, and managed to squeeze myself into my clothes. I said nothing to Mom and Dad and went to school. The next morning, no amount of constricting my stomach muscles, breathing deep, or hopping on my tiptoes allowed me to zip my skirt. I knew something was wrong—I couldn't have gained that much weight overnight. I told Mom.

"Why didn't you say something sooner?" She yelled for Dad to come.

He was furious. "Get to bed immediately. I'll do some tests." He took a blood sample and a urine specimen to his hospital. The results showed I had glomerulonephritis.

"What's that?" I asked, thinking it would be a different kind of illness that would require two weeks in bed. I didn't feel sick and I wasn't worried.

"It's a kidney disease, Suzi. You probably got it from your tonsillitis. The strep infection probably never cleared and just settled in your kidneys." Dad's face was almost the same color as my bed sheets. "You'll have to stay in bed."

I settled into another long and boring stint in bed, with Mom and Dad looking at me stone-faced. When I threw the covers aside and slid my feet into my slippers, Mom said, "Where are you going?"

"To the toilet."

"No, you're not," Dad said, lifting my feet back into bed. "You're to be at complete bed rest. That means no going to the toilet—Mom'll get you a bedpan. And she'll give you a sponge bath in bed when you need it." It was then that I knew this illness was different.

My bedroom was a straight shot from the front door to the back of the house. To get to my room, you'd walk through the living room between the lumpy couch on the left and two overstuffed chairs on the right. Then you'd pass through the multi-purpose dining room to my rectangular-shaped bedroom where my bed was pushed into a corner. A chest of drawers on one side of the bed served as an end table. It held a radio, a clock, a book, and a lamp with a ruffled pink shade.

The longer wall of my bedroom had a double-hung window with six panes through which I could see an old plum tree. Its dark, gnarled trunk held a network of sturdy branches covered with pointed leaves that swiped my window with every breeze. That bed was my prison for six months, and that old plum tree listened to my thoughts, shared my fears, and heard my cries.

I was sentenced to that bed when the tree dropped its crimson leaves and left it with a lacework of delicate branches. Behind them a steel gray sky striped with fine lines of rain fell in a steady, monotonous stream. The constant, repetitive splash of drops on the concrete driveway outside put me into a trance, and I lost all concept of time. Each day was like the last one, and the next held no hope of being any different. Hours became days, which became weeks, then turned into months. I no longer looked at my clock, whose hands seemed to be frozen in place. I told time by watching my plum tree.

When the skies became a shade lighter, my tree woke from its slumber and sent out a few delicate blossoms. Their paper-thin white petals gradually darkened to pink, then red, and then maroon. They were like the hand of a clock moving from one, to two, to three, and on. Sturdy leaves replaced the petals and changed no more. It was then that time stopped for me.

I read one book after another. I kept up with my classes by correspondence and fulfilled my algebra requirement. But mostly, I listened to my favorite programs on the radio: Jack Armstrong, the Jack Benny Show, Edgar Bergen and Charlie McCarthy, the Great Gildersleeve, and all the programs featuring songs by Bing Crosby, Perry Como, and Peggy Lee.

Mom crossed the street from the store every day to bring my lunch and check up on me. Mr. Wirth still came to work for Mom, but only for half a day—mainly to butcher the meat and set up the display for the day. Despite having reached retirement age, old Mr. Wirth took the bus all the way from the other side of town to help Mom. He liked her that much.

Fred was usually the first one to come home from school a little before dinnertime. Mom and Dad followed soon thereafter. I'd been in bed almost six weeks when Fred came into my bedroom, shoulders slumped. Ella Fitzgerald was singing *It's Only a Paper Moon* over the radio.

"What's the matter with you?" I asked.

"Catherine Anne and I broke up," he said, sitting down at the foot of my bed. He bent forward with his elbows on his knees, his fingers laced between them.

"Oh … I'm sorry," I said. "What happened? I thought you were in love with each other." I was excited about Fred's love affair. Sometimes I pretended that I was Catherine Anne and had a boyfriend like Fred. I liked her—she put a shine in Fred's eyes and a smile on his face, and when he felt especially happy, he'd even joke around with me.

Before Fred could answer me, Mom and Dad walked into my room. The first thing Dad said was, "Will you turn that screeching off. How can you listen to that noise? She sounds like a wounded buffalo." Dad lifted his eyes to the ceiling and mimicked the crooner, singing, *It's only a paper moo-oo-oo-oon....* Dad's uplifted chin made him look as if he were a howling wolf. "Turn that off!"

What's the use—they'll never like my music, no matter how long we live in America.

"How do you feel?" Mom asked, looking at me as if it were my last day on earth.

"Fine, Mom. I feel fine as long as I lie in bed. It's only when I start walking around that I get fat as a house."

"Tsk, tsk, tsk." Mom shook her head, her face knotted.

Fred sat up straight and said, "Why don't you let her listen to her music? She doesn't have anything else to do, lying in bed like this day after day."

"Why are you mixing into this? You have no business here." Dad looked down at Fred sitting on my bed, his eyes flashing at Fred for saying something contradictory.

"Because you mix into my business! You mixed into my business with Catherine Anne." Fred returned Dad's look, dagger for dagger.

"Oh, so this is about Catherine Anne, not about Illy's music. This is about Catherine Anne." Dad had a smile on his face as if he'd trapped Fred. "And what have *I* got to do with Catherine Anne?"

"Everything … everything!" Fred turned his face away from Dad for a moment and then looked back, straight into his eyes. "If it wasn't for you and Mom, we'd still be together. We'd be getting married. You ruined everything."

"What do you mean?" Mom asked, leaning over Fred, who was still sitting at the foot of my bed. "What did we do? You can have her if you want. If you're not seeing each other anymore, it means that she doesn't want you." Mom looked at Fred as if he were stupid. "What have we got to do with that?"

"Mom, please!" I said. My face felt warm. "Leave him alone."

"You have everything to do with that!" Fred stood up on his feet, ignoring me. "If you would have let me marry her when we wanted to, I wouldn't have lost her." Fred looked like he was about to cry. I bit down hard, grinding my teeth.

"How could we allow a young boy like you to get married—without any money and no education? Then she'd get pregnant and you'd have to get a job. And what kind of job would that be? A job like a common laborer. You wouldn't make enough money to live decently, and you'd have a miserable life. Then you'd come back to us and say, 'How could you ever have let me get married so young?' You'd never forgive us for letting you do it." Mom's hands pumped up and down at the end of every sentence.

"But he *loves* her, Mom." I said, beginning to breathe deeper. "You should have let him marry her."

"You keep out of this!" Dad turned to face me. "This is none of your business."

"It's too late now anyway," Fred said. "Once she told her parents that you didn't want us to get married, they wouldn't let me come near her."

"Why not? Don't tell me they would have wanted you two to get married." Dad laughed as if it were a joke.

Fred said, "They got mad. Her father said, 'So my daughter isn't good enough for those greenhorns! Who do they think they are?'"

"You should have let him marry her," I shouted. "Just look what you've done. He loves her and now he's lost her." I sat up in bed. Perspiration covered my brow. I had to put my fists down next to my hips and use my arms like crutches to keep myself in a sitting position.

Dad looked at me and didn't like what he saw. "Stop it now. Look how you've upset Illy. She's covered in sweat. All this fighting isn't helping her get well. What's done is done. If you want to marry her, go ahead and do it, but at least wait until you're through school. That's all we ask. Finish your education. Now get out of here."

I didn't hear anymore arguments about Catherine Anne after that, but I still didn't get any better. Fred's face went back to its old blank mask. He went to his classes at school and studied in the library at night. He came home only to sleep.

Two months later, my blood and urine specimens returned to normal, the swelling left my body, and I fit into my clothes. Smiles reappeared on Mom and Dad's faces, and I was allowed to go back to school. I was glad about that—I wouldn't have to listen to the daily fights between them and Fred if I weren't home.

I was at school only two days before I couldn't zip my skirt again. Yet another set of specimens were taken and when the results were in, Dad sat down on my bed and spoke to me with his eyes on the floor. "Suzinka, we're right back to where we started. You're passing blood in your urine again." He took my hand and held it as if to never let me go. Almost four months of complete bed rest had done nothing. His voice cracked as he said, "Most patients with this disease recover sooner."

"What about those who take longer? How long does it take them?" I asked.

Dad kept looking at the floor.

"Well?" I insisted.

"That's hard to predict," Dad said. A long silence followed—then he left my bedroom.

I went back to watching my plum tree and saw it was alive and strong with its thin crimson leaves fluttering against the gray sky. Dad hadn't told me that five percent of those who have glomerulonephritis never recover. But I must have read something in his face that made me wonder if I might die.

I thought about the death of our president, Franklin Delano Roosevelt, our hero throughout the war, who'd recently died. I remembered the pictures of the train carrying his casket through so many towns to his final resting place. I thought of the mourners lined up at stations along the route, openly weeping. I pictured the president's body dressed in formal clothes, hands crossed over his chest, lying inside his flag-draped lacquered coffin, and imagined myself inside such a box. *There is nothing I can do to keep myself from ending up in such a box.*

I didn't understand why I should die. Was God punishing me? I didn't think I'd done anything wrong. What had all those people, who died in concentration camps, done to deserve their deaths? They couldn't *all* have been sinners—certainly not the children. What had He done to save all those good people who died in such horrible ways? If He hadn't heard any of their desperate screams and pleading prayers, why would He listen to me?

I decided it would be no use to talk to God. I resigned myself to Fate and went back to watching my magnificent old plum tree. It continued to live, dropping its leaves in the fall and pushing out its tissue thin, delicate new growth in the spring.

Six months passed before my lab tests became normal and remained that way even after I'd returned to school. I would go on growing and changing, just like the magnificent old plum tree outside my window.

The Influence of Elaine

Like a robot, I went from class to class, without much interest in anyone or any-thing—until Mrs. Peck's Spanish class in my junior year. At first glance I thought her to be strange, wearing bright red lipstick on cupid-bow lips and Scottish tar-tan wool skirts around her short, dumpy body. But I learned soon enough that she was no ordinary teacher. She had the ability, in ten minutes time, to transport our entire class from its lower class neighborhood to the exotic environs of Mex-ico City, or Madrid, or Buenos Aires. While we laughed at her behind her back, we all loved her for entertaining us with local musicians who played for us during class time. And to add to her popularity, she was most generous with handing out good grades to her students,

What fun it was to see mariachis, dressed in black suits and wide-brimmed sombreros, strum their guitars and sing their Mexican songs for us. We tapped our feet to the music's rhythm and watched the light bounce off the silver but-tons on their jackets. Mrs. Peck beamed, her puffy cheeks. I wondered if any one of those barrel-bodied performers also happened to be her boyfriend.

One Thursday, she handed a test out to our class. The room was silent except for an occasional noise from someone coughing or crossing their legs. I felt a tap on my shoulder and out of the corner of my eye saw the girl in the seat directly behind me whisper, "Can I borrow your eraser? I forgot mine at home."

"Sure," I mumbled, and lifted a yellow pencil over my shoulder.

"Thanks," she replied. Mrs. Peck didn't notice.

After class, I stopped at my locker in the hallway. The girl from Spanish class walked up to me and said, "Gee, thanks for letting me use your eraser." With hips as wide as a horse's behind, she stood a head taller than me. "My name's Elaine."

"I'm Alice." I enjoyed the sound of my new name, one that said nothing about my background.

"Want to have lunch with me?" she asked, her smile broad. In an instant, I'd taken stock of the fact that she wore an ivory-colored Shetland wool sweater and a patterned, gathered cotton skirt. *She can't afford cashmere sweaters either.*

"Sure," I said.

We headed toward a coffee shop whose letters CAFÉ were arranged like a horseshoe on the front window. We bought a couple of Cokes to go with our paper bag lunches, and sat down at a table covered with green linoleum and edged in chrome. We pulled a paper napkin out of a triangular plastic holder bunched together with bottles of ketchup and mustard at the end of the table. Before biting into her bologna sandwich, Elaine said, "So, what are you doing tonight?"

"Nothing." I pulled a salami sandwich out of my paper lunch bag. "What are you doing?"

"I dunno. Maybe I'll go to the Center with my sister."

"The Center? What's that?"

"The Center ... the Center. It's a place to meet boys." Her smile pushed a pair of parentheses into her cheeks.

"Where's it at? The Center, I mean."

"Oh, it's all the way on the other side of town." She took another bite.

"I don't know anything about it."

"Of course, not. You wouldn't."

"I wouldn't? Why wouldn't I?"

"Because ..." Elaine's eyes were on a square-jawed boy in a letterman jacket outside the café.

"Why wouldn't I?" I repeated, and stopped eating my lunch.

"Because ... just because. Eat your lunch."

I'd stopped eating my lunch and leaned back in my chair. I was angry that she was keeping something from me and withdrew from our conversation, joining her in staring at the handsome kid on the sidewalk. After some silence, she said, "Because it's the *Jewish* Community Center. That's why."

"It's Jewish?" My eyes felt as if they were about to pop out of their sockets. "You're Jewish?"

"Yeah."

I leaned forward in my seat and shouted, "So am I!"

"You are?" Elaine stared at me, slack-jawed.

The smile on my face was as broad as Elaine's. *She's just like me—not rich—not popular—and Jewish!* The four-leaf clover, the rabbit's foot, and the ladybug, all rolled into one, had come my way when I met Elaine.

"Want to come to the Center with me and my sister tonight?" Elaine picked up her empty paper bag and stood up to leave.

I followed her out of the coffee shop saying, "I'd love to—I'll ask my parents."

That night at dinner I told Mom and Dad about Elaine. They asked me all the usual questions, where does she live, does she have any brothers and sisters, what does her Dad do for a living. Dad had to know her family's status—whether it was above or below ours. I didn't know the answer to any of his questions, nor did they matter to me. I only wanted to go to the Center with Elaine. The grilling didn't stop.

"What are you going to do there?"

"I dunno. I just want to be with Elaine, and maybe her sister."

"What goes on there? What do the kids do there?"

"I dunno. It's for kids my age to get together, I guess."

"Are there going to be any boys there?"

"I don't know!" I shouted and then, through clenched teeth, "I ... don't ... know ... maybe." I looked up at the ceiling.

"Well then, you can't go. If boys will be there, you can't go."

I took a deep breath before saying, "I don't know if boys are going to be there. I've never been there before."

"*Ach, Illy, dreh' nich so viel.* You can't go if boys will be there without one of us going with you."

"How come Elaine can go, and I can't? Her parents let her go."

"We don't care what Elaine can do. We only care about you. What kind of parents are they anyway, letting a girl go to a place like that all by herself?"

"She's going with her sister." I said, leaving the room. I knew there wasn't anything I could say to change their minds. It had been months before Mom noticed that all the girls my age wore lipstick and then allowed me to wear it too. I knew it would be at least that long before Mom and Dad would consider allowing me to go to the Center. I telephoned Elaine and told her I couldn't go.

In the week that followed, Elaine and I had lunch together every day. On Friday, she asked if someday I could come over to her house after school. When I asked Mom, there was that usual hesitation, when she'd try to think of some reason why I couldn't go. We went through the same question and answer session I'd become used to. When I told her all the girls at school were allowed to visit one another, she finally relented.

Elaine lived as far from Washington High in one direction as I did in the other. The main thing about Elaine's home was that it was dark. Nestled between tall pines with trunks as big as drums, little light could make it through to the inside of her house. In the living room, the couches and chairs were upholstered in a deep plum color. The mahogany dining room table stood on four massive legs, polished to shine like glass. A beveled glass sideboard displayed gold-edged china dotted with cherries.

Elaine told me the elegant furnishings in her house were a wedding present from her mother's wealthy family. But now her mother had to work as a secretary to support her family while her dad—who liked to go to the racetrack—drifted in and out of a series of jobs. All that information allowed Dad to be *better* than Elaine's Dad, and made it possible for us to be friends.

Whereas going to school had been a humdrum affair before I met Elaine, having her as a friend made all the difference in the world to me. I had someone with whom I could eat lunch, walk the halls, and gossip about classmates. It had been such a long time since I'd lost the friendship of Dolores that I'd almost given up having anyone like her in my life. As it turned out, I felt closer to Elaine than I ever had to Dolores—we were so much more alike.

In time I was allowed to spend the night at Elaine's house. I met her older sister, Gloria, who worked in a beauty shop, and her younger sister, Ginny, who dreamed of becoming an opera singer. Her mother, a tiny woman with a pointed chin that looked like the bottom of an ice cream cone, welcomed me with a smile as wide as Elaine's. At dinner time, she opened a can of red salmon and made croquets for all of us—out of only one can. *They must have even less money than us.*

After dinner, Gloria said, "You guys want to go to the Center tonight?"

"Yeah, let's," Elaine said, her eyes bright.

"I can't," I said. "My folks won't let me." I looked at Elaine. "You *know* I can't."

"Why don't you call and ask them again? Tell them Gloria is coming with us."

"I don't know that it would make any difference."

"Just try, why don't you?" Elaine insisted.

"Okay. I'll try." The phone rang at home but no one answered. "They must be out for a walk."

"Well, I'm going to go," Gloria said, walking to the hall closet for her raincoat. "Are you guys coming?"

"Yeah, we're coming." Elaine got up from the table. "Wait for us." Then, turning to me, she said, "Come on, Alice. Your folks wouldn't mind if they knew we were going with Gloria. She's already graduated high school and working. They won't mind. Let's go."

I hesitated. *If Dad knew I went to the Center without his permission, he'd be mad.*

"Are you coming, or not?" Elaine bobbed her head and frowned.

Here's my chance to be like other girls my age—like an American girl.

"Wait up a minute," I said, grabbing my coat and following the others out the door.

The Center was a somber looking two-story cube with four tall narrow windows facing the front. We entered to a medley of sounds—water splashing from the swimming pool, rhythmic cracks from Ping-Pong balls, echoes from dribbling basketballs, and Frank Sinatra crooning *If I Loved You*. We followed the music into a large rectangular room. A handful of boys and girls standing along the walls watched three couples dance cheek-to-cheek in the center of the room. Gloria found the dark-skinned, wavy-haired boy she was looking for and retreated to a corner.

Elaine saw a girl she knew and said, "Come on, Alice." I tagged behind and met her friend. We exchanged a few words, and then swung around to look at the boys. Not one was as tall as me, and certainly not anywhere near Elaine's height. I wanted to dance, but not with any of the *shrimps* in the room.

The record ended and everyone moved from one person to another, like bumper cars in an amusement park. In one corner, a college kid put a record of Dick James singing *I'll Get By* on the turntable. A few bars into the song, a muscular boy with broad shoulders and a handsome face approached Elaine and asked her to dance. Dimples appeared in her cheeks. When they stepped into the middle of the room and faced one another, it was evident that she was six inches taller than he. I leaned against the wall and wondered how she could be happy with someone so short.

Mom and Dad never knew that I'd gone to the Center. I didn't tell them about that night or all the subsequent Thursday nights at the Center that followed. I suppressed the guilt I felt for not being entirely honest and counted on their loving me if they ever found out, despite this subterfuge.

Appreciating Mom

The movers carried our old scratchy couch into our new house on Northeast 15th Street. I wished it had been a brand new sofa, one that didn't feel like you were sitting on a scouring pad. But Mom and Dad couldn't afford new furniture, having barely enough money to pay for the house. Our new home bordered one of the nicest neighborhoods in Portland. There, big two-story homes with massive stone chimneys sat on jade green lawns. Rhododendron and camellia bushes, tall as trees, and azaleas big as boulders, flashed a medley of red, pink, and white blossoms.

But our house wasn't like any of those. Set up twenty steps from the sidewalk, our little home had only a small, carpet-sized patch of grass in front of a picture window. Its best feature was the rock garden that dropped like a floral curtain down to the sidewalk. It was our fourth move in six years, and by far the nicest home we'd lived in since coming to America. And it was one that Mom and Dad owned, not rented. We didn't even mind listening to the roar of cars whizzing by at all hours.

Dad finally passed his exams and received his license to practice medicine in the state of Washington. With it came a regular job—doctoring the shipyard workers in Vanport, Washington. Dad was one of the original doctors who worked for Henry J. Kaiser when he founded the Kaiser Permanente Health Plan. Dad's salary as a pediatrician was sufficient to allow Mom to retire from the grocery business. His career finally gave him the respect and status that he had fought for ever since we arrived in America.

After Mom had sold the store, she didn't spend her time going to luncheons or being a clubwoman. She got interested in gardening and landscaping. She took up tailoring and made all her own suits. She even learned how to do mosaics and donated her art pieces to charity. Mom was not one to sit, with her feet raised on a stool, eating chocolates.

On a warm sunny day in October, one that everyone called Indian summer, I came home from school to find Mom on her knees in the rock garden. A sack of planter mix stood by her side, and she held a small spade in her gloved hand. She wore a full-body apron down to her hips, which covered a smudged floral housedress. I wished she wouldn't garden right out in front of our house, where every-one could see her in those dirty clothes, working like a farmhand. None of the rich kids' mothers ever did that—they hired somebody else to do it for them.

"Hi, Mom." I bounded up the steps to the front door, two at a time, so that nobody I knew would see me next to her, my pleated tartan skirt bouncing on my ankles.

"There's some doughnuts on a plate in the kitchen, if you want." She lifted her head to glance at me as I passed by.

The screen door creaked and banged behind me as I slid through the front door. In the kitchen, I grabbed a doughnut and stuffed a too-large bite into my mouth. Savoring the sugar on my tongue, I rounded the corner into the hallway to my bedroom and stopped in the doorway. There, spread out at the foot of my bed on top of my old pink chenille bedspread, were two short-sleeved, round-necked cashmere sweaters, one navy blue and the other forest green.

A gust of air escaped from my lips, as if someone had hit me in the stomach. The wad of dough in my mouth lost its taste. I dropped my books next to the sweaters, making the springs of my bed screech. I licked my fingers and touched the blue sweater. It felt soft as a baby's scalp. *Cashmere!* They were like the sweat-ers the good-looking, popular girls at school wore. I dashed out of my bedroom and out the front door.

"Mom! What are those sweaters doing on my bed?" I shouted, so Mom could hear me over the traffic din.

"They're for you. I bought them for you." Mom straightened up from her crouched position.

"But ... they're cashmere," I said, knowing they cost at least twice as much as my wool sweaters.

"I know." Mom was on her knees, looking like she was praying at church. With her gloved fists on her hips, she smiled and said, "Do you like them?"

"Of course, I like them. But ... they're expensive." I walked down the ten steps to be at her side and sat down. "What'll Dad say?" I pictured him yelling at Mom, calling her stupid and a spendthrift.

"Oh, don't worry about Dad. He won't say anything. He won't even know the sweaters are cashmere." Mom stood up, climbed over some white candytufts that looked like cotton balls, and sat down next to me. Still wearing her muddy gloves, she banged a clump of dirt off her spade and said, "He wouldn't know the difference between cashmere and burlap."

"But Mom … the money. He'll know how much money you spent. And he'll get mad." The thought of Dad's stubby eyebrows twitching and shiny drops of saliva gathering in the corners of his mouth put goose bumps on my arms.

"No, he won't know." Mom took off one muddy glove and put her hand on my knee. "He won't know because I bought them with my own money, money he doesn't know anything about. I've saved it over the years and put it in my own little bank account."

"But Mom … how did you know I've always wanted to have a cashmere sweater?"

"I knew. Don't think I've always been blind to what's going on with you. Don't think I didn't know how you've felt all these years in Portland, being an outsider, having no money, and with parents like Dad and me. No matter how hard we try, and no matter how long we're in this country, we'll always be the greenhorns. But you … you can be American. You can get an education and take care of yourself. You can do better than sneaking a few dollars here and there like I have to do."

"Mom …" I put my arm around her shoulders and pulled her close. "Mom, thanks. I love the sweaters." Her eyes welled up as I kissed her cheek.

"I'm glad." We stood up together. "Now don't say anything to Dad about this, and especially about my bank account."

"Don't worry." I turned and went back up the steps and into the house. In my bedroom, I sat down next to the sweaters so slowly that not even the slightest grating sound came out of the springs.

I felt as if a brick had fallen on my chest—so that I could hardly breathe. I asked myself how I could have been so angry with Mom for wearing out-of-style European clothes, when she had no money to buy any others. How could I have been so ashamed of her with her German accent, when no refugee spoke any better? How could I have thought her uneducated and stupid the whole time Dad was out of work, and she was the one who supported our whole family? How could I have disliked her for the way she looked with her bunions and inverted bite, without noticing the love in her warm, dark eyes and the determination in her strong jaw?

I blinked away the moisture in my eyes and sighed. I slipped the navy blue sweater over my head and snapped a string of imitation pearls around my neck. I walked over to the mirror hanging on my closet door and noticed that the navy blue of the sweater made my eyes look like the sapphire blue of Lake Shasta. She even knew that.

I locked eyes with those in the mirror and decided that I would never live the life that was forced on Mom. I wouldn't pay the price of being put down regularly for the security a marriage might give me. I would be able to take care of myself. I would become the woman Mom would have been, if only she'd been given the chance.

Tante Dora

Onkel Max

Elaine

MomandDad-1948

House at Northeast 15th and Knott Street

Alice at UCLA sorority

Falling for Karl

It was my first real job. I wore a spotless white dress and blue apron, its U-shaped skirt trimmed in white eyelet. Two bobby pins held a white cap, starched stiff as cardboard, on top of my head. That was the uniform the dessert girl behind the counter at Manning's Cafeteria in downtown Portland had to wear. I cut cakes and pies into a designated number of pieces—weighed on a scale to insure the portions would be identical—then stood behind the cafeteria line to serve our customers.

On my third day at work, I was called into the back room by one of the cooks. *Didn't I cut my last apple pie in seven exact pieces?* I found a middle-aged woman wearing an olive green raincoat and Red Cross shoes waiting for me. She held a manila envelope under her arm and looked at me with blurry eyes through thick glaucoma glasses.

"Are you Alice Fell?" she asked, her voice as low as a man's.

"Yes."

"I'm from the union."

"Union?"

"Yes. You have to join the union if you want to work here." The blur behind her glasses moved a little.

"But this is just a summer job. I'm only fifteen. I'll be back in high school in three months."

"Doesn't matter to me if you'll be back in school or not. You can't work here unless you sign up for the union." She pulled a white application form out of her manila envelope and handed it to me. "Fill this form out and leave it with your boss tonight. We'll deduct the monthly dues from your paycheck." She walked away from me without waiting for an answer.

I didn't want to join the union. It might have made sense to me if I were planning a career at Manning's, but not when I was going to college so that I wouldn't have to spend the rest of my life serving desserts. But I knew there was nothing I could do. I'd either join the union or lose my job. I left the completed application with my boss. It was my first lesson in compromise.

The following week, I was serving a piece of angel food cake to a customer when, out of the corner of my eye, I saw Mitzi and Trudi coming toward me, pushing their trays along the chrome bars.

"*Servus*, Illy," Mitzi said with a smile and bob of the head. "Your mother told me about you working here. I think it's wonderful." I smiled back, and noticed a look on Trudi's face somewhere between admiration and jealousy.

"Hi, Mitzi," I said, wondering if I was supposed to talk to anyone in line.

"We were downtown shopping so we thought we'd have coffee here," Mitzi said. "Some friends are coming to join us, too."

"That's nice," I said. *Why does Mom have to go telling everybody about everything I do?* Mitzi's friends Adele, Gila, and Marta, all refugees, lined up behind her. They had begun to dress like American women, but there still remained something foreign about their appearance, so that one could tell they weren't born here, even without hearing their accents. Perhaps it was the way they walked—or the way they laughed—a bit too often. They greeted me with smiles and waving hands. I responded, feeling my cheeks get warm and knowing they must have become the color of Delicious apples.

Mom slid her tray along the chrome bars toward me. I leaned over a piece of blueberry pie and whispered, "What did you do that for? Why did you have to go and tell everyone you know that I work here?"

"What's wrong with that? Why shouldn't they know?" Mom said.

"Why do you have to mix into my business? Now every refugee in Portland will be here. What if my boss doesn't like it? I might even lose my job." I looked down the line and saw another customer approach the dessert station. "Go on already." I waved her down the line.

"Don't get so huffy," Mom said, pulling herself upright. "Hand me a piece of that apple pie and get a hold of yourself."

It's true that I wanted to be independent, but that's not what bothered me the most. It was the pool of shame in which I swam that followed me everywhere. It was filled with the image of my fashion-ignorant mother, my outrageous aunt and uncle, and my unpredictable, ill-tempered father. But worst of all was the shame I felt for myself, a shame born in me the day I stood in front of my class at Abernethy School, shame that I felt at being called Elsie and Sally, shame at my failure to appreciate a Frankenstein movie, or learn how to swim. It was shame at every turn, which reminded me that I was different—a fact I tried to keep secret from everyone, including myself.

"You don't have to get so upset," Mom said, looking insulted. She carried her tray to her friend's table.

That day, at coffee with her friends, Mom learned about the Friendship Club. Formed by a group of immigrants, they held regular meetings and parties. She was told that Zita Gruen was going to sing arias from *Die Fledermaus* at their next meeting, accompanied by Peter Ungar at the piano. Mom would have loved to join this particular group and been part of their social life, but that was not comfortable for Dad. His habit of finding fault with almost everybody—perhaps to make himself feel superior—prevented them from joining in. But a meeting that would feature a performance of their beloved Viennese songs was too enticing to turn down.

Mom bought a new outfit for the occasion. I planned to wear one of my cashmere sweaters and hadn't decided on the rest, when Mom said I should wear the new green corduroy skirt I'd sewn.

"Don't tell me what to wear," I said. *Why does she treat me like such a baby?* "I don't want to wear that skirt."

"Why not? It's beautiful."

"It's not—the skirt's not right. I don't want to wear it."

"What's wrong with it? There's nothing wrong with it."

"Yes, there is. I didn't cut it out right. The nap on the front two panels is different—shiny on the left and matte on the right."

"Oh that ... that's nothing. Nobody'll ever notice that."

"Yes, they will. I don't want to wear it."

"Look Illy, we spent a lot of money on that fabric, and it's the nicest skirt you have. So just wear it and don't worry so much about what other people think. It looks fine, and you can be proud you made it yourself."

It was indeed the best skirt I had, and there was no other choice but to wear it to the Friendship Club meeting. We drove to a restaurant on the outskirts of the city and entered a room filled with folding chairs, an upright piano, refreshments, and a group of well-dressed people. I followed close behind Mom and Dad so that no one could see the front of my skirt. We found the Feldmans and took our places in our chairs. Peter Ungar, a dapper looking man in a striped double-breasted suit, sat down at the piano. Zita Gruen, wearing a green, belted dress draped over her near perfect figure, stepped into the S-curve of the grand piano and faced the audience. Herr Ungar played the first few bars of the song, *Ich bin eine anstendige Frau,* and brought smiles to everyone's faces. Zita's voice went flat every so often and Peter hit more than one wrong note, but no one seemed to mind.

After the performance, I joined the others at the refreshment table, turning my back to the room to hide my skirt, and reached for a butter horn. I didn't notice that Pepi was next to me, talking to two men.

"*Ach*, Illy, here you are." He glanced at the two men and said, "This is Alice. You know … the Fell's girl." Pepi's blue eyes flashed.

"Hello," I managed to mumble, looking at two men who could have been identical twins, except that one had sparse, white hair and a lined face, while the other's full mane was the color of mahogany. A cigarette held between two fingers at his side sent spirals of gray smoke up his arm. I struggled to keep my knees from trembling.

"This is Herr Gottesman and his son, Karl," Pepi said.

"Hello." The men spoke in unison.

I said hello again before fleeing to my seat with a butter horn on my plate. My skirt now hidden under my plate, I savored the tissue-thin flakes of my pastry to the strains of *On the Beautiful Blue Danube*. I put my empty plate under my chair and, before I could sit up, a pair of men's brown oxford shoes appeared in front of me. Looking up into Karl's face, my heart skipped a beat.

"Would you like to dance?" he said.

"Sure," I said, forgetting all about how my skirt looked, or that I didn't know how to dance.

Karl put his hand around my waist and pulled me close to him. I muffled a gasp and worried that Mom and Dad saw it. With our bodies together as one, he pulled me across the floor in time to the music. Even though I'd never danced before, I followed him, step for step. I inhaled the smell of his tobacco, at once sweet and acrid. I felt his strong arm around my waist, his warm cheek against my forehead, and forgot about Mom and Dad or anyone else in the room. I was on fire.

When the record stopped, we dropped our arms, stepped apart, and stood silent, until Karl said, "Do you want a drink?"

With our glasses of punch in hand, we walked toward my seat. "This is Karl Gottesman," I said, standing next to Mom and Dad's chairs.

Dad said, "I know. I met your father just now. Your family is from Berlin, right?"

"Yes." Karl was not afraid to look Dad in the eye.

"I understand they came in 1936."

"Yes. We did." Karl stood erect.

Don't grill Karl as if you were a policeman.

"Lucky for you. You probably got your things out," Dad said.

Now he's fishing to find out how much money they have.

"We brought our Persian carpets and a few Rosenthal china pieces—not enough to live on. Dad and I are trying to sell cheese and the noodles my mother and sister make."

"Oh … noodles … uh-ha."

Good! Dad can think he's 'better.'

Mom interrupted with, "Bobi, shouldn't we be going home?"

After that evening at the Friendship Club, I spent the rest of the summer wishing Karl would call me. I knew Mom and Dad wouldn't let me go out at my age, but just the same, I wanted Karl to ask me to go to the movies or out for a hamburger. But Karl never called. I spent the summer working at Manning's. Sometimes though—when I was home alone—I'd put one of our 78 rpms on the phonograph and dance around the room with my eyes shut, my right arm raised to hold Karl's imaginary hand, my left arm resting on his phantom shoulder, and my head tilted against a ghostly cheek smelling of tobacco.

Freedom of Choice

During the summer I worked at Manning's Cafeteria, cutting up spongy lemon cakes and apple pies, while Fred was wheeling patients up and down the halls of Coffey Hospital. Dad had gotten him the job, hoping it would make him more enthusiastic about becoming a doctor. It didn't. Fred needed the money for dating girls, and it was better not to ask Dad for it. Still, he had other problems, such as Mom watching his comings and goings whenever he went out with a girl.

"Mom, I wish you wouldn't wait up for me when I go out," Fred said one morning at breakfast after a date.

"Why shouldn't I?" Mom said with her eyes half-open. Puffs of steam floated up from her oatmeal as she swirled her spoon through it. "I couldn't sleep until I knew you were home safe."

"I'm a grown man. When are you going to stop treating me like a baby?" Fred leaned against the kitchen counter, clutching his cup with both hands as if to warm his fingers.

Mom got up and walked toward Fred in her loose-fitting blue duster. She put her hands on his cheeks, looked up into his eyes, and said, "Fredi, you'll always be my baby, no matter how old you are. Just remember, nobody will ever love you more than your mother."

Then Dad flipped *The Oregonian* newspaper up and down as if to straighten its fold. It made such a sharp, loud crackling sound that they both looked at him. Mom took her hands off Fred's face and sat down.

The next time Fred went out, Mom asked, "So, who did you go out with last night?"

"Some girl I met. You wouldn't know her."

"I expected it to be a girl. Does she have a name?"

"Of course, she has a name."

"So, is her name a secret?"

"Her name's Nancy." Fred set his jaw and looked out at a passing car.

Dad looked up from his newspaper and said, "Is she Jewish?"

"No-o-o—she's not Jewish."

"So, why do you bother to go out with her?"

"Because it doesn't matter to me if she's Jewish or not. I'll go out with whoever I want." The legs of Fred's chair loudly scraped the floor, as he pushed away from the table and left the room. As a spectator to the drama happening between Mom and Dad and Fred, I was having a look at what might well be in store for me when I got older.

Fred kept on going out with Nancy, and Mom and Dad kept trying to break them up—just as they'd done with Catherine Anne. They found fault with anything they knew about her, even some things they made up—such as her being "easy." Fred shouted, "How can you say that? You don't know one thing about her. How would you even know if she'd been with men before she knew me?"

Fred brought Nancy home one Sunday after their tennis game at Mt. Tabor Park. I knew they'd met on the courts, hiked the park's wooded trails many afternoons, and at night, would park their car at the top of the mountain so they could see the sparking city lights of Portland below. I thought it was romantic, and was proud of the fact that Fred would tell me about Nancy when he wouldn't tell anyone else.

When Mom opened the front door, I saw her head bounce back as if she'd been punched in the jaw. Nancy was almost as tall as Fred at six foot one, with a fashion model's figure. Her hair was as light as sunshine, turned up like a J at the shoulders. She and Fred, with his dark coloring, looked as if they came from opposite ends of the earth. Fred was still in shorts and a V-necked cable knit sweater, while she wore a belted dress with an accordion-pleated skirt. One couldn't miss the pair of legs on her that would have bested those of Betty Grable. Mom forced a smile and, between clenched teeth, said, "Please come in."

While serving coffee and blueberry pie, we did our best to keep from staring at Nancy with open mouths. I thought she was movie-star beautiful, looking like Rita Hayworth with blonde hair. Mom asked if she liked sugar and cream with her coffee. All her answers were one or two words, followed by silence that was filled with the constant drone of cars whizzing by outside our house. Then Dad began grilling, "So, where's your family from?"

"Corvallis," she said.

"What do they do there?" Dad said.

"Farming."

"Uh-huh," Dad said.

"You have brothers and sisters?" Mom said.

"One sister," Fred answered, relieving Nancy.

"What kind of work do you do?"

"Secretarial."

"Oh," Mom and Dad said in unison.

No one said anything more. Mom and Dad had run out of questions. Fred pulled Nancy close and said, "Isn't she gorgeous?" She looked at him and smiled for the first time, showing square teeth lined up like Chiclets.

"Yes … gorgeous …" Mom said, her jaw rigid. She reached for the cups and saucers on the coffee table. "I'd better clear these up." Fred read the signal and said they'd better get going, too.

Mom and Dad went to work on Fred the minute he came home. Dad asked him how he could go out with a simple farm girl with no education. Mom asked how he could talk to her when she can't say more than two words at a time. Then Dad said what they did on dates didn't require any talking. That's when Fred got mad.

"Why don't you just leave her alone?" Fred grabbed his jacket and stormed out of the house, slamming the door behind him.

Every muscle in my body tensed when Mom and Dad fought with Fred. I'd been almost as excited as Fred was about his having a girlfriend as stunning as Nancy. It didn't matter to me that she wasn't Jewish and couldn't talk. I thought Fred had a right to go out with whomever he wanted.

Mom and Dad thought everything Fred did was wrong, while I seemed to be no trouble at all. They didn't have to worry about me and boys while I was in high school—no one asked me out. I would have given anything for a date to go downtown to the "mini theater district" on Broadway. The sparkling marquee of the half dozen movie houses, lit up by hundreds of electric lights, was like magic for me. Mom said we could go together some night, but I'd have been mortified to be seen out with her. We did go to some Sunday matinees, where I kept my back to the street so as not to be seen with my Mom. But once inside the safety of the dark theater, I transported myself into the stories of the *Treasure of Sierra Madre* with Humphrey Bogart, and pretended to be Loretta Young in *The Farmer's Daughter*. Those movies were worth taking a chance of being spotted by a classmate.

It was not until I was a senior and about to graduate from high school that a kid in my Shakespeare class, as socially inept as me, shuffled up to me in the hall one day and asked, "Wanna go to the prom?" Since I was shy of eighteen by only three months, Mom and Dad said I could go. The fact that this boy's father would be taking us there and picking us up, also helped convince them that my virginity would be kept intact. Mom made my sea green taffeta formal dress, luckily in the off-shoulder style all the girls would be wearing. I was excited to go out on my first date.

Larry Le Montt was a tall, handsome kid who's slicked down brown hair made him look like a seal breaking out of water. His greatest accomplishment was playing the trombone in the school band, whereas mine was membership in the Spanish Club and National Honor Society. Graduating as one of the top students in my class of five hundred kids didn't help me one iota in feeling accepted by my classmates. It only made Mom and Dad happy knowing their daughter was *Gescheit*.

Larry bought me a corsage made of three white carnations whose petals looked as though they'd been trimmed by zigzag scissors. I wished it had been a single orchid, either fuchsia or white, like the other girls had. On the dance floor, we held one another at arms length and jockeyed around while the music played. It was nothing like dancing with Karl. But I was satisfied with the fact that, at least, I had attended my prom. After graduation in January, I never saw Larry Le Montt again.

Since I wouldn't be going to college until September, I went back to work as a salesgirl in a downtown department store. The brightest part of that summer was meeting Elaine after work and going to the Center with her. Two things had changed about our nights at the Center since graduation. First, I no longer had to keep my visits a secret from Mom and Dad, since I was almost eighteen and eligible to start looking for a husband. Second, Elaine and I expanded our search for boys from the Teenage Room to other parts of the building.

Elaine was the first one to score. She met Sam Benveniste playing ping-pong. After driving her home one Thursday, he kept asking her out. Then it was my turn. I met Herb in the lobby. Since he was still in his shorts and shirt after having played basketball, I was able to see that he was tall and thin with broad shoulders and muscular legs.

"Where'd you come from?" he said, looking down at me as if I were the prize in a Cracker-Jack box.

"From work," I said, wondering if he could dance like Karl.

"How come I've never seen you here before?" he said, his face lighting up with a smile.

"I dunno."

"Well, I'm glad you're here tonight." I knew he liked what he saw. We talked for a while and after having a Coke he said, "Can I give you a ride home?"

"Sure." *Wait 'till I tell Elaine.*

Once they knew Herb was Jewish, Mom and Dad didn't object to my going out with him. Even though he never turned my knees to rubber like Karl had done, I was proud to have him as a boyfriend. He was the president of his fraternity at college and a member of that "popular" group of kids that I'd always wanted to be part of. Like the key to a bank vault, dating him was my entry into the clannish Portland American Jewish community. But I didn't know that, every time I went to one of their parties, I'd still feel, *I'm not like them—I'm a green-horn.*

Toward the end of summer, Herb asked me to go to the University of Washington in Seattle with him, promising we'd be "pinned." I knew that having Herb's fraternity pin on my sweater meant a ring on my finger to follow. I wasn't ready for that. I was still playing catch-up on learning how to date—something I hadn't done in high school. I wasn't ready for *love.*

On a sticky evening when the humidity made it impossible to stay in the house, Mom sprung out of her chair and said, "Why are we sitting here sweltering? Let's get out of the house and take a walk."

We were halfway around the block when Dad said, "So, what's Herb studying in Seattle?" His hands were clasped behind his back, European style, reminding me of how he looked when he took me to the Prater.

"I dunno," I said. "I think just all the classes you need to graduate."

"What's he going to do after he graduates?" Mom asked.

"I dunno. Get a job, I suppose."

"What does his dad do?" Dad asked.

"Sell insurance, I think," I said, not really sure. We'd never talked about his dad.

"Uh, huh," Dad said, looking at the sidewalk in front of him. It was the same "uh-huh" I heard when Nancy said her father was a farmer. Dad took a few more steps and then said, "I would think a girl as pretty as you would want to be married to somebody who could do something better than sell insurance. A girl like you could get anybody, even a doctor or lawyer."

We crossed the street into the next block and Mom said, "You're only eighteen and you have plenty of time to find someone better."

Mom and Dad hadn't known about Herb inviting me to Seattle, nor did they know that I had decided not to go there. Many Portland Jewish kids went to college in Seattle, and Eugene as well. My going to either one of those campuses would have been like taking all the problems I'd had in Portland to college with me when I was trying to get away from them. But I resented their deciding for me that Herb was not good enough for me. I wanted it to be me who'd decide one way or another.

I focused on Berkeley instead, but before I could campaign for such a move, I was offered a scholarship at Reed College in Portland, considered by many to be one of the best small colleges in the country. It would have been unthinkable for me to turn it down. After graduating in January, I went back to work until September, when I enrolled at Reed as a freshman.

In the meantime, Fred was getting ready to graduate from medical school in June. He walked into the house one day carrying a suit on a hanger over his shoulder and headed for the bedroom. Mom and I followed him like a pair of chicks behind a hen.

"So, what's this all about?" Mom stood flat-footed in the middle of the room.

"It's a tux for my senior class formal dance on Saturday night. They're having it at Jantzen Beach—very fancy." Fred looked at me and smiled.

"Fred, that's great. Are you going with Nancy?" I was excited for him.

"Of course." Fred's grin covered his face.

"That *schikse* again? You stopped talking about her for a while so I thought maybe you'd stopped seeing her," Mom said, fists on her hips.

Fred's grin disappeared. "I stopped talking about her because there's no way we can have a decent conversation about her. And you'd better stop calling her a *schickse*. I'm going to marry her."

"What?" Mom looked as if someone had poured a bucket of ice water over her head. "Have you lost your mind?"

"No, I haven't," Fred said. "You may not want to admit it, but I'm a grown man and can do whatever I want."

"And ruin your life!" Mom shouted, her face pomegranate red. She left the room. Fred stood next to his tux, his arms limp at his sides. I sat on his bed and felt his pain.

Dad didn't like Fred marrying Nancy anymore than Mom did. I thought they were right about Nancy being a simple girl, but she was as beautiful as anyone I'd ever seen and Fred was in love with her. Neither Mom nor Dad would attend the wedding, which made it impossible for me to be there either. That hurt Fred deep, and I was sorry for him. He was married in a judge's office with only his best friend and Nancy's sister as witnesses. Afterwards, he left for San Diego and never lived in Portland again. It seemed as if Mom and Dad had pushed him right out of their lives.

Will that happen to me?

If I Were at Berkeley

I was a "day-dodger" at Reed—one of those students who lived at home, commuted to school, and didn't participate in any school activities. On campus, I never noticed the acres of emerald lawns that rolled up to stately Tudor buildings that sat on top of hills like dignified royalty. I didn't walk along the winding paths, dotted with magnificent cedars and pines that smelled like fresh bars of soap. It took weeks before I found the trail that led to a spring-fed lake behind the dormitories, where migratory birds spread their wings and showed us the rainbow colors in their feathers.

Since I was on campus only for my classes, I didn't make any friends. The only exception was a boy who offered me a seat in his car pool to school. I waited on the corner of Fifteenth and Knott, dressed in a yellow oilskin slicker to fend off our never-ending rain, until his old Ford pulled up to the curb. On the first day of car pool, I saw that my ride to school would involve sitting in an open-air rumble seat next to a Japanese boy dressed in an identical slicker. We must have looked like a pair of large bananas sticking out of the back seat as we drove off down the street.

I was dropped off at the corner again at three o'clock, at which time I retreated to my bedroom to study. On one such day, I heard Mom open the screen door at the front of the house. I came to help her bring the groceries in and arrived just in time to see a box pop out of an overflowing bag onto the carpet. It was filled with blueberries, which spread over the entire entry like the flow of lava into a valley. Dad, sitting in the living room and seeing what had happened, shouted, "Now, look what you've done!"

Mom, with a look of pain on her face, crouched down to put the berries back into their carton. Then she raced into the kitchen, clutching her groceries and shouting over her shoulder, "Don't worry. I'll clean it up."

When she returned with a bottle of soda and a rag in her hand, Dad said, "How stupid can you be? You can clean from today until forever; soda will never take those stains out of the carpet."

I returned to my bedroom. Through my open door, I heard Mom say, "If this doesn't work, I'll use a spot remover. Don't worry, I'll get it out."

"Why shouldn't I worry? You'll never get it out. You've ruined the carpeting!"

My head began to pound, and I shut the door to my bedroom. *I wish I were at Berkeley.*

Half an hour later, Mom knocked on my door and asked if I wanted to have a cup of coffee. The whites of her eyes were marked with fine red lines, the lids swollen.

"Mom," I said. "You've been crying."

"No. No. It's nothing." She attempted a weak smile. "You're imagining things."

"I'm not, Mom." I opened my bedroom door. "Come in."

Mom sat down on the side of my bed, kneading a moist handkerchief. "I didn't want you to see me like this. But sometimes he's just too cruel."

"I know, Mom," I said, sitting down next to her.

"Sometimes I think I can't stand it anymore." I put my arm around her shoulders. "It's not like he didn't warn me about his bad temper. I knew it before I was even engaged. I knew it from the moment he treated Uncle Jack so badly."

"What do you mean? What happened?" I thought about Uncle Jack, Mom's youngest brother, who was the most easy-going and most likeable of Mom's four brothers. I couldn't imagine anyone treating him badly.

"Well, Dad and I had a rendezvous to meet in the Prater at a certain time. It turned out I had to work late at my job in the bank and couldn't be there. I had no way of getting in touch with your Dad and didn't know what to do. Then I remembered Jack was home. I telephoned him and told him to meet Dad for me and tell him why I didn't show up."

"So what's wrong with that?"

"It was an hour later than the time we'd agreed upon. Dad was mad as a hornet. He started to yell at Jack as if *he'd* done something wrong. Jack apologized over and over, but Dad's anger was boiling. Since he couldn't strike out at Jack, he grabbed hold of his own shirt and ripped it apart. Jack was shocked. He didn't know what to do. In his own sweet way, he simply turned around and walked away."

"My God," I said. Then when I thought about how Dad looked when he was mad at any one of us, I could believe Mom's story.

"Of course, he felt terrible after that. He knew he had a bad temper and that he could explode sometimes," Mom said, rolling her handkerchief into a tiny pillow. "But he loved me and I knew that to be true." Mom wiped her eyes. "He said he wanted to marry me, but not unless I was sure I could handle his outbursts. He said if I could stay quiet and not talk back to him when he was mad …

if I could just let him vent until the temper passed … if I could do that, we could be happy together." She looked down at her hands.

"How could you make a promise like that?" I asked, knowing that *I* couldn't have done it.

"I was just eighteen-years-old and here I had a man, *a doctor*, in love with me—a simple, uneducated girl without a dowry. I was so young then. I thought that love could overcome any obstacle." She paused. "I think I've done pretty well." She lowered her head and wiped her nose. "… but sometimes I feel like I can't take it anymore. I just want to run as far away from him as I can get."

"Why don't you, Mom?" I felt an ache in my chest.

"How could I do that?"

"You could get a divorce."

Mom looked at me as if I'd told her to take a spaceship to Mars. "And then what would I do—all by myself without any money?"

"You could get a job and take care of yourself. You made money before—you could do it again."

"That's ridiculous, Suzi. What could I do now—an older woman without an education? Be a waitress?" Mom shook her head.

"Yes. Wait tables if you have to. It's still better than having someone treat you like Dad does."

"I can't do that," Mom said, sitting on my bed, defeated. "Despite everything, I know in my heart that he loves me."

I said no more. But I decided then and there, that no man would ever treat me like that. I would get an education and be able to take care of myself, if I had to.

Mom left my room and I went back to reading *The Odyssey*, an assignment for my Humanities course, a study of western history and literature. I was fascinated by this class, not only for its lectures, but also for a fellow student, a fair-skinned kid whose hair was as black and shiny as a panther's coat. Besides his good looks, I was mesmerized by the agility with which he seemed to glide across the room without a single dip or rise.

During a ten minute break one day, I found myself standing next to him in the hallway. He stretched to make himself as tall as he could be, with his hands stuffed into his pockets as if he were in a mighty yawn. When he returned to his normal height, he looked at me and said, "You like this class?"

"I think it's great," I said, startled.

He smiled. "What're you gonna write your term paper on?"

"Gee, I dunno," I said. "Maybe Charlemagne—or Aristotle—but most likely Charlemagne. I think the whole class will be writing about Aristotle. How about you?"

His name was Dick Brennan, the son of a successful Portland lawyer. He had graduated from high school at the top of his class, a quality important to me. Two weeks later, he asked me if I'd go to Reed's Thanksgiving Dance with him. As fast as the blink of an eye, I said, "Yes."

At four o'clock that afternoon, I climbed out of the rumble seat of my car pool Ford and wondered how I should tell Mom and Dad about Dick. I remembered how they'd called Nancy a *shikse*. I was sure they'd think I was crazy to go out with a *shaygitz*. I walked slowly, tip-toeing between the water-soaked, walnut tree leaves plastered on the sidewalk. One false step onto a leaf could turn my foot into an ice skate and land me on my butt. Having primed myself to be careful in the street, I remained guarded as I got ready to tell Mom and Dad about Dick.

That night at the kitchen table, bordered by checked window panes of black, I cut into a piece of stuffed pepper. With my eyes still on the knife and fork in front of me, I said, "I have a date to the Thanksgiving Dance at school."

"What?" Mom stopped eating. The roar of cars passing down our street filled the room.

"Who're you going with?" Dad said.

"A kid in my Humanities class—his name's Dick Brennan."

"Brennan? Brennan?" Dad said. "Brennan's an Irish name. He couldn't be Jewish."

"I know," I said.

"So, why are you going out with him? Why start something you can't finish?" Mom said.

"I'm not going out to marry him. I'm just going out to have a good time," I said, putting my fork down and adding, "to be like everybody else." I pushed my chair away from the table and left the room.

At the dance, I was in Dick's strong arms, feeling as content as a cub in its den. At the same time, there was a cloud over my head. I felt like Eve in the Garden of Eden, tempted to eat the apple, knowing full well that it would lead to trouble. Dick drove me home and parked the car in front of my house. I expected he would pull me close for a kiss, but that didn't happen. Perhaps he sensed my turmoil. I gave him no reason to ask me out again. I wasn't ready to have a fight with Mom and Dad over a date. *If I were at Berkeley, though, I'd go out with Dick again.*

Thanksgiving and Christmas came and went and we finally had New Year's Day to celebrate. Aunt Dora and Uncle Max were coming to dinner, and the mouth-watering aroma of fried chicken was perfuming our house. A 78 rpm record of *The Merry Widow* was spinning on our turntable—*Da geh' ich zum Maxim, dort bin ich sehr intim.* All of us were in our "at home" clothes—no need to dress up for *them.*

We were in the middle of eating our chicken when Uncle Max said, "You won't believe what she did this time. She went out and bought herself a string of pearls, not fake pearls, but *real* pearls."

"Why shouldn't I have pearls? I work as hard as an ox all week long. I deserve them." Aunt Dora pulled her chair out and banged it down on the floor in anger.

"Because you have no place to wear them!" Uncle Max thumped the table with the palm of his hand. "Are you going to wear them to the store … with your moth-eaten sweater and butcher apron? Where are you going to wear them … to a fancy ball?"

"*Chochim groisick!* You think you're so smart." Aunt Dora sneered at him.

The name calling became more and more insulting. I sat with my elbow next to my plate and my hand on my forehead, making circles in my mashed potatoes with my fork. I wished I could erase their images from view and shut off their diatribe like I could the power button on a radio. *If I were at Berkeley, there'd be no Aunt Dora and Uncle Max to be ashamed of.*

After the holiday break, I went back to my routine at Reed. One day our car pool driver needed to stay at school until five o'clock. Since my last class ended at three, I went to the library to study. My nose was buried in Homer's *Odyssey* when I heard someone say, "Well, look who's here."

"Karl!" I was excited the instant I heard his voice. "What are you doing here?"

"I'm taking some classes to finish the requirements for my Bachelor's degree." He sat down next to me, one elbow on the table, his hand on two books balanced on his knee. "I'll be through in June."

"Really? I just started here. I'm a freshman." *How stupid. If I'd just started, obviously I'd be a freshman.*

"Great. Reed's a wonderful school." His smile put crows' feet at the corners of his eyes. "Want to get some coffee?"

"Sure." I collected my books and stood up, measuring the breadth of his shoulders.

In a corner of the cafeteria, with dishes clanking and kids chattering, Karl and I talked on and on—him, about how he came from Berlin and me, about coming from Vienna. He talked about his sister, and I told him about Fred. He talked about his Dad's importing business, and I described Dad's lengthy struggle to get a medical license.

Karl pulled a pack of Camels out of his pocket and offered me a cigarette, looking me in the eye. I imagined I was Lauren Bacall in the film *Key Largo*, and Humphrey Bogart was holding a cigarette under my chin. I said no thanks and watched him light up, his eyes squinting against the smoke. I studied him thoroughly—the cut of his hair, the lines in his cheek, his mannerisms, the way he rested his ankle on his knee. The ring of a bell, sharp as a knife, brought me to my senses.

"Oh my Gosh," I said, springing to my feet. "That's the five o'clock bell. I've missed my ride home."

The corners of his mouth curled up. "I can drive you home."

He parked his car in front of our house and put his right arm across the back of my seat. I looked up at our picture-view window and saw Mom peeking through the Venetian blinds ... *just like she'd done at two o'clock in the morning when Fred was dating.* Karl looked down at me and said, "That'll be two dollars and thirty-seven cents."

"I don't have that much on me," I said, smiling.

"Then I'll have to come back and collect it."

"Guess so," I said, picking up my books. I stepped out of the car and bent over to look back into the cab. "Thanks for the ride."

Inside our living room, Mom said, "Who was that? Who drove you home? Don't you get dropped off at 15th and Knott?"

"That was Karl. I missed my ride and he brought me home." I walked past her down the hall toward my room. She was right behind me.

"Karl? Karl Gottesman?" She followed me and leaned against the doorjamb, folding her arms at her waist. "Where did you find him?"

"I found him at Reed. He's finishing his senior year." I plopped my books down on the bed and jumped on it to the sound of squealing springs. "Now what else do you want to know?"

"Don't be smart with me." She shifted her weight off the doorjamb onto her feet. "I only wanted to know how you got home. You were late. I was worried." Mom's hands fanned out at her waist. "What's wrong with that?" She turned and went back into the kitchen.

Karl called two days later and asked me out to see *The Fountainhead*. At the movie, he reached for my hand while Gary Cooper was kissing Patricia Neal. I muffled a gasp—but didn't pull it away. Driving home, the pace of my speech and my heart were beating in allegro time. Karl drove past my house and parked under a tree in pitch-black darkness. His arm slid over the back of my seat and he pulled me close to his side. I smelled the sweet, biting aroma of tobacco. His lips moved toward mine slowly, testing me. When they met, a current of excitement ran through me like a bolt of lightening. I put my arms around his neck and returned his kiss.

The minute I stepped into my house, I faced Mom in her nightgown and slippers. "Where have you been?" she said. "It's late."

"You knew I was out with Karl. And it's not that late."

"Did you have a good time? What did you do? Where did you go?" Mom was on her feet and following me into my bedroom—just as she had done with Fred.

Karl and I went out steadily from then on, and everyone had something to say.

"He's a nice boy," Mom said.

"He comes from a good family—a German family," Dad said as if that was the best kind.

"Good looking, too," Aunt Dora said, making her double chin wiggle.

"They must have gotten their money out if they came in 1936," Uncle Max said.

"What a catch," Mitzi said, smiling at my good fortune. "It should only happen to Trudi."

In May, Karl told me he'd been drafted into the Army and would go to Germany after he graduated from Reed. Before he left, he took me in his arms and said, "Wait for me."

It was the first sign that the thrill I felt in dating—something I'd never experienced in high school—was taking a serious turn. That scared me. I wasn't ready for anything serious. What I felt was physical attraction and appreciation for all his good qualities—not love.

By this time the entire Portland Jewish refugee community knew that we were "an item." Mom and Dad could hardly contain their delight. A day didn't go by without their remarking about our good fortune. At times their prattle caused me to take two aspirin. I hated their pushing me toward marriage as much as I had resented their pulling me away from Dick and Herb. I wanted it to be *me* that would decide yea or nay about who I'd date and who I'd marry—not Mom and Dad.

If I were at Berkeley, they'd have no say in it.

Making My Move

No matter how hard I studied, my grades in chemistry teetered between a "B" and a "C." With the final exam looming over my head, I thought looking at Dad's freshman chemistry book might help. When I asked to borrow it, he was glad to let me use it. He was happy to see that I was serious about my studies—something he didn't get from Fred. He crouched down at his bookcase, like a Japanese man waiting for a train, and said, "Here it is." It had been placed on its side, along with two other books, to act as a bookend.

I studied Dad's text along with my own and managed to end the semester with a final grade of "B." Perhaps Dad's book helped. I never knew. After I used it, I put it back into the bookcase.

During the summer that followed, I went to work again as a salesgirl. Only this time, I didn't have Elaine to keep me company during my free time. She'd gone to California, married, and had gotten pregnant, all within six months. The flirting she'd practiced at the Center had paid off.

Also, Karl was gone. I received his letters from Germany. It was clear that he was interested in me. I didn't know how I felt about that. I was excited about my newfound success and power in being able to "get" a guy. But I was afraid to "have" him, not knowing what to do with him.

He sent me presents from Europe. The first was a silver bracelet with a heart-shaped charm engraved with the letters KARL. It felt like part of a set of hand-cuffs on my wrist. Next, a thin gold necklace arrived. That gift seemed like a noose around my neck. I softened when a cocoa-colored cocker spaniel puppy made by the famous Rosenthal porcelain factory, arrived. Its adoring, dark eyes almost melted my heart, until I realized it might have been sent to decorate our home one day. I was not ready to be tied to anyone.

I went to work like a robot, did my job, came home, and spent my evenings with Mom and Dad. Without Karl or Elaine to fill the empty hours, and the prospect of returning to Reed looming over my head, I felt no pleasure or enthusiasm for anything.

One day after work, I stripped down to a pair of shorts and an off-shoulder cotton blouse, picked up a *Life* magazine, and settled into a leather chair in the living room. It was one of those summer days when the temperature and humidity spread over Portland like a suffocating blanket. An air conditioner, meant to cool the whole house, roared in the dining room, but the fruits of its labor stayed mostly in that room.

Dad came in the back door carrying his jacket. His drenched, white nylon shirt clung to his skin. His face was so red that it looked like he had a rash. Puffy bags hung under his eyes, like heavy drops about to run down his cheek. He'd made a house call the night before, and now the lack of sleep showed on his face. He hung his suit jacket across the back of a dining room chair, and said, "Whew, what a day!" Rounding the table past his bookcase, he glanced at it and said, "By the way, what did you do with that chem book you borrowed?"

"I put it back," I said.

"No. You didn't," he said, sinking into a sofa chair in the living room.

"Yes, I did."

"Aaaa-lice," he dropped his chin and stared at me—warning me not to challenge him. It was the stance he often took before an explosion of temper and attack on his adversary—much like an aura before an epileptic fit. "Don't argue with me. You lost my book and you're just too ashamed to admit it." He stood up, put his thumbs under his belt, and paced across the floor as if he were a lawyer in front of a jury.

"I didn't," I said, getting to my feet.

"Don't lie to me," he said, facing me eye-to-eye, his finger wagging back and forth in front of my face. "You're lying."

I felt every muscle in my body harden. I swallowed hard, dropped my chin, and frowned before saying, "Dad, I don't lie! I know I put that book back. Sometimes you can be wrong, too, you know."

"What?" Dad's eyes opened wide in shock. "How dare you speak to me that way? What's gotten over you? No one speaks to me like that." His face was inches away from mine, his eyes aflame.

"That's because everyone is afraid of you," I said. "It's because Mom taught Fred and me to shut up any time we wanted to speak back to you. It's not because we've always agreed with you." Dad sank back into his chair, and this time it was me who hovered over him. "Think about it … how could anyone *always* be right? This time …" I took a deep breath. "This time you went too far. Calling me a liar is just not fair."

His attack on me awakened an anger within me that had been dormant for years. It had grown every time we had to swallow saying anything to contradict him or express a different opinion from his. I stomped to the bookcase in the dining room and checked the shelf where it belonged. I saw a stack of notebooks and loose papers piled one upon another that had obviously been flung down haphazardly. I picked them up, and found Dad's chemistry book. I picked it up, walked back into the living room, and threw it into his lap. "Here's your book," I said and kept walking straight out the front door with my heart hammering and the skin on my arms tingling.

I walked around the neighborhood for over an hour. During that time, my mind tried to grasp what had just happened. I asked myself if, by striking back at Dad, I'd lost his love. *Was it worth that price?* I realized then that I was not like Mom—I wouldn't be able to keep on submitting to Dad—right or wrong—indefinitely. *It would be better if I were out of Portland.*

When I returned, Dad sat in a dining room chair, reading *The Oregonian* and drinking a glass of iced coffee. Our overworked air conditioner roared, trying to keep up with the heat. As I passed through the room to get to the kitchen, he said, "I found out one thing today … you're a lot like me." Dad never did apologize to me and I said no more about it.

The following Sunday, a day that still felt like we were in the Amazon jungle, Mom suggested we all go to the beach for lunch. We packed a picnic basket and drove to Seaside and parked a block from the beach. We opened the car door and were greeted by a blast of cold, damp air. It was hard to believe how much colder this little town on the Pacific shore, only an hour's drive away from Portland, could be. Mom and I faced the wind, our tartan bandanas flapping over our heads like birds' wings before we tied the ends under our chins.

We struggled against the strong air current to the beach, where a handful of people walked barefoot at the water's edge. Others huddled on blankets, fully dressed in long pants, jackets, and head coverings. Occasionally, the wind grabbed a stray piece of paper, lifted it up, and flipped it back and forth like it was a kite, before allowing it to float back down onto the sand.

We spread our blanket by an old petrified tree trunk, using it as a back rest while our legs stretched out in front of us in six straight lines. We ate our sandwiches silently, listening to the roar of waves crashing into the shore and watching their white foamy bubbles disappear in the sand. Two hundred yards out to sea, a huge black rock shaped like a haystack stood firm, its top streaked white by seagull droppings. The birds' raucous squeaks pierced the air as they swung left and right, white wings spread wide, searching for a stray anchovy in the bubbling tide pools below. The scene before us was tranquil and peaceful one minute, wild and stormy the next. We ate our lunch, soaking up the beauty around us. My emotions, like the scene before us, swung back and forth from intense anxiety to relative calm.

We strolled down the town's main street after lunch, studying the displays in the curio shop's windows. We saw sea shells, star fish, abalone ash trays, and chunks of quartz in every color of the rainbow. Mom ducked into a shop and returned with a bag of blue agate stones for a class in mosaics at the Center.

"What do you need that for?" Dad said.

"For my class," she answered. "Don't worry. They don't cost that much."

"If it was up to you, you'd spend every dime we have."

The bickering between them continued, progressing through the usual steps. The only thing that varied was how nasty Dad would become and how hurt Mom would be. If he wounded her deeply enough, she would cry. Those tears always ended the conflict. Dad would put his arms around her, and then tell her that he didn't mean anything, and didn't she know how much he loved her.

My annoyance at listening to their continual squabbling spurred me to say, "Dad ... Mom, I've decided not to go back to Reed next year. I want to transfer to the University in Berkeley."

"What?" Dad looked stunned. "You can't do that. Did you forget about your scholarship?"

"I didn't forget, Dad. I just don't want to go back to Reed."

"But ... what about Karl?" Mom said. She reached for my arm, stopping my gait. "He'll be coming home in just a few months." She looked into my eyes, "You can have him, you know." The worry lines appeared on her forehead.

"I'm not sure I want him, Mom."

They looked at me, stunned. I hesitated and swallowed before adding, "I just want to get out of Portland."

"Why? What's wrong with Portland?" Dad said.

I couldn't answer them without telling them they were part of "what's wrong with Portland." I couldn't hurt them like that. Getting into the Pontiac I said, in an almost inaudible voice, "Nothing is wrong with Portland." Then louder, "Every other kid in Portland is allowed to go away to college. Most of them go to either Seattle or Eugene. I don't want to go there. I want to go to Berkeley next year."

Dad slid into the car behind the steering wheel and said, "Not with my money, you're not."

I wasn't surprised by that. I didn't think Dad would let me go so easily. But I also knew that if I gave in to him then, I'd be giving in to him always—starting with choosing a husband and ending—perhaps never.

"Then I'll go without your money. I can always get a job."

"*Ach,* you're talking crazy. Who will take care of you? What if you get sick? You know you can count on at least one strep infection every winter ... out of the question. You're staying home."

No, I'm not. We drove back to Portland without saying another word—our Pontiac now a chamber of silence.

I had surprised myself. I blurted out in the heat of the argument that I'd go to work, without thinking about whether or not a salesgirl earned enough to support herself. I hadn't thought about my regular bouts with strep infections. I hadn't thought about not knowing anyone in Berkeley. I hadn't thought about any of that, but it was too late to go back now. *I'll stay home and work until I've saved enough money to go to Berkeley. But I will go to Berkeley.*

After our day at Seaside, the line in the sand between Dad and me had been drawn. The only sounds at dinner were the scrapings of knives and forks on our plates and an occasional request for a salt shaker. Mom and Dad retreated into the living room and I into my bedroom, except when I needed to go into the kitchen to take two aspirin for a headache.

Two weeks later, I came home and headed for my bedroom. Passing the kitchen door, I saw Dad embrace Mom, her head buried in his shoulder. She held a crumpled handkerchief under her nose. My footsteps made them turn their faces toward me. A network of pencil-thin red lines covered the whites of Mom's eyes.

"What's the matter?" I asked, walking into the kitchen.

Mom and Dad parted and Mom said, "Nothing." She turned her back to me, facing the sink.

"What do you mean, 'nothing'?" I said. "Why are you crying?"

"This doesn't concern you," Dad said, his voice deep. "Just go to your room."

"Please, Illy ..." Mom sounded like she had a cold. "Please ... leave us alone."

Several days after that, Dad called me into the living room. He paced up and down with his hands clasped behind his back—a sure sign that he was upset about something. He said he didn't like the idea of a young girl eighteen-years-old going off to a big city all by herself—it wasn't safe. He didn't know I'd decided to stay home and work until I had enough money to go to Berkeley without his support.

He stopped pacing and faced me. "How about going to Los Angeles where Fred could keep an eye on you?"

My heart began to race. Fred—who consoled me like a parent when I lost my best friend at school ... Fred—who was the only one to understand how I felt as an outsider ... Fred—who showed me why I had to leave Portland ... Fred would never cause me any problems.

"Will you pay for me to go to UCLA?" I said.

Dad hovered over me, making me feel like a little girl again. He cleared his throat, looked at Mom, and said, "Yes."

It was then that I understood why Mom had been crying in the kitchen. Mom understood the power of her tears. Challenging Dad forced each of us to develop our own courage and cunning to get our way. Mom used her tears. Fred and I would run away.

I was ecstatic over being able to leave Portland. I arranged for my transcripts to be transferred to UCLA. I selected the clothes I'd be taking with me. I bought my train ticket to Los Angeles and asked if I could stay with Fred and Nancy until I found housing on campus. I was no longer creeping about in a cocoon of gloom.

But the price for Dad's compromise was his bitter send-off. When we said our goodbyes, his parting words to me were, "You'll be back. You won't be there long. Something will happen ... something always does ... and you'll come running home."

The New Rules

I wore my navy blue cashmere sweater—the one Mom had bought with her own secret money. I was covered in a thick film of salty perspiration, and it wasn't entirely due to nerves. I was sitting in a sorority house in Los Angeles during "rush," the week when they selected their new members. It was one hundred degrees in Los Angeles, and I'd taken only clothes appropriate for the cold weather we would have had in Portland in September.

I hadn't intended to join a sorority, but it was the only housing available to students on the newest of the University of California campuses. A week later, I stood in a reception line at one of the two Jewish houses at U.C.L.A., Sigma Delta Tau, being presented to the community at-large. I wore my sea green high school prom formal, and stood between a wavy-haired beauty and a frog-eyed girl with buck teeth.

"Alice," the good-looker on my left said. "I'd like you to meet Mr. and Mrs. Pearlmutter."

I extended my white-gloved hand to a well-dressed diminutive couple, turned to the unfortunate girl on my right, and said, "Arlene, I'd like you to meet Mr. and Mrs. Mulepetter."

"What?" Mrs. Pearlmutter exclaimed. Several guests in front and behind her in line gasped. The girl with too many teeth in her mouth burst out laughing. I must have turned every shade of red in the color palette—bathed in shame once again. Perhaps this incident was to foreshadow what my sorority days would be like.

I moved into a triple room in my sorority's three-story stucco house with two other girls. Margie had all the good looks of a high school cheerleader without the bubbly personality that should have gone with that position. She'd never forgiven her parents for moving her from Chicago to Los Angeles, thereby parting her from the "most popular" group of kids at her former school forever. While she wore her sadness on her sleeve, my other roommate, Amy, seemed to be smiling all the time. With dark, curly ringlets framing her face, she was engaged to her high school sweetheart. All three of us had no interest in the sorority activities, having joined only to have a place to live. We formed a separate unit, floating about the house as if we were encapsulated in a soap bubble.

I learned the rules of the house and obeyed them the best I could. I wore my sorority pin over my heart every day, didn't chew gum on campus, didn't stay out after curfew, and attended our parties. Knowing no one to invite as my date, I had to agree to be fixed up with a succession of blind dates. The resulting bouts in the back seats of cars with one or another overly eager fraternity boy added to my growing addiction to aspirin. I didn't realize I had exchanged Mom and Dad's rules for those of the sorority.

In November, Fred called to invite me to dinner. He pulled his car up in front of my house and I jumped in, saying, "Where's Nancy?"

"Get in and I'll tell you." Fred's fingers were wrapped around the steering wheel, his knuckles like white marbles. He turned his head away from me as he checked the street for oncoming traffic. "Nancy and I are getting a divorce."

"What?" My jaw dropped.

Fred stopped at the traffic light on Sunset Boulevard and looked at me. "Apparently she's having an affair with the dentist she works for." Fred clenched his jaw, sending ripples up his cheeks.

"Oh Fred, I'm so sorry," I said, feeling his pain. *Nothing goes right for this poor guy.*

Fred called me often after that—sometimes on the spur of the moment in the middle of the week, asking me to go out for coffee with him. He'd lost all interest in playing tennis or bridge, and didn't want to meet any girls. Instead of Fred looking after me, it was I who became the crutch under his arm.

I wasn't surprised when my roommate said, "There's someone in the living room asking to see you." I thought it was Fred again until she added, "Have you been keeping him a secret?"

"What are you talking about? I don't know anybody in L.A.," I said. "Did he tell you his name?"

"No, but he sure looks good in that uniform," she said.

"Karl! It must be Karl!" I bolted off my bed, dashed to the bathroom, put on some lipstick, brushed my hair, and tucked my shirt into my pants. I ran down the hall and slowed my step before going down the stairs so that he wouldn't see me rushing toward him.

"Karl—what are you doing here?" I said, admiring him in his dark green uniform, now with three stripes on his sleeve. He looked different somehow. Perhaps a bit more muscular in the shoulders—or maybe he held his head higher. *This is no fraternity boy!*

"I'm on furlough. I don't report back to the base until the end of the month, so I thought I'd surprise you." He studied me as if he'd never seen me before. Several sorority sisters passed us on their way to the kitchen, staring. I imagined them thinking, "what a catch."

I wanted to kiss him right then and there. He smiled, reading my mind. We went to dinner in Westwood at an Italian restaurant with red-and-white checkered tablecloths. A candle, stuffed into the top of an empty Chianti bottle, flickered between us like a loosely connected light bulb. Karl pulled a Camel out of a pack in his pocket and lit it. Its sweet, woodsy aroma, almost like that of a wellstoked fireplace, excited me. We ordered a glass of wine and looked at one another, holding hands across the table. "Little Alice from Portland doesn't need an ID anymore," he teased.

I wished we were alone, in his car, parked in some dark, secluded place. "Not anymore. Little Alice is a big girl now."

Having Karl across the table from me, after having dated a succession of fraternity boys, made me more aware of all of his good qualities than ever. If he had given me a bracelet or necklace then, I'd have been glad to wear it. We drove along Pacific Coast Highway after dinner and parked the car. Karl told me about his job as a translator in Germany, but my mind wasn't on his words. It was on his hands that I wanted to touch me, on his muscular arms that I wanted to hold me, on his lips that I wanted silent, kissing me. The sky was filled with white dots, glistening like glowworms. The ocean waves roared as they rolled into shore and disappeared on the sand. I was in Karl's arms at last, kissing him.

"I've missed you," he said, leaning back in his seat behind the steering wheel.

"I've missed you, too."

Karl's arm was around my shoulder, his eyes on the moonlit white foam on the beach. "If I save up my vacation time, I could be home the summer after next."

"That would be great," I said, before his lips met mine.

When we looked at one another again he said, "How about you transferring back to Reed?"

I felt a thud in my stomach. I didn't want to go back to Portland. But I didn't want to lose Karl either. "I hadn't thought about it, really," I said. "I'm not crazy about Reed."

"You wouldn't be at Reed for long. As soon as you graduate, you could move on to a next part of your life."

I laced my fingers together and looked up at him. "I thought I'd finish my schooling in California. Had you ever thought about living here?"

"What? And walk away from the business that my dad and I worked so hard to build up? That wouldn't be too smart."

"Of course not." I forced a smile. Our lips met again, but my heart ached.

Mom and Dad called the day after Karl left and asked about his visit. *How'd they know he was here?* They said they'd heard it from Mitzi, who'd heard it from Adele, who'd heard it from Zita. They wanted to know what happened—what we did—what he said—did he ask you to come back to Portland—what did you say? The long arms of Mom and Dad pushing me to Karl, and to Portland, had reached me all the way in Los Angeles. I gave them one or two-word answers and took two aspirins.

Something Will Happen

"Who're you taking to the Fiesta Fling Friday night?" Margie asked. She was sitting on the floor of our bedroom, drawing a nude on a large white board for her Life Drawing class. Her artistic talent was so obvious to everyone that she was made Art Director at the sorority after having been in the house only two weeks.

"Some blind date, I guess. I don't know anyone in L.A.," I said, making a face that must have looked like I'd bitten into a lemon. "Who're you taking?"

"Some kid who's in my art class. He's not much to look at, but he's nice. We're friends. I won't have any trouble from him. Don't you know anyone?"

"No," I said, not mentioning my statistics professor, who'd asked me out to dinner. Even though I worried that my turning him down would affect my "A" grade in his class, I couldn't bring myself to spend an evening with the pudgy, colorless man with eyeteeth like a dog. He did, however, have character, and I maintained my grade.

The Fling was just the latest in a series of parties and dances we were forced to attend, or be fined. That would have been all right with me, but I had to worry about Dad seeing the extra charge on my monthly bill. It was better not to test Dad. Being in California cost him so much more than if I'd gone to Reed. Margie and Amy also felt the same about our social events, but we all attended them dutifully. Early the next morning, they both left for the weekend, as did almost everyone else in the house.

That Saturday, I slept in late and missed breakfast. I went into the kitchen to fix a cup of black coffee—all other foods were under lock and key. Our housemother, a widow of about sixty years with dyed red hair and long, raspberry red fingernails, came into the room. Her job was to supervise the girls at the sorority at night after curfew and on the weekends.

"Are you staying at the house tonight?" she asked with a smile.

"Yes, I have nowhere to go. My brother is away skiing."

"Oh," she said, as she filtered the last drop of her coffee into the cup. "Well, have a nice time," she said, leaving the kitchen.

I walked several blocks into Westwood Village and bought myself brunch at a small café. Afterwards, I did some window shopping along the boulevard and returned to the house. I spent the afternoon studying in my room to the background noise of my dorm mates chattering, taking showers, making phone calls, and playing bridge. The noises diminished in the late afternoon, and when I tried to find someone to have dinner with, I found the dorm empty.

At eight o'clock, after another meal alone, I trudged up Hilgard Avenue with our large, three-story stucco house in sight—large, somber, and foreboding. Devoid of a single shrub or blade of grass to break its starkness, it looked like an alcazar. Once inside, I was engulfed in a cloud of silence. There wasn't a sound to be heard upstairs, in the living room, or in the kitchen.

I passed the housemother's room and looked for the beam of light that normally lay at the bottom of her closed door like a white snake. It wasn't there. She must have left despite my telling her I'd be there that night. I climbed the stairs to my third floor dorm room, hoping to find one of the girls in a bathroom or reading in a bedroom. Silence. I knocked on a few doors and called, "Is anyone home?" No answer. Quiet. The hair on my arms stirred.

I stood in the hallway and remembered the words our president spoke at our last club meeting. "For your information, there's been a rape on campus. It was a girl at the Tri-Delt house who came home after curfew hours. She'd forgotten her key and was ringing the front door bell when someone grabbed her from behind and dragged her into his car. So, be careful. Don't come home late." My heart beat against the wall of my chest as if to repeat, "Be careful," in rhythmic time. My fear grew with each passing minute. I felt as if I were in Frankenstein's castle waiting to be attacked. I got into bed, propped a pillow against the sea green wall behind me, and picked up a book. I read a few words without grasping their meaning.

From downstairs, I heard CREAK—as if someone had stepped on a floor board. I sat up in bed and dropped my book on the floor, my body stiff with fear. Quiet again. Then, a car's headlights lit up the wall to my left for an instant, as if it were done with the flip of a cape, erasing the shadows cast by the leaves outside my window. All was still again. I took a deep breath and let it our slowly, then picked up my book and leaned back against my pillow.

After ten minutes, I heard BANG! I thought the rapist was in my house. I pulled the covers over my head, hoping he wouldn't know anyone was under the pile of rumpled blankets on my bed. It looked much like Margie's and Amy's beds. I remained in that position, as if frozen in place, remembering Dad's words, "Something will happen ..."

I wish I were home.

I lost consciousness some time thereafter. When I finally dared to peek out from under my blanket, my room was flooded with light. It was morning, and nothing had happened to me. I survived the night, unscathed except for my head, which felt as if it were in a vice. I ventured downstairs and fixed a cup of black coffee, strong as espresso, and took two aspirin. With my hands wrapped around my mug like a koala bear's paws, I wondered how I could have been so stupid.

The CREAK was probably from a floorboard in this old, rickety house. The BANG must have come from wind pushing that tree in the alley against our house. Something happened, all right, but I won't go running home.

I went back to the routine I'd settled into before—attending meetings, going on blind dates, observing the curfew, wearing my pin, and on and on—all the rules that I thought would secure my membership in the sorority and a bed in a dormitory. But about a month later, my "big sister," the girl assigned to facilitate my way to full membership, asked me to meet her in the living room.

"Hi, Alice," she said, motioning me to sit next to her on a couch. I focused on her two dark eyes, eyes that looked like they might pop out of their sockets at any moment, and wondered what kind of assignment she'd give me for our next fraternity exchange. I'd failed the last one, the one placing me in the club choir. It came to light that I couldn't sing anything right. Every musical note that came out of my mouth was flat—no other way but flat. I was promptly discharged.

"Hi, Rhoda," I said.

"Hi," she said again, and cleared her throat. She looked down at her hands, allowing me some relief from her eyes, before shooting them up at me again, saying, "The board wanted me to talk to you." She hesitated. "They wanted to know if you're happy here." She exhaled, lowered her shoulders, and studied me as if she were my psychiatrist.

Happy? Happy? Well, no. I'm not. I don't really want to be here in this sorority. I'd rather be at Berkeley. Then I remembered my need for that bed on the third floor and said, "Of course I'm happy. Why do you ask?"

She smiled, narrowing her eyes somewhat, and said, "Well, some of the girls are worried about you. Is everything all right?"

"Of course, it is. I'm fine. Tell them not to worry." I lied.

"I'm so glad," she said, relieved to have done her duty.

I returned to my room and took two aspirin.

The weeks that followed were filled with term papers and tests, exchanges and parties, black coffee and aspirin in the kitchen late at night, and bridge games on the floor of our dorm room until three o'clock in the morning—until the day I was waiting for the traffic light to change on the curb at Hilgard Avenue. I hadn't finished a term paper on Ana Pauker, the Romanian Communist Party leader, which was due in a couple of days, so I skipped dinner and went to the library to catch up on the work. At about nine o'clock I was overcome with one of my frequent crashing headaches and took a double dose of aspirin to help me get through the evening. I worked until the library closed at ten o'clock, and then walked home. I made it as far as Hilgard Avenue.

As I stood on the curb waiting for the light to change, I began daydreaming about Karl and living in Portland. I pictured Dad standing in our living room, saying Karl's father wasn't such a big shot; "How much money could he make already selling noodles?" I imagined Karl meeting Aunt Dora and Uncle Max, and wondered how I could keep them a secret. My head began to pound. When I looked at the traffic light again, it was out of focus.

I blinked, hoping my eyelids would act like windshield wipers and clear the haze. Nothing changed. The light was so dim that I wasn't sure which color was lit up. *I can't see! What's wrong with me?* I took a deep breath and looked at my feet. They were a blur. *My eyes are okay ... I don't even need glasses.* I heard footsteps approach and stop next to me. A large gray boulder shaped like a person was at my side for a short while before I heard footsteps moving away from me.

I began to breathe fast and deep, as if I'd been running, and reached for the lamppost on the corner to steady myself. *What's happening? What'll I do?* I heard the screech of brakes followed by a car door slamming shut once and then again. Then footsteps and the clanking of something—perhaps keys—I couldn't tell what. I tried to focus on the steps and clatter that were coming ever closer to me. I could make out two boulders that looked like they might be people.

"I'm Officer Rodriguez. Are you all right?"

Oh my God, it's the police! I responded immediately, "No. I mean yes! Thanks. I'm all right ... just a little dizzy." I hooked my arm around the lamppost. "I get these dizzy spells sometimes. They'll go away in just a few minutes. I'll be all right." I forced a smile.

"Think we should take her in?" the other boulder said.

I couldn't let that happen. They'd call Dad right away. There had to be some other way. I didn't want anyone to know about my not being able to see. "No, no ... please don't do that. I get these spells all the time. Let me just sit down here on the curb."

One of them grabbed my arm to help me sit down. "Sure you're going to be all right?" he asked.

"Yes, yes. I'm sure. Thanks anyway." I tried to make myself sound unconcerned and cheerful. "I get these spells all the time. I'll be on my way in about five minutes."

"All right, then. We'll pass by here again in about ten minutes to make sure you got home all right." With that, the two boulders retreated, the equipment at their waists clanking as they walked, and drove off.

Sitting on the curb, I crossed my arms over the top of my knees and dropped my forehead on them. *I've got to do something before they come back.* But I couldn't think of what to do.

Fred! That's it! I've got to get a hold of Fred! I decided that if the police returned, I'd have them drive me to Fred's apartment. He could help me find out if something was wrong with my eyes—or my head. *Maybe I'm crazy like Aunt Dora.* Knowing that Dad wouldn't need to know about this incident, my deep breathing became more shallow, and the pounding in my head less intense. *Yes ... Fred will help me.* I looked at the traffic light again and could guess at the colors. *Maybe I can get back to the house before the police get here.*

Safe in my room at last, I lay prone on my bed staring at the ceiling, my fingers laced behind my head. Even though I began to be able to see better and better, I called Fred and told him I was sick. Within ten minutes, he was in the sorority living room, sitting next to me on a floral couch. He was dressed in his hospital whites and looked like an attending physician in an emergency room. His face stern and without any emotion, he asked me all sorts of questions.

"Illy ... you idiot! You had an overdose of aspirin," he said. "Why, the hell, did you take so much of that stuff?" He looked at me with the same concern and love he'd shown me when I'd lost my friend Maria as a thirteen-year-old.

"I dunno, Fred. I guess everything came crashing in on me at the same time—Karl ... mid-terms ... the sorority ... going out with all those goons. I just couldn't get rid of my headaches."

"Well, you'll have to find another way to do it, because aspirin can be dangerous ... as you just found out."

"I guess so." We stood up together. I kissed Fred on the cheek and held his hand as I'd done so often when he took me to the park in Riga, and walked him to the front door. "One more thing ... promise me you won't say anything to Mom and Dad about this."

"Don't worry, I won't."

My headaches didn't disappear. But from then on, I rationed the number of aspirins I would take to control them—much as an alcoholic might limit the number of drinks he'd allow himself when trying to kick the habit. This worked quite well until the middle of the next semester, when I came down with a sore throat and fever. Another strep infection, I thought. I took the medication Dad gave me to take to California and prepared myself for a two week bout of tonsillitis.

I went to school as usual, but began to feel tired most of the time. One morning I stepped into the shower before breakfast, as was my custom. It felt refreshing, the drops bouncing off my body like tiny hands massaging my skin. I heard the soothing sound of water splashing on the tile floor around my ankles, and I breathed deeply, enjoying every sensation—until I felt nothing.

"Alice … Alice … what's wrong? Wake up!" Margie shouted as she shook my limp body on the bottom of the shower floor. I opened my eyes. "Amy! AMY!" she shouted. "Come help me."

I had passed out, and when I came back to my senses, I could hardly walk across the hall to my bedroom to lie down.

"I'm calling your folks," Margie said.

"NO!" I shouted.

"What else can I do? There's no medical clinic on campus. You know that."

"I know." I sat up in bed, feeling weak as a newborn pup, and knew I couldn't bear weight. "Call my brother."

When Fred got through analyzing all my lab work, he told me I had infectious mononucleosis. I had all the symptoms—swollen glands, an abnormal blood count, and extreme fatigue.

"It sometimes takes months to recover," he said. There was no other choice but for Mom and Dad to take care of me in Portland. He gave me this news in my dorm room with Margie and Amy standing by, mute. I sat with my hands clutching the edge of the bed, my head hanging as if my neck muscles were paralyzed, and with tears cascading down my cheeks.

Dad's prediction, "you'll be back," finally had come true.

Fitting In

A gust of wind blew the sheer, chevron-patterned curtains into my bedroom. Violet, rust, and mustard-colored zinnias, large as grapefruit, floated aimlessly on the drapes framing the window. Mom had sewn them for my bedroom as soon as she knew I'd be coming home to recuperate.

I lay in bed most of the time, with only enough energy to read and listen to the radio. I needed someone to hold my arm to get to the bathroom for fear of falling. The thought of collapsing in the shower was fresh in my mind, so Mom solved the problem with vigorous and thorough sponge baths. Meals were brought to me in bed on a tray. I had been reduced to an infantile level.

"Here … I've made you some rhubarb," Mom said, entering my room one afternoon. She found me flat in bed, like a beached whale. I mustered up all the energy I had and raised myself onto my elbows. Inside the bowl on her tray I saw a dark, reddish liquid, thick as syrup. Short, light green fibers floated inside the bowl—just looking at it made my stomach cramp. "Mom, I don't like cooked rhubarb—not as a pie, not as compote, not in any way."

"Please, Illy," she said. "Just taste it. It's good. It's high in protein and that's what you need." She scooped some of the stewed fruit onto a teaspoon, bent forward, and held it up to my lips. "Come on … taste it."

"Mom, take it away. I don't know where you got the idea that there's protein in rhubarb," I said, turning my head to the side and falling back down onto my bed.

Having no support for her lie, she burst out laughing. And I, lying in a room of mismatched patterns and a bowl of goo in front of me, let out a guffaw of my own.

Meanwhile, there seemed to be an extra bounce in Dad's step and a constant smile on his face. He didn't need to worry about my recovering—it was assured. The only variable was the length of time it would take. He re-established his authority over me as my physician and as my father. He monitored my blood tests, looked into my throat, and felt my lymph nodes. He watched my energy level and supervised my diet, except for the slip-up with Mom's rhubarb. His control over me was complete, a situation which preyed on my mind as much as the mononucleosis devastated my body. I thought about nothing other than returning to California.

Several weeks passed before I regained my health and returned to L.A. for summer school to make up the credits I'd lost by dropping out of the spring semester. I lived in my sorority house with a half dozen girls who were doing the same thing. Fred was gone. He'd been drafted into the air force and sent to Korea. I was alone for the most part, giving me plenty of time to think and make some decisions.

After summer school ended, I went home to await the start of the fall semester. I hadn't been there but a day or two, when the phone rang. "Hi … it's me. I'm home for good this time. When can I see you?"

"Karl!" I was excited. "Tonight," I said.

He picked me up at eight-thirty and drove to a night club, where we spent the night dancing and drinking bourbon and sodas. He was out of uniform but looked just like he did when he'd impressed my sorority sisters in L.A.. What had changed was me. I was no longer the teenager who went rubber-kneed at the sight of this handsome, eligible young man. My head was full of getting back to California and I knew that Karl would not be part of that picture. The fire that had burned so fiercely was now reduced to a few smoldering embers. We kissed goodnight on the landing to my front door, but it was not the same. Walking away from me, he said, "I'll call you."

Mom and Dad were delighted to see me going out with Karl again. Mom said, "He's such a gentleman—such a good upbringing." She had been impressed by the cheese and cracker basket he'd brought to the house when he'd picked me up. His family had moved on from peddling noodles to establishing a flourishing import-export business.

"They're doing very well, I hear," Dad said. His attempt to lure me into living in Portland by marrying into a financially successful family was not lost on me.

"I know," I replied, biting into a piece of Jarlsberg cheese and saying no more.

Our date had rekindled Mom's hopes, and she was feeling good. "Why don't we go out to dinner tonight?" she said. "It's so hot—I don't want to make the house even more unbearable by cooking."

Mom and Dad had come around to having dinner out once in a while, despite the fact that it was more expensive than eating home. Dad's position with Permanente had given them a bit of financial security. We went to a neighborhood family restaurant with green Naugahyde upholstered booths and linoleum covered tables—no tablecloths. We slid into our seats and ordered their specialty—meatloaf, mashed potatoes, and gravy.

We'd been talking about Fred and the girlfriend he left behind in L.A., when I changed the subject. "Mom … Dad, I'm not going back to L.A. next month."

"What?" Dad put his fork down and frowned at me.

"You're going back to Reed—you're going to get serious about Karl," Mom said, hoping she'd guessed right.

"No … no … no," I said. "I'm going to transfer to Berkeley."

"Berkeley?" Dad leaned forward and lined his fingers up over his mouth—a sure sign of total concentration.

"What about Karl?" Mom said.

"*Ach*, stop already with Karl all the time," Dad said, with a tone of voice that meant *you're talking stupid again.* Then, looking at me, he said, "I thought you'd forgotten all about Berkeley."

"I never forgot about Berkeley, Dad," I said, leaning against the back of the booth with my arms folded at my waist. "I just got sidetracked when you offered to pay my way at UCLA. But Fred isn't going to be there anymore, and I just don't belong in a sorority. I think it's time for me to go where I wanted to be in the first place."

A thick cloud of silence hung over our table. I put my fork down and looked out the window. Mom and Dad looked at one another. Finally, Dad said, "What can we say … if you think you'll be happy there, maybe you should transfer. We can't *force* you to stay in Portland—or marry Karl. We want only the best for you. You have to do what you think will make you happy. You know how much Mom and I love you."

Ever since I'd exploded over the chemistry book, Dad seemed to talk to me in a different tone of voice. He seemed to know that the equation of his saying *you'll do as I say* was no longer answered by my saying *okay.* His acceptance of my wishes to return to California was no surprise to me. The gracious way it was done, however, moved me deeply. While he was speaking, my throat tightened and I could hardly utter the words, "I love you, too."

The next time I went out with Karl, I told him I was going to Berkeley in September. My words were like a bucket of water pouring on the few remaining embers that still smoldered between us.

It was raining on the day I boarded the train to Berkeley, but my mood couldn't have been sunnier. I took a taxi to Durant Street, where a number of homes had been converted into university-approved housing. I paid the driver in front of the Victorian house that would be my home for the next two years. Its front door, a light shade of oak, was inset with an oval-shaped, leaded glass window picturing a bouquet of roses tied with a bow. Inside, the musty smell of an old, well-worn house greeted me. A rug runner covered a spiral staircase of stained mahogany wood. After checking in, I climbed up to the second floor and entered my room. Brown bedspreads of heavy cotton, almost like awning material, covered our beds—no doubt chosen so they wouldn't show dirt and could withstand heavy laundering. A small window let in so little light that the lamps needed to be lit in the middle of the day. Three girls sat cross-legged on the floor in the space between the beds.

One of them, a chunky, smiling girl, sprang to her feet and said, "Hi, my name's Arlene Minassian. You must be my roommate." She wore pants and a pullover sweater two sizes too large—covering an overly endowed chest.

"I think so," I said, warming up to her broad smile. "I'm Alice."

"Hi," she said. "Come on in. This is Betty." She pointed to a freckle-faced redhead. "She's from Walla Walla." I knew it to be the apple capital of the state of Washington. "And this is Marilyn. She's from New Mexico and has a full scholarship—lucky girl." Marilyn had dark, ruddy skin, with thick, black hair around her fleshy face. *An American Indian.*

"Hi, everybody," I said. "I'm from Portland.

"Come have some dolmades. My Mom made them with my grandma's old Armenian recipe and shipped them down from Fresno," Arlene said.

"Thanks." I plopped myself down on the floor and pulled a stuffed grape leaf out of a jar. Whatever nervousness I felt in coming to Berkeley disappeared as I tasted the spicy, tart juices of that Armenian delicacy in the company of the girls in that room.

I walked down the hall toward my room a few days later and passed a door through which I could hear someone playing a record of Vivaldi's *Four Seasons.* Surprised to hear anything other than a song on the Hit Parade, I knocked on the door. A girl with ivory-colored hair, like a newborn chick's feathers, opened it. She was as wide as she was tall. Everything about her was round ... her body, her rosy face, and her ice-blue eyes.

"Hi," she said. "You musht be ze new girl von Portland. I'm Magdalena." *Her accent sounds a little like German—but it isn't.*

"Hi. I'm Alice," I said. "I was surprised to hear the Vivaldi. I thought there wouldn't be another person in Berkeley, beside me, who'd like that kind of music."

"Vell, you're not," she said, smiling. "Come in ... shit down."

Magdalena's phonograph was pushed up against the wall of her room—a stack of Mozart, Beethoven, and Brahms records were piled next to it. I sat down on the floor and leaned against the wall, feeling welcome and at home.

The next time she invited me to listen to her records, I asked her about her accent. She told me she was a Jewish refugee from Holland. She'd lost her parents in the war and was raised by a distant cousin in Los Angeles. She didn't say how her parents had died, and I didn't want to open up that wound by asking. I told her about myself—which sounded like a walk in the park compared to what she had been through. I felt close to my roommate Arlene, but Magdalena and I understood each other on a different level.

Magdalena often joined the rest of us for a hamburger or pizza at Larry Blake's restaurant on Telegraph Avenue, an easy walk from our house. We'd go there whenever our dinner at the house was close to inedible or when we needed a snack after studying at the library at night. Our diets were also supplemented by packages from our mothers—not only dolmades from Fresno, but also red corn fry bread from New Mexico and apples from Walla Walla. My package arrived about two weeks after school had started. Our entire group of five was in my room when I opened it.

"Hamentaschen!" I exclaimed, slack-jawed.

"Hamentaschen?" Arlene asked. "What's that?" Everyone gathered around me to get a closer look inside my box.

"I've never seen a cookie like that before," Betty said, looking at the over-sized, triangular pastry.

"What's that inside them?" Marilyn asked.

"It's poppy seed filling. Sometimes Mom fills them with prunes … but I really like poppy seed better," I said. "Want to try one?"

"Are you kidding?" Magdalena reached inside my box. "I wouldn't pass up the chance. But why are you getting them now when it isn't even Purim?"

"Because Mom knows how much I like them. She makes them whenever she likes—whether it's Purim or not," I said.

Arlene reached inside my box. "What's Purim?" she said, before biting into her cookie.

"It's a Jewish holiday," I said.

"Jewish?" Arlene stopped chewing and looked surprised "You're Jewish?" She looked as stunned as Elaine had been at our high school hangout.

"Yup, I am," I said smiling, and savoring the sweet crunch of its tiny black seeds in my mouth. "I sure am."

Even though each one of the girls in my boarding house came from different ends of the earth, we formed a bond that made us appreciate who we were. We ignored the rabble-rousing kids handing out politically charged pamphlets at Sather Gate, and commiserated with one another over the difficulties of our studies. I discovered a special liking for social sciences in Dr. Shibutani's sociology class. It was there that I met a kid with pewter-colored eyes who made me forget all about Karl. I fit into this patchwork of cultures and distanced myself from the frightened, anxious girl I'd been, and began to become the Alice I was meant to be in the first place.

EPILOGUE

After completing a Bachelor's degree and a Master's degree in Social Welfare at Berkeley, Alice taught the importance of social and emotional issues in patient care to the house staff at the University of California Hospital in San Francisco. She met her future husband, a physician, at the hospital. Her father did not meet him until after she'd become engaged. They settled in southern California where they raised three children.

Mom and Dad followed Alice to California after Dad's retirement. A role reversal took place in their old age, as they became her charge, and she their care-taker. Troubled throughout his lifetime, Fred remained in Los Angeles, where he practiced medicine and experienced the turmoil of four marriages. Aunt Dora and Uncle Max also moved to southern California upon their retirement.

Karl built up his family's import-export business and became extremely suc-cessful. He married, had two children, and died at an early age, the victim of lung cancer. Elaine remained in California and, after raising two children, succumbed to breast cancer. Trudi stayed in Portland with her parents. She completed a Master's program in education and taught elementary school until her retire-ment. She has two children and remains Alice's lifelong friend.

978-0-595-40339-4
0-595-40339-5

Printed in the United States
92536LV00003B/151-198/A

9 780595 403394